POLITICAL IDEAS

OF THE AMERICAN

REVOLUTION

Published by Samuel Walker, Boston

Signing of the Declaration of Independence

UNIVERSITY PAPERBACKS

POLITICAL IDEAS
OF THE AMERICAN
REVOLUTION

BRITANNIC-AMERICAN CONTRIBUTIONS TO
THE PROBLEM OF IMPERIAL ORGANIZATION
1765 TO 1775

By RANDOLPH G. ADAMS

Director of the William Clements Library

Third Edition
With Commentary by Merrill Jensen, Ph.D.
Professor of History, University of Wisconsin

BARNES & NOBLE, INC. • New York

Publishers • Booksellers • Since 1873

Printed in the United States of America

PUBLISHER'S STATEMENT

RANDOLPH G. ADAMS wrote this volume in 1919 to fulfill requirements for a doctoral dissertation at Trinity College (now Duke University). The first edition was published in 1922 as the initial publication of the Trinity College Press (which later became the Duke University Press). The text was considered a significant contribution to the history of the American Revolution because it developed the author's view that the Revolution could not have occurred but for Britain's insistence that it was impossible to distribute imperial authority and still retain sovereignty.

A second edition, with minor corrections by the author, was issued in 1939 by Barnes and Noble, Inc. in cooperation with the Facsimile Library, Inc. and under the editorial direction of Alec J. Hammerslough, founder and president of the latter organization.

The volume remained in continuous demand among students and scholars in the fields of American history and political science. Copies of the second edition became scarce, highly prized, and difficult to obtain. Consequently, this third edition has been made available, incorporating numerous emendations which the late author had prepared or approved and had authorized Mr. Hammerslough to make. Publication of the new edition was facilitated by the cooperation of the late author's son, Thomas R. Adams, librarian of the John Carter Brown Library of Providence, Rhode Island, for whose constructive suggestions and careful examination of the revisions the publisher is most grateful. In all other respects the text has been preserved intact as it appeared in the second edition. An Introductory Note and a Commentary, both written by Professor Merrill Jensen, of the University of Wisconsin, have been included in order to bring the discussion up to date in the light of recent historical research.

The publisher is also indebted to Professor Samuel Eliot Morison, distinguished historian of Harvard University, for his encouragement and advice. It was Dr. Morison who, in 1922, wrote in the *English Historical Review* concerning the first edition of this work: "It is an able and well-written piece of work. . . . Some of the chapters in themselves are enlightening essays." Dr. Morison's evaluation has been confirmed during the intervening decades, for the volume has since become an indispensable reference in historical literature of the American Revolution.

CONTENTS

A NOTE TO THE READER

—by Merrill Jensen

AMERICAN POLITICAL theorists between 1763 and 1776 did far more than debate the theoretical questions arising from their relationship to the British Empire. They also dealt with fundamental problems as old as those that troubled the citizens of the Greek city–states in antiquity, and as new as those which concern the whole world in the middle of the twentieth century. The questions of the relationship of local to central governments, of the nature of law and written constitutions, and of the role of democracy in political society, were problems then and are problems now.

The argument over the division of power between local and central governments resulted in two quite different national constitutions in the United States between 1776 and 1787, but the adoption of the Constitution of 1787 did not settle the issue of sovereignty, nor have innumerable laws and Supreme Court decisions from 1787 to the present been able to do so. It was once said that the Civil War had finally established national supremacy over the states; yet the mid–twentieth century has seen the revival of a "States rights" feeling that threatens to become as violent over the issue of segregation in the schools of the nation as it was over the issue of slavery in the mid–nineteenth century. The division of power between central and local authority continues to agitate the world as a whole in the work of the United Nations organization today, as it did earlier in the century in that of the League of Nations.

The Americans began the fight against "colonialism" and thus set an example for other colonial peoples that has been followed

1

ever since. The Spanish–American colonists won their independence early in the nineteenth century. During the twentieth century India has won her independence, and the new republic of Indonesia has been erected upon the ruins of the Dutch Empire in the Far East. Today the French colonies in Africa are carrying on a relentless struggle for their freedom.

The American Revolution provided two other political concepts which have been widely put into practice in the modern world: these are the idea of democracy and the idea of a written constitution. Ever since 1776, revolutionists have followed the American example. The French, the Spanish–American, and the Russian revolutionists, among others, have adopted written constitutions and have proclaimed their ideals in these and other documents. Japan, with a history stretching back through thousands of years, was given her first written constitution by her conquerors in 1945, and is now trying to work within its bounds.

For such reasons it is easy to see why people have sought lessons and guidance from the experience of the American Revolution, as Randolph G. Adams does in this book. Unlike, him, however, many would–be "teachers" of the peoples of the world, arguing from the basis of American experience, are all too often ignorant of the complexities of the very experience they try to expound, and hence their lessons have little utility for anyone, even Americans. Often, moreover, such "teachers" are disappointed by the apparent unwillingness or inability of other peoples to learn from American experience, however eloquently expounded. A word of warning and a caution are therefore in order.

Most imitators of American experience, or those who seek to learn by it, or to teach others about it, when applying this experience to the problems of world organization, democracy, or written constitutions, seem to have little comprehension of the complexities of political societies. Above all, such people lack understanding of how deeply rooted in the history of any nation are its own political ideas and attitudes, many of which are more felt than verbalized, and hence difficult to reconcile with the experience and problems of other nations.

To understand the political theory and practice of the Americans of the eighteenth century, one must realize that the English colonies in America inherited a tradition of individual and legislative rights from England that was unknown or little regarded by other nations and their colonies at the time. Furthermore, these English colonies had had the experience of more than a century of virtual self-government before they won their independence. The Spanish colonies in America had neither this tradition nor this experience. Therefore, although they copied American constitutions and ideals on paper when they had won their independence, nothing in their history equipped them to understand the meaning of those ideals or forced them to adhere to it in times of adversity or crisis. From that day to this, many Spanish–American nations have had dictators in fact or in name without ever once abandoning the paper ideals which they copied from eighteenth–century Americans. Russia has a written constitution and universal suffrage, but few outside of Russia would call her actual government a democracy. Nothing in Russian experience, either before or after the Revolution of 1917, enables most Russians to understand American political traditions. The difference between the autocracy of the Tsars and that of the Communist Party is one of name rather than of essence. Likewise, the "democratic" constitution of Japan has been imposed on a society which had been feudal for untold generations and remains so today.

Nations can escape neither their history nor their inherent social and political attitudes. Political revolutions may disturb the surface of a political society, but any alteration of fundamental attitudes takes generations, not decades. Anglo–American political traditions are the result of centuries of evolution. The long span of years between Magna Charta in the thirteenth century and the Declaration of Independence in the eighteenth was necessary to achieve the latter. Perhaps as many more centuries are needed if those nations which have adopted some of the Anglo–American traditions and practices on paper are to make them an integral part of their own political life.

COMMENTARY

—by Merrill Jensen

$\mathbb{P}$*olitical Ideas of the American Revolution* was the first book ever
devoted solely to the subject. In a sense it was a tract for the
times. Randolph G. Adams, like many others at the end of World
War I, was concerned with the problem of international organization as embodied in the League of Nations. He makes this clear
to begin with by asserting that first of all the book is a contribution
to international law, that secondly it is a chapter in British imperial
history, and that lastly it is a fragment of the history of the United
States. Many writers following World War I, in their search for
the "lessons" that history might "teach" concerning an international
organization, turned to the history of the United States after the
Revolution, with special emphasis upon the trials of the Confederation Period and the United States Constitution of 1787. But Adams'
approach was unique in that he turned to the theoretical debate
between the American colonies and Great Britain before 1776 in an
attempt to discover such "lessons." (In this sense the book is still
unique; the proponents of "Union Now" during and after World
War II have continued to appeal to the character of the American
Union formed in 1787 in their search for arguments, justifications,
and analogies to solve the problems of the relationship between a
central world organization and the constituent sovereign governments.) Adams, too, at the time he wrote, was concerned with the
British Commonwealth of Nations which was then working toward
that form which exists for the most part today.

Because of his particular interest, and hence his self—imposed
limitations, he offered a special interpretation of the political theories

5

before 1776. Furthermore, he assumed that there was an essential change in the nature of political thought after 1776, that the problem before this date was the relationship between the colonial and the British governments, and that the problem after 1776 was the creation of governments within the United States. Had he carried his study beyond 1776 he would have found that neither the history nor the political theory of the age can be so divided. In theory and in practice the problem was the same: it was the problem of the relationship between local governments and a central government. There was no basic difference between colonial legislatures debating with Parliament, and state legislatures debating with the Congress of the United States. Americans used the same ideas and arguments after 1776 that they had used before; there was merely a difference in context. Furthermore, most of the political ideas of the age were familiar to Americans at the beginning of it, political ideas which were deeply rooted in their colonial past and were a part of their heritage of political thought and feeling from the mother country, and, indeed, a part of the body of political thought that was an integral part of the history of Western civilization.

The purposes of this "Commentary" are, therefore, to point to the political thought which was a part of the American tradition when the disputes with Great Britain began in 1763, to indicate certain areas that are worthy of further study, and to give an account of some of the writing that has been done since the first publication of this book. Taken in conjunction with Adams' contribution, it may present a somewhat broader perspective on the problems of the political thought of the American Revolution before 1776.

THE ENGLISH HERITAGE

The Americans who debated the nature and foundation of their rights and privileges with the mother country after 1763 were for the most part not dealing with new ideas. What they were doing was reformulating and reiterating ideas which had been a part of their English heritage, and to which they had appealed over and over in the course of a century and a half of experience as colonists in the New World. Whether those ideas concerned the theoretical foundations of government, the rights of legislatures and legislators, the rights of individuals, or questions of representation and taxation, they had been known and used in one way or another throughout the course of American colonial political history. Onʲˇ

the context in which those theories were used, and the intensity with which they were stated, were new in the years between 1763 and 1776. In fact, many of the basic patterns of political thought in the eighteenth century had been well established during the course of the seventeenth century.

The first English colonists in America brought with them political theories which were derived in part from the constitutional and political history of England. The first colonies were founded at a time when the great debate between Crown and Parliament was beginning in England: the debate over the distribution of power between the executive and legislative branches of government. The American colonists on the whole supported the claims of Parliament as opposed to the Crown. And as their own legislatures developed in the seventeenth century, they consciously modeled themselves on the House of Commons, and used theories of parliamentary rights in their struggles with the governors and the proprietors of colonies. They insisted upon freedom of elections, freedom from arrest during sessions, freedom of speech in debate, and the right to petition for redress of grievances. They likewise argued that as elected representatives of the voters, they should control all taxation and the expenditure of money raised by taxation. There were many difficult battles in the colonies between tiny legislatures and royal and proprietary governors, but, on the whole, the legislatures won out. By 1763 every colonial legislature regarded itself as a miniature House of Commons, and its members were as jealous of their rights and privileges as any British member of Parliament.

A second heritage of the American colonists from England was that collection of ideas concerning the rights of individuals which were summed up in the phrase "the rights of Englishmen." From the beginning the colonists claimed those rights and the colonial charters guaranteed them. The early charters declared that children born in the colonies, or on the high seas going to or coming from the colonies, "shall have and enjoy all the liberties and immunities of free and natural subjects . . . to all intents, constructions, and purposes whatsoever, as if they and every of them were born within the realm of England."[1]

---

[1] From the Massachusetts Bay Company Charter of 1629 in Merrill Jensen, ed., *English Historical Documents*, IX (*American Colonial Documents to 1776*, London and New York, 1955), 81–82. (Hereafter cited as EHD, IX.) In this and other quotations from contemporary sources, spelling, capitalization, and punctuation are modernized.

The American colonists knew what the guarantee meant and they appealed to it throughout their history, and with great fervor after 1763. They therefore insisted on the right of petition as individuals (and for the redress of grievances) either to the king or to his representative, the royal governor of a colony. They insisted that they should be free from arrest and imprisonment except upon specific charges and by due process of law. They claimed the right to trial by a jury made up of one's peers residing in one's own community. They claimed exemption from all taxation except by action of their elected representatives in their colonial legislatures. Such were the "rights of Englishmen" claimed in every American colony, whether it was a royal colony like Virginia, a corporation colony like Rhode Island, or a proprietary colony like Maryland.

The rights of colonial legislatures and legislators and of individuals as colonists and Englishmen were thus firmly fixed in American minds long before the crucial debate began with the mother country in the years after 1763. Such ideas had been an integral part of the colonists' English heritage, and they were to remain an enduring part of the American political tradition in the years after independence. The bills of rights in the first state constitutions and the Bill of Rights attached to the United States Constitution of 1787 were part and parcel of English constitutional experience and political thought which can be traced back as far as Magna Charta in the thirteenth century.[2]

TAXATION AND REPRESENTATION, 1763–1776

The immediate occasion for the theoretical debate after 1763 was the attempt of Parliament, for the first time in colonial history, to raise money by direct parliamentary taxation. In the course of a century during which Parliament had passed laws regulating the trade of the whole British Empire, certain duties had been imposed on the shipment of products into and out of the colonies. Although small sums had been collected, it was recognized that the purpose was regulation and not revenue. But in the Revenue Act ("Sugar Act") of 1764, Parliament frankly proposed to use regulatory duties

[2] For an excellent account of the colonial heritage from England see Charles F. Mullett, *Fundamental Law and the American Revolution, 1760–1776* (New York, 1933), Chapter 2, "English and Colonial Sources of Fundamental Law."

for the purpose of raising revenue in the colonies. Although the purpose was new, the method was old, and the colonists did not quite face the principle it raised. But the passage of the Stamp Act in 1765 presented the issue of principle with utter clarity. The Stamp Act ran counter to a tradition dating back to the first legislature founded in America: the House of Burgesses in Virginia.

That legislature, which met for the first time in the summer of 1619, had been called together by a business corporation, the Virginia Company. All the colonists in Virginia were considered members of the company, with the purpose of giving them a share in the management of their own affairs. Despite its origin, the first House of Burgesses consciously modeled itself on the House of Commons. It elected a speaker, questioned the qualifications of delegates, and passed laws, all in the best parliamentary tradition. Five years later, knowing that the Virginia Company would soon lose control of the colony, the Assembly made its wishes felt. In a petition to the Privy Council the members spoke of how their "slavery" had been converted into "freedom" and of how they were now "cherished under a just and moderate government. . . ." They requested that any future governor sent by the king should not be given absolute authority but should be restrained by the "consent" of the Council. "But above all we humbly entreat . . . that we may retain the liberty of our General Assembly, than which nothing can more conduce to our satisfaction or the public utility."[3] At the same time the Assembly passed an act stating that "the governor shall not lay any taxes or impositions upon the colony, their lands or commodities, other than by the authority of the General Assembly, to be levied and employed as the said Assembly shall appoint."[4] Thus in two short statements in 1624, the first legislature in America claimed in essence what the colonial legislatures were to insist upon in thousands of words after 1763. Only the "enemy" was different; it had become Parliament, and "liberty" had become "right."

As other colonial legislatures were established during the seventeenth century they, too, claimed the sole power of raising taxes, and they cited the record of English experience in support of their

---

[3] *Journals of the House of Burgesses of Virginia, 1619–1658/59* (Richmond, 1915), 26–27.

[4] W. W. Hening, *The Statutes at Large . . . of Virginia. . . .*, I (New York, 1823), 124. This act was passed repeatedly and later the Council was included with the governor in the prohibition. See ibid., I, 171, 196, 244.

claims. When James II replaced the New England legislatures with the Dominion of New England, ruled over by a royal governor and council who proceeded to levy taxes, there was bitter protest. Englishmen, said the people of Massachusetts, cannot be taxed except by their own consent given through their elected representatives. Men like the Reverend John Wise of Ipswich were jailed for telling the people not to pay taxes levied by appointed officials, and in the course of the struggle New Englanders appealed to English history all the way back to Magna Charta to justify their refusal to pay "unconstitutional" taxes. The Dominion of New England ended when James II was driven from the throne in the Revolution of 1688–1689 in England, and the colonial legislatures were restored.[5]

The final triumph of Parliament over the Crown in the Revolution settlement of 1689 was regarded by Americans as a victory for the principle of legislative supremacy, but for the supremacy of their own legislatures, not that of Parliament, over the colonies. Where taxation was concerned, it mattered not whether the legislature was an old one as in Massachusetts, or a new one as in New York. New York had never had a legislature under the Dutch, and after its conquest by the English in 1664, it was ruled as a conquered province by the Duke of York. When the Duke finally authorized the meeting of a legislature in 1683, it at once prepared a "Charter of Liberties and Privileges." This was as complete a statement of the English heritage of the rights of legislatures and of individuals as anything proclaimed after 1763. On the issue of taxation, the "charter" declared that "no aid, tax, tallage, assessment, custom, loan, benevolence, or imposition whatsoever shall be laid, assessed, imposed, or levied on any of his Majesty's subjects within this province or their estates, upon any manner of color or pretence, but by the act and consent of the governor, council, and representatives of the people in General Assembly met and assembled."[6]

The Assembly of Maryland was as vigorous as any other in the colonies despite the disadvantage it had. The charter gave the pro-

[5] Viola M. Barnes, *The Dominion of New England* (New Haven, 1923) is a full account of this experiment in British colonial administration.

[6] 30 Oct. 1683. Reprinted in EHD, IX, 229–30. The charter was vetoed by the Duke of York when he became King James II in 1685. When the New York Assembly was at last permanently established in 1691, it repassed the "charter" with only minor changes. This too was vetoed but by the middle of the eighteenth century the New York Assembly had in practice gained nearly every "right" and "privilege" it claimed in 1683.

priètor almost dictatorial powers, the only limitation on him being the requirement that he call the people together to assent to his laws. From the beginning in the 1630's the Maryland Assembly claimed all the prerogatives of the House of Commons, and particularly the right to levy all taxes. In the 1730's in the course of a bitter fight against the Proprietor's fixing of fees by proclamation, and of his taking certain fines and forfeitures for his own use, the Assembly told the governor that the Proprietor could not have greater prerogatives than the king. It appealed to the settlement of "the happy Revolution" in 1689 which made it illegal for the Crown to raise money except by grant of Parliament. The Assembly told the governor that it is "the peculiar right of his Majesty's subjects not to be liable to any tax or imposition but what is laid on them by laws to which they themselves are a party. . . ." When the governor tried to argue, the Assembly told him that "the people of this province are the subjects of Great Britain and entitled to all the rights, privileges, and liberties of . . . their mother country . . . that the basis on which their privileges are principally founded is the right they have of not being subject to any payments, whether they be taxes, duties, imposts, fees or any other denomination whatsoever, but what shall be raised, settled, and appointed by the laws to which by themselves or their substitutes, they give their consent, is a matter we conceive, can admit of no contradiction."[7]

When Americans objected to parliamentary taxation after 1763, they were thus using long–established patterns of theory to oppose a new threat to the claims of colonial legislatures. One of the first protests came from the Boston Town Meeting in May, 1764, when it drafted instructions to the town's representatives in the colonial legislature. It told them that the proposed stamp act "annihilates our charter right to govern and tax ourselves. It strikes at our British privileges which, as we have never forfeited them, we hold in common with our fellow subjects who are natives of Britain. If taxes are laid upon us in any shape without ever having a legal representation where they are laid, are we not reduced from the character of free subjects to the miserable state of tributary slaves?"[8]

A few months later the Virginia House of Burgesses petitioned the House of Commons against the proposed stamp tax, declaring

[7] Proceedings of the Maryland Assembly, 21 May–5 June 1739 in *Archives of Maryland,* XL (Baltimore, 1921), 336, 367, 381, 392.
[8] EHD, IX, 666.

that "it is essential to British liberty that laws imposing taxes on the people ought not to be made without the consent of representatives chosen by themselves. . . . This privilege, inherent in the persons who discovered and settled these regions, could not be renounced or forfeited by their removal hither, . . . it was secured to them and their descendants, with all other rights and immunities of British subjects by a royal charter. . . ." Such being the case, the Burgesses confessed themselves unable to discern how they could be deprived of "that sacred birthright and most valuable inheritance by their fellow subjects, nor with what propriety they can be taxed or affected in their estates by the Parliament, wherein they are not, and indeed cannot, be constitutionally represented."[9]

In May, 1765, after the passage of the Stamp Act, the Virginia House of Burgesses passed the resolutions that set off the colonial revolt which effectively nullified a law of Parliament. The resolves asserted that the first settlers had brought with them all the rights and immunities of the people of Great Britain and that these had been transmitted to posterity; that by the royal charters given the colony they were entitled to all the privileges and immunities of people living in England; that taxation of the people by themselves or their representatives was "the distinguishing characteristic of British freedom, without which the ancient constitution cannot exist"; and that the people of Virginia had always had the right to govern themselves in matters of taxation and internal police and had never forfeited that right.

Two further resolves breathed complete defiance and, although not adopted, were soon in the newspapers for the American people to read. One of them declared that the Virginia legislature had the exclusive right to levy taxes and that the attempt to vest that right in any other body was "illegal, unconstitutional, and unjust, and has a manifest tendency to destroy British as well as American liberty." The other resolution said flatly that the people of Virginia did not have to obey any laws imposing taxes except those passed by the Virginia legislature.[10] Other legislatures were less strident than that of Virginia, but by the end of 1765 most of them had gone on record as claiming that the only constitutional taxes were those levied by the elected representatives of the people of the colonies.

[9] 18 Dec. 1764, EHD, IX, 669–70.
[10] 30 May 1765, EHD, IX, 671–72.

The Stamp Act Congress of October, 1765, was a rather conservative body but in its Declarations it summed up the prevalent theories concerning American rights to self–taxation. It was essential to the freedom of a people, and the undoubted right of all Englishmen, that no taxes should be imposed upon them without their consent, given personally or through their representatives. The people of the colonies were not and could not be represented in the House of Commons and no "taxes ever have been, or can be constitutionally imposed on them, but by their respective legislatures."[11]

By the end of 1765 the Americans had set forth their basic argument on the subject of taxation. There was some confusion for a short time on the question of whether or not the Americans could be or should be represented in Parliament, or whether they were "virtually" represented in that body. Much of the confusion on the American side was due to the contradictory pamphlets of James Otis. The first well–known pamphlet of the period was Otis' *The Rights of the British Colonies Asserted and Proved,* published in the summer of 1764. In it Otis admitted that Parliament had complete power over the colonies but he argued that Parliament did not have the right to tax the colonies unless Americans were represented in Parliament. Early in 1765, apparently frightened by possible charges of disloyalty, he withdrew even the claim to representation in Parliament. In two further pamphlets he declared that Parliament was the supreme power in the empire and that it had the right to "impose taxes on the colonies, internal and external, on land, as well as on trade." As for representation, he asserted that in effect the colonies were represented in Parliament.

He openly praised the official defense of the Grenville ministry prepared by Thomas Whately, one of George Grenville's spokesmen. This pamphlet took up the American argument that colonials could be taxed only by representatives of their own choosing, and insisted that the inhabitants of the colonies *were* represented in Parliament. It claimed that the Americans were in the same situation as nine–tenths of the people in Britain, since they, too, did not vote for representatives. The Americans and such Britons "are virtually represented in Parliament," for every member of it sits, not as a representative of his own constituents but "as one of that august

[11] "The Declarations of the Stamp Act Congress," 19 Oct. 1765, EHD, IX, 674–75.

assembly by which all the Commons of Great Britain are represented."[12]

It was soon clear that James Otis did not reflect American opinion, even in his own colony of Massachusetts. In October, 1765, the Massachusetts House of Representatives resolved that the people of Massachusetts "are not and never have been represented" in Parliament.[13] The Stamp Act Congress summed up prevailing American opinion when it declared that "the people of these colonies are not, and from their local circumstances, cannot be represented in the House of Commons in Great Britain."[14]

The idea of "virtual representation" got equally short shrift. Anonymous newspaper writers went to work to prove the idea false. The people of Anne Arundel County, Maryland, called it "fantastical and frivolous nonsense," and Daniel Dulany of Maryland, in one of the most widely read pamphlets of the period, effectively and finally disposed of the idea. While Dulany denied that Parliament had the right to tax the colonies, he made a distinction between the power of taxation and the power of legislation. Like several of the American legislatures and the Stamp Act Congress, he agreed that the American legislatures were subordinate to Parliament in such matters as the regulation of trade.[15]

William Pitt read Dulany's pamphlet and made much of its ideas in the great debate in the House of Commons on the Stamp Act in January, 1766. "Taxation," he said, "is no part of the governing or legislative power. The taxes are a voluntary gift and grant of the Commons alone. . . ." Parliament had no right to tax the colonies; only their own legislatures could do so. As for "virtual representation," it was "the most contemptible idea that ever entered into the

[12] *The Regulations Lately Made* . . . (London, 1765). Most of James Otis' pamphlets have been republished by Charles F. Mullett in *Some Political Writings of James Otis* (University of Missouri Studies, IV, nos. 3 & 4, Columbia, 1929). Ellen Brennan, "James Otis: Recreant and Patriot," *New England Quarterly,* XII (1939), 691–725, is a thorough study of Otis' wavering attitude in his pamphlets.

[13] *Boston Evening Post,* 4 Nov. 1765.

[14] EHD, IX, 674.

[15] For a discussion of "virtual representation" and of Dulany's pamphlet, *Considerations on the Propriety of Imposing Taxes in the British Colonies . . .,* see Edmund S. and Helen Morgan, *The Stamp Act Crisis: Prologue to Revolution* (Chapel Hill, 1953), Chapter vi. In this and other chapters will be found the most extended account of political theories during the Stamp Act crisis.

head of a man; it does not deserve serious refutation."[16] When Parliament passed the Declaratory Act in March, 1766, it dropped all idea of "virtual representation" as a basis for the assertion of power over the colonies. In fact, it is doubtful whether more than a few Englishmen ever considered it seriously. Parliament operated on the same assumption that Governor Bernard of Massachusetts had made the year before. As he reviewed the argument over "virtual representation" he came to the conclusion that the right of Parliament to make laws for the colonies was founded on "its being the supreme imperial legislature, to which all members of the empire, whether represented or not, are subject in all matters and things and in manner and form as shall be judged most convenient for the whole."[17]

A second area of theoretical confusion relates to the question of "internal" and "external" taxes. In January, 1767, when Charles Townshend promised the House of Commons that he knew how to raise revenue in America, he declared that the distinction between internal and external taxes was ridiculous in the opinion of everyone except the Americans.[18] William Pitt had not thought it ridiculous in January, 1766, when he insisted that Parliament had no power to levy internal taxes within the colonies. When George Grenville said that he could not understand the difference, Pitt told him bluntly that internal taxes were for the purpose of raising revenue and that external taxes were for the purpose of regulating trade.[19] The Townshend Revenue Act did lay "external" taxes in the form of import duties on certain manufactured goods entering colonial ports, and Americans at once objected. Ever since then most writers have held to the view that the Americans shifted the theoretical foundations of their opposition between 1765 and 1767. It has been said that they objected to "internal" taxes in 1765 while admitting the right of Parliament to regulate trade, and hence the right of levying "external" taxes, only to deny Parliament that right after 1767. Randolph G. Adams in the present volume states the conven-

---

[16] Hansard, *Parliamentary History*, XVI, 99.

[17] To Lord Barrington, 23 Nov. 1765, Edward Channing and A. C. Coolidge, eds., *The Barrington—Bernard Correspondence* (Cambridge, 1912), 97.

[18] Lord Shelburne to William Pitt, 1 Feb. 1767, in W. S. Taylor and J. H. Pringle, eds., *The Correspondence of William Pitt. . . .* (4 vols., London, 1838–1840), III, 184. See also the letter quoted by Adams, p. 96 of the present volume.

[19] Hansard, *Parliamentary History*, XVI, 106.

tional view in his discussion of the three "stages" of the taxation controversy.[20]

Recently this idea has been rejected. Instead, it is asserted that the colonies did not shift their grounds but consistently denied the power of Parliament to lay any taxes for revenue, whether "internal" or "external."[21] There is something to be said for this new interpretation, but it needs qualification. It is clear of course that Americans did not want to pay any parliamentary taxes, whatever the form. But it is also clear, if one looks at theoretical statements from the point of view of the political history of the period, that not all Americans were in official agreement on the subject. The fact is that statements expounding political theories were as often the reflection of local politics as they were of the basic convictions to which men adhered.

Americans between 1764 and 1766 did talk about "internal" and "external" taxes, and on the whole they meant what William Pitt meant in 1766 and Charles Townshend meant in 1767. Some legislatures made the distinction and some did not. Thus the New York Assembly in October, 1764, made a sweeping statement. It was the "natural right of mankind" to be free from all taxes except those levied by themselves or their representatives. Parliament had the right to regulate trade and to levy duties in the course of such regulation. But the duties on trade in the Revenue Act of 1764 were for the purpose of raising revenue. "All impositions," the Assembly stated, "whether they be internal taxes, or duties paid, for what we consume, equally diminish the estates upon which they are charged" and "the whole wealth of a country may be as effectually drawn off, by the exaction of duties, as by any other tax upon their estates."[22] The great landlords who dominated the New York Assembly feared that Parliament would lay a tax on land in the colonies. Many of their vast holdings had been acquired illegally and they had for the most part avoided the payment of local taxes and royal quitrents for them. Hence, they adopted the broadest theoretical statement possible to avoid the danger which seemed to threaten them. Later,

[20] See below, p. 91.

[21] Edmund S. Morgan, "Colonial Ideas of Parliamentary Power, 1764–1766," *William and Mary Quarterly,* 3rd ser., V (1948), 311–41. Curtis Nettels upholds the orthodox view and is answered by Morgan, ibid., VI (1949), 162–70.

[22] Edmund S. Morgan, ed., *The New York Declaration of 1764* (Old South Leaflets, no. 224, Boston, 1948).

however, when the ordinary citizenry of New York began to take "natural rights" seriously and to use it to justify demands of their own, the landlord–dominated Assembly viewed the idea with horror.

While the New York Assembly was talking of "natural rights," the Massachusetts legislature was also preparing a petition against the Revenue Act of 1764. But in Massachusetts the political situation was different, and consequently the theoretical statement was also different. The popular leaders of the town of Boston wanted to base theoretical opposition to the Act of 1764 on the ground of the "right" of the people to vote their own taxes, whatever the kind. They persuaded the House of Representatives to adopt a petition based on "right." The upper house, the Council, was dominated by Thomas Hutchinson, who was convinced that Parliament had the "right" to levy taxes upon the colonies. He was able to shape the wording of the petition so that any mention of "right" was entirely omitted. Instead, the Massachusetts petition against the Revenue Act of 1764 and the proposed Stamp Act was based entirely on "privileges" granted to the colonies, and it argued against British measures on purely economic grounds. In Massachusetts, therefore, the official theoretical statement was entirely due to the balance of political power. As power shifted into the hands of the popular leaders, theoretical statements also shifted.

Political pamphleteers, too, changed their arguments with changing times, though none so conspicuously as James Otis. In 1764, in *The Rights of the British Colonies,* he said that "there is no foundation for the distinction some make in England between an internal and an external tax on the colonies." By the first is meant a tax on land and the things on it, by the latter a tax on trade. If Parliament can tax trade, as in the Revenue Act of 1764, then it can lay a stamp tax and a tax on American lands.[23] But in 1765, in his *A Vindication of the British Colonies,* he asserted that "the Parliament of Great Britain has a just and equitable right, power, and authority, to impose taxes on the colonies, internal and external, on lands, as well as on trade. This is involved in the idea of a supreme legislative, or sovereign power of a state." Of course, such taxes may not be expedient or equitable, nor reasonable, unless Parliament allows actual representation, but Parliament does have the power.[24]

[23] Mullett, *Some Political Writings of James Otis,* 75–76. The original text, which referred to taxes on trade as "internal" and taxes on land as "external," is obviously confused.

[24] Ibid., 132–33, 139, 141.

What Americans objected to was taxes in any form levied by any body except their own legislatures. Whether they mentioned words like "external" and "internal" is largely beside the point. In 1767 Townshend took advantage of the American admission that Parliament had the right to regulate trade and to levy duties for that purpose, but he went beyond the regulation of trade because he proposed to raise money to be used for political purposes in the colonies. The New York legislature had pointed out the answer in 1764 when it said that any act to raise revenue, whatever its guise, was a tax measure, and hence could be rightfully passed only by the elected representatives of the people, that is, by the colonial legislatures.

John Dickinson met the new challenge in his *Letters from a Farmer in Pennsylvania*. He admitted freely the right of Parliament to regulate trade but denied it the right to raise money in the form of duties on trade. In the Townshend Revenue Act "we may observe an authority expressly claimed to impose duties on these colonies; not for the regulation of trade; not for the preservation or promotion of a mutually beneficial intercourse between the several constituent parts of the Empire, heretofore the *sole objects* of parliamentary institutions; *but for the single purpose of levying money upon us.* . . . This I call an innovation; and a most dangerous innovation." It would make no difference if the money were collected by means of export duties in Britain rather than as import duties in the colonies. He scoffed at those who argued that the Stamp Tax was wrong because it was an "internal" tax and who argued that Americans must submit to the Townshend Act because it was an "external" tax. "To this I answer with a total denial of the power of Parliament to lay upon these colonies any tax whatever. . . . To the word 'tax' I annex that meaning which the constitution and history of England require to be annexed to it: that it is, an imposition on the subject for the sole purpose of levying money. . . . It is true that impositions for raising a revenue, may hereafter be called regulations of trade, but names will not change the nature of things." If we are not watchful, "a new servitude may be slipped upon us under the sanction of usual and respectable terms."[25]

John Dickinson's answer won wide acclaim among Americans

[25] R. T. H. Halsey, ed., *Letters from a Farmer in Pennsylvania, to the Inhabitants of the British Colonies* (New York, 1903), Letters II, IV, VI, pp. 18–19, 37, 62.

and abolished any doubt on either side of the Atlantic as to dominant opinion in America. Britain abandoned the Townshend Revenue Act in 1770, keeping only the tax on tea to maintain the principle of "right." Most Americans nullified it in practice by abandoning the use of tea or smuggling it from other countries.

THE CROWN, PARLIAMENT, AND THE COLONIAL GOVERNMENTS

Although it was direct parliamentary taxation of the colonies after 1763 that began the final dispute between Britain and the American colonies, the overriding constitutional issue of the age was the precise status of the colonial governments within the British Empire, and ultimately, the relationship between the British legislature and the colonial legislatures. The latter had not always been the case. At the beginning of the seventeenth century the colonies were the undisputed domain of the Crown. In theory and fact English America belonged to the monarch and no colony could exist legally without a royal charter, or in the course of time without its equivalent in the form of a commission to a royal governor. The charters and commissions were in every sense written constitutions outlining the form of government and granting political and economic rights and privileges. The colonial governments thus derived their constitutional authority by grant from a higher authority, the Crown, which delegated a part of its power to a subordinate political state.

One central issue throughout the colonial period was whether or not the Crown could take away that which had once been given. In time, the Americans insisted that their governments were theirs as a matter of "right," while the British insisted that they were a grant of "privileges" which, in theory at least, could be revoked at any time. This had been done in certain cases during the seventeenth century. Through court action the Crown brought about the revocation of the Virginia Company charter in 1624 and of the Massachusetts Bay Company charter in 1684, and thus converted those two colonies into royal colonies ruled directly by the Crown. During the quarter century after 1689 Parliament made several attempts to abolish all colonial charters by an act of Parliament, but the attempts failed. However, most of the chartered colonies had been converted into royal colonies by 1763. In each royal colony the monarch was head of the government exercising his power through a governor appointed by him. In the course of disputes with such royal governors, it made no difference whether a colony had a charter or not; the colonists appealed to "charter rights" and to the "rights of Englishmen" in defense of their own claims to authority and in denial of the governor's claims as represented in his commission and instructions from the King.

The same pattern is to be found in the remaining proprietary colonies, Maryland, Pennsylvania, and Delaware, where the proprietor appointed the governor, and even in Connecticut and Rhode Island, which retained their status as self–governing republics throughout the colonial period and elected their own governors. The fact is that virtually every colonial assembly was thoroughly familiar with the constitutional methods and political theories which the House of Commons had used in its battles against the prerogatives of the Crown during the seventeenth century. They knew too that the Revolution of 1688–1689 had marked the final triumph of Parliament over the Crown and that never thereafter could the monarch act alone, particularly in matters of taxation and the expenditure of money. The colonial legislatures fought their governors, whether royal or proprietary, as vigorously as Parliament had fought the Crown. They were thoroughly familiar with the "constitutional blackmail" practiced by Parliament; namely, the acknowledgment of legislative rights and privileges by the Crown before voting taxes to operate the government. And they used the same methods with enormous effectiveness to gain control of most of the workings of colonial governments and to take over much of the power legally possessed by the governors. Because they voted the taxes to operate the colonial governments, the elective legislatures demanded control of the expenditure of the money they raised, and by the middle of the eighteenth century they had won as effective a victory in questions of taxation and expenditure as the House of Commons had in England. The governors, like the King in England, however wide their legal powers might be, could function only by submitting in large measure to their legislatures.

When Parliament after 1763 began interfering as never before in the affairs of America, the question was: did Parliament have the same power over the King's domain in America that it won over the King's domain in Great Britain as a result of the Revolution of 1688–1689? Parliament insisted that it had. As early as 1649 the Commonwealth Parliament asserted its supreme authority over the colonies, and in 1689 William and Mary swore when they were crowned that they would govern not only England but the overseas dominions according to the laws of Parliament. From 1660 onward Parliament had legislated for the colonies. In the Acts of Trade and Navigation it shaped the patterns of their trade as well as those of the commerce of England. During the first half of the eighteenth century Parliament adopted laws to restrict colonial manufactures. In 1751 it went so far as to forbid the issue of legal tender paper money by the New England colonies. In such laws, and many others, Parliament had been regulating and shaping the economic life of the colonies for a century before the final crisis began.

Increasingly after 1763 Americans were to insist that such legislation was illegal and unconstitutional and eventually to assert that Parliament was only the Parliament of Great Britain, not of the colonies, that each colonial legislature within its own territorial domain was equal to Parliament. This idea, like most of the others involved here, had roots running back to the seventeenth century and particularly to New England, where Massachusetts, Connecticut, and Rhode Island had started out as self–governing corporations. The people of Connecticut and Rhode Island remained inconspicuous, but the Puritan fathers of Massachusetts looked upon themselves as the rulers of what amounted to an independent republic and they openly ignored English efforts at control after the restoration of Charles II in 1660. Among other things, they refused to obey the first three Acts of Trade and Navigation until the pressure became too great. Then in 1677, the General Court of Massachusetts adopted the acts by laws of its own. The next year the legislature blandly informed English authorities that as far as the Navigation Acts were concerned, "we humbly conceive, according to the usual sayings of the learned in the law, that the laws of England are bounded within the four seas and do not reach America. The subjects of His Majesty here being not represented in Parliament, so we have not looked on ourselves to be impeded in our trade by them. . . ." However, the legislature went on, when it learned that the King wanted the laws obeyed by Massachusetts, "which could not be done without invading the liberties and properties of the subject until the General Court made provision therein by a law," the legislature had passed such legislation.[26]

<hr>

[26] N. B. Shurtleff, ed., *Records of the Governor and Company of the Massachusetts Bay*, V (Boston, 1854), 200.

The legislatures in the 1760's did not alter the basic content of the ideas expressed in the 1670's by Massachusetts; in fact, they did not go so far. Instead they admitted that they were subordinate to Parliament. The first of the Declarations of the Stamp Act Congress summed it up when it said that the Americans "owe the same allegiance to the Crown of Great Britain, that is owing from his subjects born within the realm, and all due subordination to that august body, the Parliament of Great Britain."[27] In 1764 and 1765, Americans, at least officially, made a distinction between the power of taxation and the power of legislation. Taxes were the free gift of a people and could be granted only by their own representatives. Parliament therefore could not levy taxes upon Americans, for they were not and could not be represented there. The regulation of trade necessarily belonged to Parliament because there had to be a superintending power for the whole empire.

This was the official position taken by legislatures, by many of the pamphleteers, and by the Stamp Act Congress. Legislative bodies, however, lagged behind popular opinion and they did so because virtually every colonial assembly contained men who like Thomas Hutchinson believed in the supremacy of Parliament over the colonies, or men who believed that chaos would ensue if each colonial legislature were left unchecked by a superior legislative authority. By 1765, however, there was a far more radical view in existence which found expression in anonymous writings in the colonial newspapers and in the resolutions of town meetings and of the Sons of Liberty. This view was summed up during the Stamp Act crisis by Governor Francis Bernard of Massachusetts. The basic cause of trouble, he wrote, was that the precise nature of the constitutional relationship between Britain and the colonies had never been defined. "Hence it is that ideas of that relation are formed in Britain and America so very repugnant and contradictory to each other. In Britain the American governments are considered as corporations empowered to make by-laws, existing only during the pleasure of Parliament, who hath never yet done anything to confirm their establishment, and hath at any time a power to dissolve them. In America they claim (I mean in the public papers) to be perfect states, no otherwise dependent upon Great Britain than by having the same King; which having complete legislatures within them-

27 EHD. IX. 674

selves, are no ways subject to that of Great Britain; which in such instances as it has heretofore exercised a legislative power over them, has usurped it. In a difference so very wide who shall determine? The Parliament of Great Britain? No, say the Americans (I mean the violent and foolish of them); that would be to make them judges in their own cause. Who then? The King? He is bound by charters and constitutions equal to charters, and cannot decree against his own grants. . . . there is no superior tribunal to determine upon the rights and privileges of the American colonies."[28]

It was clear by the end of 1765 that the more radical Americans were setting forth what Adams calls a "Commonwealth" conception of co-equal legislatures within the Empire, with the King as the sole bond among them. Seven years later, Thomas Hutchinson supported Bernard's analysis of popular opinion in America when he wrote that the opinion was broached at the time of the Stamp Act and "ever since cultivated until it is become general, that the people of the colonies are subject to no authority but their own legislatures and that acts of the Parliament of Great Britain, which is every day in print, termed a foreign state, are not obligatory."[29]

In the summer of 1774 Thomas Jefferson summed up the popular opinion which had been growing ever since the Stamp Act, although seldom if ever expressed by colonial legislatures, in a series of resolutions adopted by the freeholders of Albemarle County, Virginia. The first resolution said "that the inhabitants of the several states of British America are subject to the laws which they adopted at their first settlement, and to such others as have been since made by their respective legislatures, duly constituted and appointed with their own consent; that no other legislature whatever may rightfully exercise authority over them, and that these privileges they hold as the common rights of mankind, confirmed by the political constitutions they have respectively assumed, and also by several charters of compact from the Crown."[30] This statement was separated two years in time from Jefferson's Declaration of Independence; in idea it was contemporaneous.

[28] To Lord Barrington, 23 Nov. 1765, *Barrington–Bernard Correspondence*, 96.

[29] To Lord Dartmouth, 23 Oct. 1772, British Public Record Office, C. O. 5/761.

[30] Julian P. Boyd, ed., *The Papers of Thomas Jefferson*, 1 (Princeton, 1950), 117.

The British answer to such ideas had been given in 1766 in the Declaratory Act and the British never wavered in theory thereafter, however much they wavered in practice. The act asserted that the "colonies and plantations in America have been, are, and of right ought to be, subordinate unto, and dependent upon the imperial Crown and Parliament of Great Britain. . ." and that they "had, hath, and of right ought to have, full power and authority to make laws and statutes of sufficient force and validity to bind the colonies and people of America . . . in all cases whatsoever." The act concluded with a futile gesture declaring all the proceedings and resolutions of colonial legislatures denying the authority of Parliament to be "utterly null and void to all intents and purposes whatsoever."[31] The next year Parliament spelled out theory in practical terms when it passed an act suspending the New York Assembly until it should agree to abide by Parliament's Quartering Act of 1765.[32] In 1774, in the Massachusetts Government Act, Parliament took the final step in intervention within a colony when it altered the terms of the royal charter of 1691.[33] In 1774, Lord Dartmouth, secretary of state for America, went far beyond the Declaratory Act when he wrote that "the supreme legislature of the whole British Empire has laid a duty (no matter for the present whether or not it has the right to do so, it is sufficient that we conceive it has). . . ." If Americans say they will not submit to the laws of Parliament, "they say in effect that they will no longer be a part of the British Empire. . . ."[34] By 1774 the American and British positions on the power of Parliament were irreconcilable. The British by 1774, as Dartmouth showed, had stopped arguing about "right": they proposed to use armed force to maintain their conception of sovereignty over the colonies. The Americans met force with force and settled the issue by winning their independence.

The debate over the constitutionality of parliamentary legislation for the colonies has continued into the twentieth century. In the 1920's Charles H. McIlwain re–examined the dispute from the point of view of a constitutional historian and came to the conclusion that the American colonists were right in their contention

---

[31] EHD, IX, 697–98.
[32] EHD, IX, 705–6.
[33] EHD, IX, 781–83.
[34] To Joseph Reed, 11 July 1774, William B. Reed, *Life and Correspondence of Joseph Reed* (2 vols., Philadelphia, 1847), I, 72–74.

that Parliament had no authority outside the realm of Great Britain. He argued that the claim of Parliament to imperial dominion was an act of usurpation beginning with the act establishing the Commonwealth by the Long Parliament in May, 1649.[35] On the other side, Robert L. Schuyler insisted that the British position between 1763 and 1776 was right and that Parliament had always legislated constitutionally for all the King's dominions. In fact, there was no King without Parliament, and no Parliament without the King.[36]

THE DEMOCRATIC TRADITION IN POLITICAL THOUGHT

The Declaration of Independence appealed to "the laws of nature and of Nature's God" and proclaimed that "all men are created equal, that they are endowed by their Creator with certain unalienable rights, that among these are life, liberty, and the pursuit of happiness. That to secure these rights, governments are instituted among men, deriving their just powers from the consent of the governed, that whenever any form of government becomes destructive of these ends, it is the right of the people to alter or to abolish it. . . ." In thus appealing and proclaiming, and in abandoning their former appeals to charter rights, to the British constitution, and even to the "rights of Englishmen," the Americans turned to another political tradition that was as old as their history.

Forty–nine years after he drafted the Declaration of Independence, Jefferson remembered that when Americans were forced to take up arms, "an appeal to the tribunal of the world was deemed proper for our justification. This was the object of the Declaration of Independence." Its purpose was "not to find out new principles, or new arguments, never before thought of, not merely to say things which had never been said before; but to place before mankind the common sense of the subject, in terms so plain and firm as to command their assent. . . . Neither aiming at originality of principle or sentiments, nor yet copied from any particular and previous writing, it was intended to be an expression of the American mind. . . . All its authority rests then on the harmonizing sentiments of the day, whether expressed in conversation, in letters, printed

[35] *The American Revolution: A Constitutional Interpretation* (New York, 1923).

[36] *Parliament and the British Empire* (New York, 1929). Chapter 1.

essays, or in the elementary books of public rights, as Aristotle, Cicero, Locke, Sidney, etc."[37]

The appeal to natural law, to the law of nature, and to the sovereignty of the people was as old as the writings of the ancient Greeks and as fresh as the writing in American newspapers in 1776. As Jefferson said, writers from Aristotle to Locke were "elementary books" for Americans of the eighteenth century.[38] Americans, too, were familiar with the ancient word "democracy" and they knew what it meant. The first English colonists had differed sharply as to whether or not democracy was a fit form of government for mankind. Some of them, like the Puritan leaders in Massachusetts, were bitterly opposed to it. The Reverend John Cotton said in 1636 that "Democracy I do not conceive that ever God did ordain as a fit government either for church or commonwealth. If the people be governors, who shall be governed?" John Winthrop, the greatest leader of the colony, said that "where the chief ordinary and administration [of government] is in the people, there is a democracy," and that "democracy is among most civil nations accounted the meanest and worst of all forms of government . . . and histories do record that it hath been always of least continuance and fullest of troubles."[39]

The Puritans were religious dissenters, but there were far more radical groups of English dissenters who came to the colonies. These were people who believed that state churches were false churches, who believed that the only true churches were voluntary associations of men who thought alike, and who usually organized a church by signing a compact or covenant with one another. It did not take such people long to transfer their conception of a true church to the political sphere and to conclude that a valid government could be created by a group of people without asking any higher authority. This is what the Plymouth settlers did when they drew up the Mayflower Compact. So, too, did the settlers of Connecticut when they drafted the Fundamental Orders of 1639, and the various Rhode Island towns when they formed their governments in the

[37] Jefferson to Henry Lee, 8 May 1825, P. L. Ford, ed., *The Writings of Thomas Jefferson* (10 vols., New York, 1892–1899), X, 343.

[38] See Mullett, *Fundamental Law and the American Revolution,* Chapters 1 and 2, and B. F. Wright, *American Interpretations of Natural Law* (Cambridge, 1931).

[39] EHD, IX, 167. 169–70.

1630's and 1640's. The assumption that a group of people could create governments for themselves was contrary to both the law and the "constitution" as Englishmen understood it, but in distant America it was possible for small and inconspicuous groups of people to put the idea into practice.

Believers in the formation of government by means of compacts, ordinances, or constitutions adopted by the people of a community, did not always believe in democracy. Certainly the people of Plymouth did not, and it is doubtful that the people in Connecticut did. Their practice was democratic but their theory was not. However, it was only a short step from democratic practice to democratic theory, and this step was taken by the people of Rhode Island. In 1641, a meeting at Newport declared that "the government which this body politic doth attend unto in this island . . . is a democracy or popular government." When the several Rhode Island towns formed a confederation in 1647, they declared the government to be "democratical; that is to say, a government held by the free and voluntary consent of all, or the greater part of the free inhabitants."[40] Roger Williams, though primarily concerned with the separation of church and state, offered a philosophical basis for democracy in 1644. The civil power, he argued, may establish whatever form of civil government it pleases to maintain the civil peace of people so far as concerns their bodies and goods. While "civil government is an ordinance of God," he goes on to say that "the sovereign, original, and foundation of civil power lies in the people (whom they must needs mean by the civil power distinct from the government set up). And if so, that a people may erect and establish what form of government seems to them most meet for their civil condition. It is evident that such governments as are by them erected and established have no more power, nor for no longer time, than the civil power or people consenting and agreeing shall betrust them with. This is clear not only in reason, but in the experience of all commonweals where the people are not deprived of their natural freedom by the power of tyrants."[41]

In practice, of course, the American governments were based on royal charters and commissions, even in Connecticut and Rhode Island which received royal charters in the 1660's, but the ideas set

[40] EHD, IX, 168, 226.

[41] From *The Bloody Tenent, of Persecution, for Cause of Conscience* (1644) in EHD, IX, 174.

afloat during the early days of the colonies did not die out. Early in the eighteenth century the Reverend John Wise, who had been jailed for telling his people to refuse to pay taxes to the Dominion of New England in the 1680's, wrote two pamphlets in which such ideas were set forth in detail. Wise declared that "the original of civil power is the people"; that "when the subject of sovereign power is quite extinct, that power returns to the people again. And when they are free, they may set up what species of government they please"; that "Salus populi, or the happiness of the people is the end of its being, or main business to be attended and done." As for democracy, Wise declared it to be the oldest form of government and that it was created when a number of free people came together and entered into a covenant agreeing to unite, and then formed a second covenant by which "a popular form be actually established."[42]

Whatever Wise's personal convictions (and some doubt has been cast on his having been genuinely democratic) he nevertheless gave currency to ideas that had been heard in the past and were to have a remarkable resurgence after 1763. While colonial legislatures argued about charters and taxation, there was a growing statement and restatement of far broader political generalizations. Sometimes these came from anonymous writers in newspapers and pamphlets; sometimes they were expressed in town and county meetings. Anonymous writers and lesser bodies had either more courage or more conviction than the legislatures, and they appealed to ideas like "natural rights," "laws of nature," "laws of reason," and "higher law," to the "compact" idea of government, and to the idea that all government is based on the "consent" of the people.[43]

In complete contrast to the formal Declarations of the Stamp Act Congress were the resolutions of a town meeting at New London, Connecticut, December 10, 1765. The meeting resolved:

"1st. That every form of government rightfully founded, originates from the consent of the people.

"2d. That the boundaries set by the people in all constitutions are the only limits within which any officer can lawfully exercise authority.

[42] EHD, IX, 177–81. From *A Vindication of the Government of the New England Churches* (1717).

[43] See the discussion of the natural rights philosophy in Carl Becker, *The Declaration of Independence* (New York, 1922), Chapter 2.

"3d. That whenever those bounds are exceeded, the people have a right to reassume the exercise of that authority which by nature they had before they delegated it to individuals."

The people of New London then went on to state that any tax imposed on English subjects without their consent was "against the natural rights and bounds prescribed by the English constitution," that the Stamp Tax was such a tax, and that therefore it was the duty of every person in the colonies to oppose its execution. If they could get relief in no other way, they should "reassume their natural rights and the authority the laws of nature and of God have vested them with."[44] Here was the basic content of the Declaration of Independence ten years before it was written.

The notion of "voluntary compact" and "consent" was a constant theme of the more radical writers from 1765 on, and notably of Samuel Adams, whose various pen-names but thinly disguised his newspaper publications. He quoted authorities such as Locke to justify his contention that the original colonists "entered into a compact . . . with the king of England, and upon certain conditions, become his voluntary subjects, not his slaves." And they did not promise to be subject to the control of the parent state, nor could it be shown they were bound to obey the acts of Parliament. "The legislative of any commonwealth must be the supreme power. No body can have a power to make laws over a free people, but by their own consent, and by authority received from them. . . ." Samuel Adams made it clear that, so far as he was concerned, the people of Massachusetts had never given that authority to Parliament.[45]

As British officials and Americans read resolutions like those of New London in 1765 and the writings of Samuel Adams and other pamphleteers, the conviction naturally grew that some Americans were aiming at independence from 1765 onward. Legislatures of course denied that this was their aim, for they were in conspicuous positions and such ideas constituted treason. It is doubtful, too, that most legislators approved of the idea; and many of them did not approve until almost literally forced to do so in 1776 or until they were displaced by revolutionary bodies controlled by men who

---

[44] EHD, IX, 672–73.

[45] "Valerius Poplicola," *Boston Gazette,* 28 Oct. 1771, reprinted in H. A. Cushing, ed., *The Writings of Samuel Adams* (4 vols., New York, 1904–08), II, 256–64.

did want independence. But the idea was implicit in the concepts of "compact," "consent," "natural rights," "the law of nature," and "fundamental laws," if not in the appeals to charters and the "rights of Englishmen" which were so common in legislative resolutions.

Of course, anonymous newspaper writers could and did go much farther than official bodies. In 1772 a writer in the *Providence Gazette* declared that, if no attention were paid to American complaints, "we should be justified in the sight of the world, if we sought a remedy in another way; I mean set up a government of our own, independent of Great Britain."[46] A Massachusetts writer in January, 1773, said that "no people on earth have a right to make laws for the Americans but themselves." If Britain continues to try to do so, "we shall become a separate state."[47] We can hope for no justice from Parliament, said still other writers; the only solution is to form an independent state.[48] Another writer after the First Continental Congress declared: "Let us neither think, write, speak nor act without keeping our eyes fixed upon the period which shall dissolve our connections with Great Britain." This man made it clear that all just government derived its power from the people and he proclaimed that the history of kings "is nothing but the history of the folly and depravity of human nature."[49]

Thus, when Jefferson drafted the Declaration of Independence, he picked ideas out of the air, as he said much later, and they, too, like other political ideas, had long been a part of the American heritage. The idea of the sovereignty of the people became the formal justification of the war for independence and an integral part of all American political thought since then, but it was not an idea which was accepted by all Americans who fought for their independence. They accepted it as a necessary theoretical foundation for what they were doing, but many of them tried to avoid its practical implementation in the creation of governments for the newly independent states. Thus the conflict over basic principles of government which had been a part of the colonial heritage, and which was given new point in the debates with Britain between

[46] 22 Aug. 1772.

[47] *Boston Gazette,* 11 Jan.; *New York Journal,* 21 Jan. 1773.

[48] *Providence Gazette,* 16 Oct. 1773.

[49] 14 Nov. 1774, reprinted in EHD, IX, 818–19.

1763 and 1776, continued to be a vital part of the political thought of the American revolutionary era after 1776.[50]

[50] The most recent and most scholarly account of American political theories from 1763 to 1776 is contained in part three of Clinton Rossiter, *Seedtime of the Republic: The Origin of the American Tradition of Political Liberty* (New York, 1953). In general Rossiter emphasizes the "conservative" character of American political thought and insists upon the fundamental "agreement" of Americans after 1776. Like many other writers he virtually ignores the "democratic" thought of the period. It is true of course that the political consequences of the Revolution were mainly "conservative" so far as forms of government were concerned, but it is a mistake to ignore the role of democratic ideas in the Revolutionary era. Even if they did not dominate it, they were an integral part of the history of the times. For a discussion of this point see Merrill Jensen, "Democracy and the American Revolution," *The Huntington Library Quarterly* (Summer, 1957). For the part played by democracy in the writing of the first state constitutions see Elisha P. Douglass, *Rebels and Democrats: The Struggle for Equal Political Rights and Majority Rule During the American Revolution* el Hill, 1955).

POLITICAL IDEAS
OF THE AMERICAN
REVOLUTION

PREFACE TO THE SECOND EDITION

THIS BOOK HAS A curious history. It was written for the most part in a back room of the old Philadelphia Library Company, just after I had returned from the War in 1919, and was making an effort to get back into academic life. It was frankly intended as a doctoral dissertation and as such, lay in typescript for a year or so. Then my friends, William K. Boyd and William T. Laprade wanted a manuscript with which to start a "Trinity College Press" in North Carolina, in order to anticipate their old friends at Chapel Hill who were also starting a "University of North Carolina Press." I believe their plan succeeded, and this book was the first to appear from what has since become the "Duke University Press."

Although, when it came out, the volume bore all the marks of inexperience, including a shoal of minor textual errors as well as errors in quotations and typography, it was very kindly received, notably by C. H. van Tyne in the *American Historical Review* and by S. E. Morison in the *English Historical Review*. I shall never cease to be grateful to these gentlemen. Equally kind were R. L. Schuyler of Columbia and C. H. McIlwain of Harvard, who had both, evidently, in preparation at the time, books on the same subject which my little volume rather anticipated. Both then confined their immediate publications to works smaller than had been intended, Professor Schuyler's being an article in the *Political Science Quarterly*, "The Britannic Question and the American Revolution," and Professor McIlwain's being his little gem, *The American Revolution, a constitutional interpretation*, New York, 1923, which took a Pulitzer prize. Neither of these gentlemen was obliged to recognize even the existence of my book, much less to admit it had merit.

Seventeen years ago, the book had a certain timeliness because it related to the constitutional organization of the present British Commonwealth, a matter which was ill understood by the laity in America until delegates of the British dominions appeared in Paris in 1919, asserting their equal right with the representatives from Great Britain. Now, in the 1930's, another part of the book seems equally apposite. The re–valuation of the function of the judiciary in the American system, particularly with reference to the power to pass on the constitutionality of legislative enactments, brings into sharp focus once more the theory of Iredell that when the legislature attempts to alter the constitution, it destroys the basis of its own existence, since the legislature is a creature of the constitution. In America at least, the Fathers intended that the law should be superior to the majority, and they certainly intended to have the courts pronounce on the constitutionality of legislative statutes.

R. G. A.
Ann Arbor
April, 1939

1

THE DOCTRINE OF STANDING STILL

IT IS IN SOME quarters regarded as a mild form of heresy to write about the eighteenth century without mentioning Dr. Samuel Johnson. His phrase, "In sovereignty, there are no gradations," about epitomizes his celebrated and unfortunate essay in the field of Anglo-American politics.[1] Had anyone attempted to discuss the matter with the doctor, his boldness would probably have been rebuked with some such thunderous proclamation as the well known, "Sir! I would not give half a guinea to live under one form of government rather than under another."[2] If one still had the temerity to suggest that perhaps this was no adequate reply to the objections which the American colonists were making to the management of the empire, he would have brought upon his head the wrathful denunciation, "Sir! The Americans are a nation of convicts and deserve anything we give them short of hanging."[3] This allusion to the American colonies as penal institutions hardly helped matters, but does it not give an insight into the type of mentality against which the Americans had to work? "The last in many things: Johnson was the last genuine Tory; the last Englishman who with strong voice and wholly believing heart, preached the doctrine of standing still."[4] No apology need be made for cutting that sentence off in the middle, for Carlyle goes on to extol as a virtue the doctrine of standing still. But Carlyle was not exactly a democrat, and

[1] *Taxation No Tyranny* (London: 1774).

[2] Boswell's *Johnson* (G. B. Hill, ed.), II. 195.

[3] Boswell's *Johnson* (G. B. Hill ed.), II. 357. Maryland in particular was used as a dumping ground for English convicts.

[4] Carlyle's Review of Croker's edition of Boswell's *Johnson*.

his own solution for the British imperial problem seems to have been to rescue the self-governing dominions from the abysmal depths to which democratic institutions had plunged them and to rule the colonies by proconsular English princes who should found new houses with hereditary titles.[5] This is neither Johnson nor Carlyle at his best; but perhaps it will serve to show the kind of thinking against which the liberal thought of America was striving to find expression.

America, after the French and Indian War, was a nation which had outgrown its old political garments. To its clamor for new institutions, necessary to fit the new conditions, the restrictive policy of the old colonial system brought only more swaddling clothes. This failure of the mother country to understand conditions in the colonies precipitated armed conflict in 1775. But a revolt against toryism produces an intellectual as well as a physical contest. The latter is always destructive; but the former is not, and it seldom happens that people emerge from a struggle in which they have been compelled to put forth their best mental efforts without having enriched the field of thought. An historian of the English law has pointed out wherein British thought needed more light and more warmth. "The state that Englishmen knew was a singularly unicellular state, and at critical times they were not too well equipped with tried and rational thoughts with which to meet the case of Ireland, or some communities, commonwealths or corporations in America which seemed to have wills, and hardly fictitious wills, of their own, which became states, and United States." Then, in a footnote, he adds: "The want of a theory about Ireland which would have mediated between absolute dependence, and absolute independence, was the origin of many evils."[6] "Many evils" is a gentle reminder of a most painful chapter of British imperial history, a chapter that displays the fruit of the Johnsonian dictum, "In sovereignty, there are no gradations."

It is here that the problem of the British Empire exemplifies the fundamental problem of international politics. For it is not Ireland alone which constitutes a sad commentary on the inability of men to work out a rational theory of sovereignty. As Robert Lansing points out, nine-tenths of all international difficulties arise out of

[5] *Shooting Niagara.*

[6] F. W. Maitland, Introduction to Gierke: x.

the so-called sovereign state.[7] The thirteen colonies did not endure what Ireland tolerated, and in their refusal we may seek some evidences of "tried" if not "rational" thoughts which might meet the case of a multicellular political system. A recent monograph[8] has reproduced the theories upon which Americans worked in their efforts to construct a more perfect union of states which claimed to be sovereign. Yet, after all, the task of the delegates at Philadelphia in 1787 was somewhat simplified by the presence of certain factors which are absent in the larger problem of organizing the commonwealth or league of nations. If the Britannic political laboratory supplies any material for study and observation which can throw light on the greater problems of international politics and the organization of a league of nations, surely it is not unfitting to consider the American contributions in that day when the thirteen colonies were members of the British Empire. Britain's unquestioned success in the case of her great self-governing dominions, her unquestioned failures in the case of the thirteen colonies, and for many centuries in Ireland, and her still seething experiments in India, Egypt, and Persia, challenge and excite the curiosity of anyone who is trying to work out a theory which will mediate between those grades of sovereignty which Dr. Johnson insisted could not exist.

But that curiosity must go unsatisfied if there are no adequate historical data, if historians do not continue the story which Edward A. Freeman left unfinished. Perhaps, if there could be found a federal-thinking historian to whom history is something more than past politics, the stock of historical information might be greater. A part of the difficulty lies in the fact that the historian must take into account two forces which at first glance seem mutually incompatible. He must take cognizance of a centralizing force which is trying to devise some central agency for reminding each of the groups of society of its responsibility toward every other group. At the same time, the federal idea involves a decentralizing force which would preserve to each group sufficient authority to develop freely according to its own genius. Both of these forces are observable in the political thought of the American Revolution, and it was partly because of the inability of men to preserve the balance

[7] *Reports of American Bar Association*, XLIV. 247.

[8] J. B. Scott, *James Madison's Notes of the Debates in the Federal Convention, and Their Relation to a More Perfect Society of Nations.* 1918.

between them that the Revolution occurred and terminated as it did.

It has been pointed out that the core of modern liberalism is a new federalism, not directed wholly toward the integration of several states or groups into a larger whole, but rather toward the disintegration of the great state or group into smaller national groups.[9] For example, the efforts of the modern Britannic statesmen are not directed so much toward the creation of a greater Britain, a huge superstate, as toward the disintegration of the empire into a commonwealth of nations. In America, even some of the warm advocates of a league or association of nations have been wary of the great Leviathan-like state of states. What light the story of the American Revolution has to reflect upon this subject it is our task to find.

The economic aspect of the whole question is one which would fill many volumes, and one which cannot properly fall within the scope of such a work as this. Such economic motives as the statesmen of America and England understood in the time of the Revolution were frequently so naïve that we are probably justified in leaving what contemporaries thought very largely out of account. For example, in the controversy before 1775, Britain claimed she had spent millions in defense of the colonies, and that it was no more than fair to demand a compensating contribution from the colonies. To this the colonies responded with much eloquence, concerning their emigration to a wild and uncivilized country, their battles with and victories over the economic difficulties which beset them, and the extent to which they had sacrificed their own economic interests to the interests of the empire. Fortunately one Englishman was realist enough to remark, "Much declamation has been used on both sides. The English speak of the blood and treasure they have expended. The Americans say that they have encountered an inhospitable climate for the purposes of Great Britain, and have dedicated their lives and fortunes to her service. There is no weight in any of these declamations. Whatever was done by either was done for their own advantage."[10]

And if one would be a realist he must recognize that on the whole imperial problem, and the theories of politics allied there-

---

[9] E. Barker, *Political Thought from Spencer to the Present Day*, p. 182.

[10] *The Case of Great Britain and America: Addressed to the King and Both Houses of Parliament* (London: Phila. reprint: 1789), p. 11.

with, the sentiments of a very large group in society are best expressed by the flippant parodist who exclaimed:

> "But, Oh! God bless our honest King,
> The Lords and Commons, true.
> And if, next, Congress be the thing,
> Oh! Bless that Congress, too!"[11]

Such a group there always is, and its very existence must lessen the value of any generalizations one might be tempted to make about the prevalence or representative character of any political theories. Nevertheless, since we are committed to the task of expounding the political thought of the American Revolution, we must observe its general position and function in human thought.

The Germans speak of a "Staats–und Korporationslehre," which seems to them to be the general genus of which states and corporations are but species. Britannic history is too full of commercial corporations which are suddenly found to be functioning as national states for any one to overlook the importance of what, for lack of a better term, we may style The Science of Commonwealths and Corporations.[12]

The story of the attempt to reconcile groups, to arbitrate between group claims and the claims of associations which are now corporations, now something more, and now something less, fills many pages of history. In this great story the history of international law and the history of federal government bear upon such matters as the work of administering group interests within a state and of reconciling the interests of labor unions and churches with the rest of society, and upon trade wars and "Kulturkampfs." Of that science as a whole some future age may have more to say. Sufficient it is here to note its existence and to see how the subject of political theories penetrates the innermost recesses of our thought.

---

[11] *A Poor Man's Advice to his Poor Neighbors: A Ballad to the Tune of Chevy Chase:* (New York: 1774).

[12] The use of the word "science" in such a connection is admittedly unfortunate; but for lack of another and better term to express the idea of a body of systematized knowledge we must employ it. The German *Lehre* is hardly adequate, as in this sense it means rather "doctrine." Similarly, the word "commonwealth" instead of *Staat* enables us to get away from some connotations which do not help in group thinking. For the germ of this idea, I am, of course, indebted to Frederick W. Maitland.

2

THE BRITISH IMPERIAL PROBLEM IN THE EIGHTEENTH CENTURY

"UNTIL THE WAR which was ended by the peace of 1763, the plantations, deemed only inconsiderable and distant parcels of an extensive empire, had remained extremely obscure, offering little celebrity to the historian." Such was the opinion of an English spectator-historian who could make some pretense of being a scientific observer in the modern sense.[1] Such, moreover, is one of the reasons why one may properly turn to the period between the war which ended in 1763 and the war which began in 1775 in a search for efforts to solve the imperial problem. For that war, which ended in the expulsion of the French from North America, had revealed the colonies as no longer negligible outposts of an imperial realm, but component parts of an empire, parts which could be relied upon to furnish men and treasures for imperial defense.[2] The British imperial problem, in the eighteenth as in the twentieth century, consisted in the question of how to make the political machinery of the empire catch up to the facts of the empire. It was a question of reorganizing the structure of the empire to meet a situation in which the overseas dominions were no longer "inconsiderable and distant parcels" to be ruled through absentee Boards of Trade or negligent Colonial Offices, but were to be given a share and a place

[1] George Chalmers, *Political Annals of the Present United Colonies from their settlement to the Peace of 1763,* (London, 1780), Preface, p. i.

[2] "In 1660 the people of England and of the English Colonies in North America may be said to have formed parts of one nation; in 1760 this was no longer true." E. Channing, *Hist. of U. S.,* II. 598.

in the empire commensurate with the dignity which the late war [1756–63] had demonstrated that they possessed.

In the twentieth century, the best thought of what has been known as the British Empire is once more at work on a still existing imperial problem. Colonial conferences have become imperial conferences, and the far-sighted statesmen of the overseas dominions again have given notice that the British Empire is no longer a composite state made up of a central dominant kingdom with its several "inconsiderable and distant parcels" lying about in the four corners of the earth. To such men the British Empire is not a nation, but a league of nations, for which some suitable machinery is to be devised, and they urge the claims of those they represent with an unmistakable insistence, albeit with the same loyalty to the empire which characterized the claims of almost all the pre-Revolutionary American agitators right down to the battle of Lexington. The liberal statesmen in Great Britain in the twentieth century seem to have the same understanding of the aspirations of their overseas colleagues that made the eighteenth century English Whigs side with the Americans of their day. The chronicle of liberal thought as well as the history of the British Empire would be incomplete without the story of that earlier epoch in which liberals at home and abroad were outvoted by the Tories in a Parliament elected by the "rotten" borough system.[3]

In the ten years preceding the American Revolution, liberals on both sides of the Atlantic called for bringing the old political apparatus up to date. From this agitation emerged three distinct concepts of the nature of the empire. *First,* there were those who held to the "Theory of Colonial Dependency," who regarded Britain as the head and mistress of her dominions and the dominions as children, proper subjects for exploitation under the old colonial system. Adherents to this view believed that the Parliament then existing at Westminster was in fact an imperial parliament in the

[3] Dr. W. T. Laprade, while editing the John Robinson Papers, called my attention to a delightful illustration of what sometimes took place. "The Earl of Sandwich set down in black and white what he demanded for one of the seats at Huntington, 'I must have £2000 to be lent me for five years on my bond; and to pay the expenses of the election, which in all probability would not amount to £300. The condition offered to Captain Phipps are thinking and acting as I do on all American points.'" See: G. O. Trevelyan, *The American Revolution,* pt. III. 357n. The Earl of Sandwich, of course, was anything but a liberal friendly to the overseas dominions.

form it then had, i.e., that the Lords and Commons of Great Britain were adequate representatives of all the outlying portions of the empire as well as of the constituencies which they happened to represent on the island of Britain. They believed that this Parliament had political supremacy and overlordship above all the dominions wherever situated. *Second,* there were those who believed that there should be an imperial parliament, but that the Parliament at Westminster as then constituted was not such an assembly. These men held that the British Empire was in essence a federal state, and that as such it should have a federal parliament, representing all the dominions, with supreme jurisdiction over all the empire and paramount over all subordinate legislatures. These were the advocates of "imperial federation" in the sense in which the term is still employed. To give a name to this political form is dangerous, yet it is suggested that Freeman's term, "Federal Commonwealth," accords best with the ideas which this group held, with the additional understanding that what Freeman called the "Central Power" in the federal commonwealth be in the nature of a parliament with legislative functions.[4]

Third, there were those who held to the theory that the colonies in America were in fact states in the political sense, that they were what are commonly known as "nations," that their local legislatures were the supreme power over them, under the crown; that their sole connection with Great Britain lay in the crown; that the parliament at Westminster was but one of many co-equal legislatures, analogous, for example, to the General Court of Massachusetts Bay. The logical consequence of such a conception of the empire was complete independence, whereby the colonies would become units in international law, separate so-called sovereign states in the society or

[4] "We may then recognize as the perfect Federal Commonwealth any collection of States, in which it is equally unlawful for the Central Power to interfere with the purely internal legislation of the several members, and for the several members to enter into any diplomatic relations with other powers." E. A. Freeman, *History of Federal Government,* 2nd ed. (1893), p. 8. Historically there is no question but that this was a perfectly tenable view of the nature of the empire. William Knox wrote in 1765, "I find almost as many instances of parliament's exercising supreme legislative jurisdiction over the colonies, as there have been sessions of parliament since the first settlement of America by British subjects." *The Claim of the Colonies to an Exemption from internal Taxes Imposed by the Authority of Parliament Examined,* (London: 1765).

family of nations. A writer on the common law has pointed out that the "life of the law is not logic, it is experience."[5] This is equally true of the constitutional law of England. Even those who were soberest and clearest in thought did not follow the idea to its logical conclusion. They do not do so today. Experience had and has demonstrated the utility of the empire, despite some of its illiberal policies. When pressed for an explanation of what organ of the empire should assume control in case of war, foreign affairs, and, in the eighteenth century, the regulation of trade, the men who held to this third group replied that in such matters they were perfectly willing that Westminster should shoulder the burdens, but denied vehemently that this gave Westminster any primacy among the other nations which composed the empire. Such a political form we call the "Commonwealth of Nations."[6] And the thing the liberal thought of the Revolution foresaw, the empire has in fact become. At the recent meeting of the Imperial Conference, held in London in 1921, the same imperial problem was attacked, and the consensus of opinion of the representatives of England and the overseas dominions alike was that there was nothing particularly to be gained by calling a constitutional conference or establishing an imperial parliament, that there was nothing the dominions could do as independent nations that they cannot do now, that there is no essential thing in which the great self-governing dominions differ from the so-called independent nations of the world, and therefore it is wise to let well enough alone.[7] Such an arrangement apparently works, and each member of the imperial conference subscribed to the proposition that the empire must endure, that the constant consulta-

[5] O. W. Holmes, *The Common Law*, p. 1.

[6] The familiar distinction between a "federal union" (federal system) and a "confederation" will occur to one in connection with the second and third groups. But in fact both these terms are totally inadequate to describe the thing the Americans were aspiring to in 1774 and the thing the British Empire has in fact since become. Any orthodox work on politics will give the usual facts and terms about "federal unions" and "confederations," e. g., J. W. Garner's *Introduction to Political Science*, pp. 142–67; 191–7. But most of them totally ignore this new and vitally significant form, the Commonwealth, or League of Nations. This is all the more astonishing in view of the fact that the avoidance of periodically occurring world tragedies depends so largely on understanding this new form of political organization.

[7] *Conference of the Prime Ministers and Representatives of the United Kingdom, the Dominions and India, held in June, July & August, 1921.* (London: H. M. Stat. Office: 1921) Cd. 1474, pp. 9, 10, 22.

tions between the premiers of the different dominions must be kept up to insure the endurance of the empire, and that it was perfectly possible to operate a league of nations without reference to the illusion of independence or the spook of sovereignty.

Ten years before the outbreak of the American Revolution, a colonial governor wrote to a friend, "the patchwork government of America will last no longer, the necessity of a parliamentary establishment of the government of America upon fixed constitutional principles is brought on with a precipitation which could not have been foreseen a year ago; it is become more urgent by the very incidents which make it more difficult."[8] In fact it must have been obvious to any colonial administrator that "instead of certain constitutional law, adapted to the nature of governments, established by the sovereign or imperial state and recognized by the dependent and subordinate states, America has hitherto been governed by temporary expedients."[9] Throughout the ten years, efforts were made to attack the problem as one of imperial constitutional law. Even at the end, when considering the injustice done their fellow colonists under the Boston Port Bill, with its shutting off commerce from one of the chief ports of America, the Committee on Correspondence of Pennsylvania urged their compatriots in Massachusetts Bay that the proper method of remedying the difficulty, now amounting to a wrong, lay in an assembly of delegates "to ascertain our rights and establish a political union between the two countries, with the assent of both, which would effectually secure to America their future rights and privileges. Anything short of this will leave the colonies in their present precarious state, disunited among themselves, unsettled in their rights, ignorant of their duties, and destitute of that connection with Great Britain which is indispensably necessary to the safety and happiness of both."[10] The historically minded spectator could not fail to perceive the existence of a problem of practical political and constitutional engineering to solve which "recourse was had in vain to parchment authorities made at a distant time, when neither grantor nor the grantees of

---

[8] *Barrington–Bernard Correspondence,* 1760–1770, (Edited by E. Channing & A. C. Coolidge, 1915), p. 99.

[9] Francis Bernard, *Select Letters on the Government of America and the Principles of Law and Polity Applied to the American Colonies.* (London: 1774), p. iii.

[10] 18 June, 1774. Force, *American Archives,* 4th ser., I. 486.

American territory had in contemplation anything like the present state of the two countries."[11] Prospective Tory and potential patriot alike were thinking out some plan whereby the British imperial problem might be solved, and though the futility of their efforts may make those efforts relatively negligible for purposes of American history, they certainly have their place in the history of the British Empire. This chapter is, for reasons of convenience, devoted to the first two of the three concepts of the empire mentioned above, i.e., colonial dependency and imperial federation, while the third, more elusive, yet today more significant in history, in politics, and in international law, is reserved for another chapter.

THE THEORY OF COLONIAL DEPENDENCIES

The eighteenth century, like the twentieth, had its European war in which the overseas dominions flocked to the banner of Britain and afterwards asked for a greater share in the management of the empire and a recognition of their status as self-governing states within the Britannic Empire. But let no one be deceived by this historical parallel. At Paris in 1763 there was no Borden or Smuts to insist "that the assent of the king as high contracting power to the various treaties should in respect to the dominions be signified by the signature of the dominion representatives" so that each American colony could "preserve unimpaired its absolute autonomy" and make clear that "the Britannic Commonwealth is in itself a community or league of nations."[12]

In considering the subject of early American efforts to define the relationship between the component parts of the empire, the thought turns almost instinctively toward those efforts at colonial union and confederation which began to appear early in colonial history. But the "Plans of Union" which have received the most attention from American historians are, most of them, based upon an entirely different need and are actuated by different motives from the

---

[11] David Ramsay, *A History of the American Revolution*. (Phila., 1786), I. 54.

[12] Sir Robert Borden on "Canada's Status as a Nation within the British Empire," N. Y. *Sun*, Oct. 7, 1919; reprinted in the *Cong. Rec.*, 66th Cong. 1st. Sess. pp. 8010–8011. He states the part played by the overseas dominions at Versailles in 1919.

theories which appeared in the later period on the eve of the Revolution. Those plans, both the theoretical and doctrinaire ones of private individuals and the plans of colonial congresses, were inspired rather by the necessity of common defense against the French and Indians and were bent rather on linking up contiguous or neighboring states or provinces in a local confederation than designed to work out a formula for the organization of the Britannic Commonwealth of Nations.[13] The celebrated Stamp Act Congress called in 1765 was in one sense merely one of the last of a series of colonial conferences looking toward concerted action by the colonies. But in another sense it was something entirely new; this was no meeting of colonial governors and Indian chiefs of which the frontier town of Albany had so many times been the witness. Even the Albany Congress of 1754 had been called under the instructions of the Lords of Trade and confined its attention very largely to Indian affairs and the prospect of a North American colonial union.[14] But the Stamp Act Congress was not a paternalistic creation emanating from Lords of Trade and Plantation; nor was it concerned with measures for defending England's possessions from savage foes; it undertook to raise the question of the political constitution of the British Empire. It was in a sense a forerunner of those "colonial" and "imperial" conferences which the next two centuries produced; but it lacked representatives from Britain, and even the timorous Lieutenant Governor Colden of New York gave it scant courtesy when it met.[15] Its utterances are not significant because they are profound as much as because they are representative. Yet, in the main, it may not be entirely unfair to call it a conservative assembly. The story of what it did has been told many times.[16] Despite its character as a meeting of protest, it betrayed in all four of the documents which it pro-

---

[13] R. Frothingham's *Rise of the Republic of the United States,* pp. 107–21, contains a study of these early plans and Congresses. See also J. Winsor, *Critical and Narrative History of the United States,* V. 611.

[14] E. Channing, in *History of the United States,* II, 569–70, and *American History Leaflet* No. 14, indicates the nature of the Albany Conference and the various plans there suggested by Franklin, Hutchinson, and others.

[15] *Boston Post Boy,* Oct. 14, 1765.

[16] R. Frothingham, in *Rise of the Republic,* pp. 177–200, has worked this out. Although it might be going too far to describe it as a Tory assembly, in view of the unprecedented boldness exhibited in calling it at all, yet from progressive Massachusetts two of the three delegates were what even in that day were known as tories. See Hutchinson, *History,* III. 103, 118 and note.

duced an unmistakable adherence to the "colonial dependency" theory of the nature of the empire.

The report of the Committee on Colonial Rights admitted the "due subordination of the colonies to the crown *and parliament*."[17] The Declaration of Rights and Grievances as adopted admitted "that his Majesty's subjects in these colonies owe the same allegiance to the crown of Great Britain that is owed from his subjects born within the realm, and all due subordination to that august body, the Parliament of Great Britain"; this, in fact, was the first article of the declaration.[18] The address to the King conceded that the colonial legislatures were "subordinate," while the separate memorials to the Lords and Commons at Westminster employ the same language, thus admitting the supremacy and primacy of parliament in a manner quite inconsistent with any idea of an empire of co-equal states. Nevertheless, while admitting in theory that which overthrew any argument they might have in law, the colonial representatives "humbly conceived that this subordination is sufficiently secured by common law, by our allegiance and above all by the general superintending power and authority of the whole empire indisputably lodged in that august body the parliament of Great Britain, whose authority is clearly admitted here, so far as our circumstance is consistent with the enjoyment of our essential rights as freemen and as British subjects."[19] Here was a new note: the traditional supremacy of Parliament, so well established in English constitutional law, was declared inapplicable to imperial constitutional law. Parliament could not do anything it chose but was limited by the essential rights of British subjects. Yet the expressions of the Stamp Act Congress were on the whole conservative as befitted the sympathies of the majority of those who composed it. Far from looking toward total separation and independence it was very definitely an effort to make clear the status of colonies in an empire in which there existed an imperial parliament with whose acts a part of the empire was dissatisfied.[20]

[17] Reprinted in T. Pitkin, *Political and Civil History of the United States,* (1828), I. 448.

[18] Other Proceedings of the Stamp Act Congress are reprinted in H. Niles, *Principles and Acts of the Revolution in America* (Baltimore: 1822), pp. 457-9.

[19] Pitkin, *Political and Civil History,* I. 453.

[20] "The foundation is now laid for rendering the British Empire the most extensive and powerful of any ever recorded in history; our connection with

This admission of colonial dependency was made by potential rebels against the authority of Great Britain without the least qualm. "It was readily granted that the colonies are dependent states united under one head, and with the other dominions, form one entire empire," in which empire it was "admitted that the parliament of Great Britain as the supreme legislative power, has a superintending authority to regulate and preserve the connection between the several parts and members of the empire."[21] Such an admission, coming from one who then went on to the Lockeian formula about there being no right in Parliament to deprive the colonists of their property without their consent, shows how essentially conservative the early protestors were willing to be.

With such conservatism in America, there is no wonder that the House of Commons reveals very little advance beyond the conception of the empire in terms of "our colonies." In fact, after the Stamp Act provoked a wave of rebellious indignation throughout the colonies, the utterances on the floor of the Lords and Commons show an almost unanimous assent on the part of the English to the validity of this theory of empire. The Parliament assured the King of its support "in all such measures as shall be necessary for preserving and securing the legal dependence of the colonies upon this their mother country, for enforcing their due obedience to the laws, for maintaining the dignity of the crown and asserting the indubitable and fundamental rights of the legislature of Great Britain."[22] Naturally enough the King replied reasserting the "legislative power of *this kingdom* over *its* colonies."[23] Lord Mansfield, one of the ablest of the English thinkers, put this theory in unmistakable lan-

---

this empire we esteem our greatest happiness and security, and humbly conceive that it may now be so established by your royal wisdom as to endure to the latest period of time; this with most humble submission to your majesty we apprehend will be most effectively accomplished by fixing the pillars thereof on liberty and justice and securing the inherent rights and liberties of your subjects here, on the principles of the English Constitution." Niles, *Principles and Acts,* p. 458.

[21] "A. B." in a letter to the Boston "Centinal" (1768) reprinted in the *American Gazette;* (London: 1768), p. 45. Yet this passage occurs in the same letter with the following, "As the people are supposed to be the best judges of what will promote their good, and most interested in what concerns their own safety, it is an established maxim that no human laws can or ought to bind them unless made with their consent." p. 49.

[22] Hansard, *Parliamentary History,* XVI. 89, Dec. 17, 1765.

[23] Hansard, *Parliamentary History,* XVI. 94, Jan. 14, 1766.

guage in his assertion "that the British Legislature, as to the power of making laws, represents the whole British Empire, and has authority to bind every part, and every subject without the least distinction, whether such subjects have the right to vote, or whether the law binds places within the realm or without."[24] Whatever posterity chooses to think of Mansfield's analysis, history has to thank him for his startlingly clear exposition of the theory of colonial dependency. Fortunately Lord Mansfield's reputation in English history does not depend upon the character of his vision as a statesman of the empire. Lord Lyttleton, more temperate, yet no less explicit, explained that these "maxims which imply a subjection to the supreme government or legislature do not exclude the existence of inferior legislatures, with restrained powers subject to the superior legislature."[25]

From 1765 to 1775 the official position of the administration in England remained the same: the colonies were subject to the legislative authority of the Parliament of the British Isles.[26] Moreover, this was the theory of the liberal Burke and Chatham as well as of the less liberal North and Mansfield.[27] Even Charles James Fox believed that America was wrong in resisting the authority of Great Britain's legislature.[28] The debates in Lords and Commons during these ten years resound with classic references to the colonies of the ancient world, and while the liberals cited the tradition of the free and uncontrolled Greek and Phœnician colonies, the tories summoned to their aid the illustration of the Roman pro-consular administration and its stricter connection with the metropolis.[29] Yet

[24] Hansard, *Parliamentary History*, XVI. 174, Feb. 24, 1766.

[25] Hansard, *Parliamentary History*, XVI. 166–7. Feb. 24, 1766.

[26] Hansard, *Parliamentary History*, XVI. 94. Jan. 14, 1766. At the other end of the ten years the speech from the throne was still in terms of the dependence of the colonies on Parliament. Hansard, *Parliamentary History*, XVII., 1159.

[27] See chapter on *Some Reconsiderations of Taxation and Representation* with citations to Chatham in Hansard, *Parliamentary History*, XVI. 101, and to Burke in *Ibid.*, XVII. 1266–7.

[28] Hansard, *Parliamentary History*, XVII. 1288. April 22, 1774. So too Richard Jackson, even while opposing the Stamp Act, asserted 'Parliament is undoubtedly the universal, unlimited legislature of the British Dominions, etc." Sir Edmund Fitzmaurice, *Life of Shelburne*, I. 224.

[29] "The reasoning about the colonies drawn from the colonies of antiquity is a mere useless display of learning; for the colonies of the Tyrians in Africa and the Greeks in Asia were totally different from our system. No nation

it is probably safe to say that practically not a member of Parliament in those years went further than the theories of colonial dependency. Of course not all were so obtuse as the worthy knight who blandly inquired whether it was the purpose of Parliament to annihilate the colonial assemblies.[30] But when one member did have the vision to liken the colonies to foreign nations with whom a cause of friction would be made a subject of negotiation and not of immediate invasion such as had been done in New York and Massachusetts,[31] this suggestion was lost in the tumult of the eloquence of other honorable members, who could thunder that Boston was to Westminster as Carthage was to Rome, and hence "delenda est!"[32] The self-styled imperial parliament, including Whigs, Tories, Burke, Chatham, North, and George III as well, never seem to have got beyond the idea that the overseas dominions were "our colonies."[33]

One might have supposed that the existence of the charters in certain colonies would have given some suggestion of a different status, as being compacts or constitutions stating the terms under which men consented to submit to government at all. But far from it, it was even suggested that the charters were merely guarantees against illiberal interference by the King, and by no means invalidated the right of Parliament over all Englishmen in America.[34]

---

before ourselves formed any regular system of colonization but the Romans; and their system was a military one of garrisons placed in the principal towns of the conquered provinces. But the right of jurisdiction of the mother country over her colonies among the Romans was boundless and uncontrollable." Hansard, *Parliamentary History*, XVI. 198.

[30] Sir Francis Norton: Hansard, *Parliamentary History*, XVII. 1194, March 28, 1774.

[31] Colonel Isaac Barre: Hansard, *Parliamentary History*, XVII. 1307. March 2, 1774.

[32] Mr. Van: Hansard, *Parliamentary History*, XVII. 1178, March 23, 1774.

[33] Cf. the interesting parallel a century and a half later in which the theory still persists. Sir R. Jebb remarks, " 'Our Colonies' betrays a mind which has not yet acquired the modern perspective. The expression marks the user as mentally disqualified for Britannic statesmanship. Tried by this simple but sufficient test, the present British Cabinet (1913) has been found to yield not a single member with a modern outlook." *The Britannic Question*, pp. 71–2. James Otis inquired by what right Englishmen used this expression "Our Colonies" and [Otis] suggested that Americans might as well say "Our London." *Considerations on Behalf of the Colonists*. (London: 1765. 2nd Ed.), p. 6.

[34] "The colonies are secured by these charters from the despotism of the crown, of whom they are, perhaps, as independent as inhabitants of Great

A Tory annalist of the period, who had opportunities for personal observation of events and personal contact with the thought in governmental circles in England, expressed the opinion that a charter did not erect the community to which it was granted as "a province of the English Empire, to be regularly governed by the acts of a provincial legislature." This indeed is the essence of the Tory view and in the main the basis of the "our colonies" theory of colonial dependency, assuming that the empire was an "English Empire" which was formed by the union by statute of the two kingdoms of England and Scotland "while the coalition of Great Britain with her dependencies was established by common law."[35]

As a matter of fact, there is something to be said in defense of this position. As regards the crown colonies and other dependencies, Great Britain still stands in the relation of suzerainty which she once asserted over all her colonies. Many of them are still even "possessions, rather than colonies,"[36] and so perhaps it may be the more readily understood why at one time many people in England regarded all of the outlying parts of the empire as colonies rather than self-governing dominions.

The futile and belated efforts of Chatham and Burke to arrange an adjustment, the one just before, and the other just after the outbreak of the Revolution, show that both of those statesmen were still clinging to the old theory. In February of 1775, when Chatham startled and shocked the Lords by introducing a bill of his own for reconciliation with America, he could not get away from the fetish "that the American colonies have been, are, and of right ought to be, dependent on the imperial crown of Great Britain, and subordinate to the British Parliament." Nevertheless, he struck a new note in his further assertion that this Parliamentary supremacy was applicable to matters touching the general weal of the whole dominions of the imperial crown of Britain, "which he designated as regulation

---

Britain can be. But from this state of independence of the crown which the colonies insisted upon results the necessity of a dependence on some other power;—sound policy, and the nature of modern colonization require it. This power must be the parliament of Great Britain who hath and ought to have, a full and absolute sovereignty over all the British dominions." *The Late Occurrences in North America and the Policy of Great Britain considered.* (London: 1766), p. 2.

[35] Chalmers, *Annals*, I. 130, 140.

[36] W. H. Woodward in his *Expansion of the British Empire*, p. 296, employs this expression.

of trade and matters of naval defense of the whole empire." Recognition of colonial jurisdiction over taxation was accorded. Here was the germ of a new idea, i.e., that it was possible to limit the jurisdiction of Parliament and grant certain powers to the subordinate jurisdiction. Chatham was headed toward the idea of federalism. However, the insistence with which he emphasized that "all the subjects in the colonies are bound in duty and allegiance to recognize and obey (and they are hereby required to do so) the supreme authority and supreme power of the parliament of Great Britain" makes it impossible to get Chatham out of the "our colonies" class of thinkers.[37] Burke's bill for composing the troubles with the colonies, which he introduced in November of 1775, reflected the same theory "that the parliament of Great Britain was not representative, but the sovereign of America" and might graciously choose "by its own act for wise purposes to put the local power of the purse into other hands than its own, without disclaiming its just prerogative in other particulars." There is no question but Edmund Burke was sincerely sympathetic with the aspirations of the American colonies, but that he possessed the vision to imagine either a Federal Commonwealth or a Commonwealth of Nations, in each of which the ideal of the equality of each of the overseas dominions with the British Isles was a necessary element, is doubtful. The difficulty of defining the relationship between the colonies and Great Britain which so troubled men like Governor Bernard did not worry Burke, who contended that the "silly and wicked attempt to define it had been the first and continued cause of their present disunion." One is tempted to question whether after all this was the language of a sincere political engineer.[38]

[37] Hansard, *Parliamentary History*, XVIII. 198. Lord Shelburne, who might properly be classed with those of larger vision, even went so far as to oppose the Declaratory Act in 1766, not so much because he wanted to surrender the idea of the supremacy of Parliament as because he wanted to avoid the question altogether: Fitzmaurice, *Life of Shelburne*, I. 260 and Hansard, *Parliamentary History*, XVI. 165.

[38] Hansard, *Parliamentary History*, XVIII. 1299. Nov. 20, 1775. That the theory of Parliamentary supremacy was by no means confined to the English, is demonstrated by the appearance of the *Four Dissertations on the Reciprocal Advantages of a Perpetual Union between Great Britain and her American Colonies;* (Philadelphia: 1766), written for Sargent's prize medal at the University of Pennsylvania; all four acknowledge subordination of the colonies to the Parliament at Westminster, pp. 28, 100, 109.

THE THEORY OF IMPERIAL FEDERATION

The Parliament at Westminster threshed out the subject of "no taxation without representation" quite as thoroughly as did colonial pamphleteers and assemblies in the decade before the war, yet it is remarkable how few there were in that body to whom occurred the idea of taking the Americans at their word and granting them representation in Parliament. The geographic obstacles were obvious and played a large part in the matter; the difficulty of making the tenure of office of the American delegates coincide with corresponding periods in England; the obvious fact that a large part of the time would be consumed with discussions of purely British affairs in which the Americans would have not the slightest interest, all combined to make this solution a rather remote possibility. Moreover, one is tempted to suggest that after all there may have been something in Franklin's assertion that both sides were too proud and obstinate to take the initiative in such a scheme. Nevertheless, the solution of the problem by what is known today as "imperial federation" was suggested on both sides of the Atlantic.[39] This was the mode by which the thirteen colonies subsequently solved the same problem when they had secured their separation from Great Britain. But the problem of 1787 was a far simpler one than had been that of 1765–75. The earlier problem, essentially the same as the British imperial problem of the twentieth century, involved ethnic and geographic difficulties of no mean proportions. The presence of the befezzed deputies from Algeria in the French Chamber suggests what might have been. But the suggestions of those who advocated granting representation to the Americans ranged all the way from simply adding new members to the old body to constructing an entirely new Imperial Parliament.

It is to this group of thinkers, who believed in the possibility of a federal commonwealth of Britain, that the American, James Otis, seems to belong. Difficult as it is to extract any consistent political philosophy from the somewhat chaotic utterances of Otis, there is little doubt that at the outset he acknowledged the right of the supreme power in the state to tax its colonies. What is more, he

[39] "Imperial Federation, i.e., the creation of a Federal Parliament with an executive responsible to it." This is the modern definition of the same solution and serves the purpose of this analysis. See R. C. Jebb, *"The Britannic Question,"* (1913), p. 126, also A. B. Keith, *"Imperial Unity and the Dominions"* (1916), pp. 498–509.

acknowledged that the supreme power in this case was the Parliament at Westminster. Such an admission would seem to undermine the whole fabric of his traditionally accepted position as an exponent of the American cause. But as a fact it should be remembered that Otis fastened his attention upon the nature and composition of that parliament which, he granted, had "the same right to levy internal taxes on the colonies as to regulate trade."[40] Otis saw that Parliament as then constructed was little more representative of England than it was of the united colonies, that part of the disease of which the rebellious colonial attitude was only a symptom, was the "rotten" borough system in England.[41] When a Tory cited the essentially unrepresentative character of the British legislature as a defense of the theory of virtual representation (i.e., the theory that while Parliament did not in fact represent all the people proportionately, it represented them all virtually), the reply of James Otis belongs even more essentially in English than in American history. "To what purpose is it to ring everlasting changes to the colonies on the cases of Manchester, Birmingham and Sheffield, who return no members? If those now so considerable places are not represented, they ought to be." Moreover, if it be really true that "by far the major part of the inhabitants of Great Britain are non-electors, the more is the pity!"[42] Otis believed that a supreme parliament of the Britannic Empire ought to be able to do what the self-styled imperial parliament claimed its right to do, but he denied that the then-existing parliament was such an imperial parliament, representative of all the subjects "without as well as within the realm" of Britain.[43]

But a far more consistent and thoughtful supporter of the idea of imperial federation was the British Governor Thomas Pownall of Massachusetts Bay. He had the vision to see what the empire

---

[40] *A Vindication of the British Colonies published by Mr. Otis at Boston in 1765* (London: 1769), pp. 23, 29, 30. Originally published as *A Vindication of the British Colonies against the Aspersions of the Halifax Gentleman in his letters to his Rhode Island Friend* [James Otis] (Boston: 1765). This assertion of the supremacy of parliament is also made in *The Rights of the British Colonies Asserted and Proved* by James Otis, Esq. (London: 1766: 3rd ed.), p. 49.

[41] Otis, *Vindication*, etc., pp. 23, 29, 30.

[42] James Otis, *Considerations on behalf of the Colonists in a letter to a Noble Lord,* (London: 1765, 2nd Ed.), p. 6.

[43] James Otis, *Vindication,* etc. p. 23.

had in fact become; he understood that it was no longer fitting that a small island off the coast of Europe should send its proconsuls to the ends of the earth and expect the ends of the earth to yield submissive obedience. Whether Britons liked it or not, the fact was that "The British Isles, with our possessions in the Atlantic and in America, are in fact united into one grand marine dominion and ought therefore by policy to be united into one imperium, in one center where the seat of government is."[44] The time had come for that dominion or series of dominions to be consolidated into one empire by allowing the parliamentary representation of the dominions in that "one center where the seat of government is." His plan embraced "sending out some considerable person" who should make a detailed report as to how the matter could be arranged.[45] On the basis of this report he would have some centralized government erected, "founded on the basis of the whole, adequate and efficient to the whole," which would include the granting to the colonies "a share in the legislature of Great Britain, by having knights and burgesses of their own election representing them in parliament."[46] But the most striking feature of Pownall's proposal was the insistence with which he repeated "that there does exist, in fact, in nature, a real union and incorporation of all these parts of the British Dominions, which wants only to be avowed and actuated by the real spirit in which it moves and has its being."[47]

After being relieved as governor of Massachusetts, Pownall retired to England, where as a member of the House of Commons he continued to the end to defend the rights and aspirations of those colonies which he knew so well. It is not fair to him to class him with all of the other Tories as unable to understand the American position. In a sense he was quite in advance of some of the more eloquent and zealous champions of the American cause at Westminster, for he did not so persistently predicate the inferiority of the overseas dominions. To the end he advocated such a union between Britain and the colonies as was well known and amply precedented in

---

[44] Thomas Pownall, *The Administration of the Colonies, wherein their Rights and Constitutions are Discussed and Stated,* (London: 1768), p. xv.

[45] Ibid., p. 32.

[46] Ibid., p. xv.

[47] Ibid., p. 163. Pownall's views had been criticized as those of a deluded visionary. He replied, "I wish those declarations of power with which we mock ourselves may not be found the more dangerous delusion."

English constitutional history, "in a like manner as was done in the union of the two parts of the present kingdom," i.e., England and Scotland with their act of union of 1707 whereby representatives for Scotland appeared at Westminster in the Parliament of Great Britain. The only alternative was to govern the colonies by military occupation and to be prepared to hold America in a constant state of siege, which would cost more than the colonies were worth to the mother country and finally ruin both. Pownall's plan was frankly one of what would today be called federation, for, although he emphasized the subordinate position of the colonial legislatures as was fitting in a federal commonwealth, the co-equality of all the dominions with the kingdom of Great Britain would be secured by some contractual act of union which could not, "according to the law of nations, of justice and policy be altered without the consent of the parties."[48]

Pownall's ideas seem to have been the fruit of his experience as a colonial administrator. The Stamp Act afforded a similar opportunity for his successor, Governor Francis Bernard, to make some practical suggestions, but Bernard had presented his solution in the shape of a plan for inter-colonial union which would have consolidated the colonies into a few large provinces confessedly subject to the supremacy of Parliament as then constructed, and would have created an American nobility. The form of government in the colonies was to be made uniform, and such traces of the federal idea as appear in Bernard are very faint indeed.[49] Nevertheless, the Stamp Act controversy was not wholly barren in this regard, for from England came the suggestion that after all the only means of endearing a son to his father was to give him a proper share in his fortune and also in the management of family concerns upon his coming to maturity. Hence "if every colony were to choose such representation as they should think proper, as our counties in England do, and that such representatives were in every respect to have the same privileges as our members of counties, they would be on an equal footing." The scheme involved a certain degree of indirect election and was not very clearly thought out, but it did manifest a willingness to consider the idea of adding some new members to

[48] Feb. 20, 1775, Hansard, *Parliamentary History,* XVIII. 326–27.
[49] Francis Bernard, *Select Letters on the Government of America and the Principles of Law and Polity applied to the American Colonies* (London: 1774), p. 83. Written in 1764.

Parliament "to represent the colonies in the Parliament of England," and hence may be said to reflect the federal idea.[50]

After all this was an obvious type of solution to fair-minded Britons who understood English liberty as the Americans interpreted it, yet who could not forego the idea that somehow England should be the center of the federal commonwealth. Similar to this was Francis Masseres' scheme of imperial federation which appeared in 1770. Reasserting the supremacy of Parliament, yet acknowledging the fairness of the American contentions, he suggested that eighty members be sent to the House of Commons from overseas, duly apportioned to the North American and West Indian colonies. These representatives were to bear the title of Commissioners of the Colonies of America, and they were to have the right to sit in the House of Commons, to debate, and to vote. Such a plan, he asserted, would beyond question transform the Parliament at Westminster into an imperial federal parliament which might equitably claim jurisdiction over all the British dominions in Europe and America. The proposal of this author even comprehended the division of subjects of jurisdiction, with superior and subordinate legislatures, each with its exclusive sphere of activity, thus limiting the supremacy of the imperial body by the rights reserved to the several component states of the empire. The parliament at Westminster was thus to sit in two separate and distinct capacities: in one, with only members from Great Britain present, it would act as a local legislature for that country. In the other, with the "Commissioners of the Colonies of America" present, parliament should be the imperial and federal parliament of the British Empire. No imperial act could be passed without giving the colonial commissioners time to know that parliament was changing from one capacity to the other.[51]

Curious as it may seem, it is almost as difficult to extract any

[50] *The General Opposition of the Colonies to the Payment of the Stamp Duty and also a Plan for Uniting this Kingdom in such a manner as to make their Interests Inseparable from Ours for the Future, in a Letter to an M. P.* (London: 1766), p. 33. Another plan dated in this same year is contained in the Dartmouth Papers. It proposed that each colony send representatives to Westminster, proportioned on population, but not to exceed four per colony. *Manuscripts of the Earl of Dartmouth,* Vol. II., *American Papers: Hist. MSS. Commission.* 14th Rpt., App. Pt. X., p. 51; vid. also Ibid., pp. 204, 244, 252.

[51] Francis Masseres, sometimes spelled Maseres, *Considerations on the Expediency of Admitting Representatives from the American Colonies to the British House of Commons:* (London: 1770).

consistent doctrine from Benjamin Franklin as it is to get such a thing from the unfortunate Otis, whose mental weakness in his later years makes it difficult to tell just when his mind began to go astray. No such excuse can be made for Franklin's inconsistencies and contradictions. Perhaps it is an easy and entirely a fair thing to say that just herein lay Franklin's greatness: he did not worship the jewel of consistency. He changed his opinions as he learned, and he never stopped learning. Consequently when in 1754 we hear him say that "uniting the colonies more intimately with England, by allowing them representatives in parliament" would in fact "be very acceptable to the colonies," we need not take this as his final opinion. At any given time he was likely to be consistent, and he argued now that such a parliament, representing the American Dominions as well as Great Britain, should start off with a clean slate, with the acts of trade and navigation repealed, and that it should then re-enact only such of those acts as the parliament composed of representatives of all the dominions might deem acceptable.[52] More than a decade later, with the controversy leading to separation in full swing, we find Franklin still clinging to the idea of imperial federation, "fully persuaded that a consolidating union, by fair and equal representation of all parts of this Empire in parliament is the only basis on which its political grandeur and prosperity can be founded."[53] But he perceived by that time that Britain "is indeed too proud to propose admitting American representatives to Parliament, and America is not so humble, nor so fond of the honor to petition for it."[54] In the midst of the controversy, while he was in England, one of his English friends sent him a scheme for admitting overseas members to the Parliament upon which he expressed the opinion that the plan was a wise one, but mournfully commented that the English would hardly come to that conclusion and invite Americans to sit at Westminster before it was too late to attempt any such thing.[55] Yet as late as 1767 he held to the idea of a "consolidating union," based on the principle of what is now called imperial federation.

[52] To Governor Shirley, Dec. 22, 1754, Franklin's *Works,* (Bigelow Ed.), II. 384–5.

[53] To Lord Kames, April 11, 1767, Franklin's *Works,* (Bigelow Ed.), IV. 2.

[54] To John Ross, December 13, 1767, Franklin's *Works,* (Bigelow Ed.), IV. 59.

[55] Jan. 6, 1766. Franklin's *Works,* (Bigelow Ed.), III. 402–3.

But one of the most comprehensive of all the schemes for imperial federation was a "Plan of Union by Admitting Representatives from the American Colonies and from Ireland into the British Parliament." In this plan all of the British dominions in the western hemisphere, from Canada to the further corner of the Caribbean Sea, were to send representatives to Westminster. The thirteen disgruntled colonies in North America, the Floridas, Barbadoes, St. Kitts, Antigua, the Bahamas, the Bermudas, and all the rest down to St. Vincents and Tobago were grouped according to population so that the largest sent four members each and the three smallest combined to send one member. Nor was this all, for the scheme took in Ireland, providing for both burgesses and knights of the shire. Provisions were made for corresponding increments to the House of Lords, and the body thus constructed of overseas lords and commons was made independent of all the ordinary dissolutions of Parliament, six months being allowed for the members to assemble after any given election. This project distinctly reveals the idea of a supreme legislature and introduces the new concept of such a legislature limited by the instrument creating it. In other words, the idea of a limited supreme legislature was here emerging, an idea which the Englishman with his concept of the unlimited power of Parliament found it so hard to grasp.[56]

[56] The proposal of "Amor Patriæ" is found on a broadside which, according to Sabin, was circulated in the colonies about 1770. The copy I have used is in possession of the Library Company of Philadelphia. In volume IV, page 3, of Bigelow's edition of Franklin's works is this same proposal printed in a footnote with Bigelow's comment, "Among Dr. Franklin's manuscripts is a paper entitled 'A Plan of Union by Admitting Representatives from the American colonies and from Ireland into the British Parliament.' It is not in his hand-writing, and appears to have been communicated to him by some other person." Bigelow then cites the letters to Kames and Ross, cited supra, which discuss very generally the subject of imperial federation. More interesting, however, is the letter, cited supra, of January 6, 1766, written in reply to an unknown person, who had sent Franklin a draft of some scheme of imperial federation which is not found with the original letter. The coincidence of a letter to Franklin inclosing some such draft and the existence of such a draft, not in Franklin's handwriting, is one worth noting. Meanwhile the existence of the same thing in printed broadside form testifies to the fact that it had wider circulation than a mere correspondence between two friends. "Amor Patriæ" was Thomas Crowley, who made several similar suggestions to the Earl of Dartmouth. *Manuscripts of the Earl of Dartmouth, American Papers*, Vol. II. *Hist. MSS. Commission*, 14th *Rept.*, App. Pt., X. 34, 38, 184, 196.

The suggestion of Samuel Clay Harvey, made in the London *Publick Ledger* in January of 1775, is ingenious, if nothing else. He proposed to Lord North that the difficulty lay in finding some scheme "to remove the cause of the contention without subjugating the Americans on one hand or impairing the supreme authority of the Legislature, by an impolitick yielding, on the other." His plan was to grant the Americans representation at Westminster by apportioning to the colonies, including Canada and the larger West Indies, the same number of votes in Parliament as was held by the sum of the county representation in England. Then the Americans were to be accorded the privilege of electing whomsoever they pleased among those already sitting in Parliament as representatives of the counties, to represent them also. To the smaller West Indian islands were assigned the four members from London. By this scheme each county and London member of Parliament was to have a double vote in "business appertaining to the colonies," "one as an English and one as an American member." The scheme was, of course, designed to give the county members greater power in Parliament than the borough members.[57]

[57] This plan is reprinted in Force, *American Archives,* 4th ser., I. 1204. Another interesting plan appeared in New York after the signing of the French Alliance, but before Yorktown, which provided for a federalized but decentralized political union. The institutions already existing, the British Parliament and the American Continental Congress, were to continue to function as they were at that time (1780?). The latter was to have added to it an upper House of Lords, appointed by His Majesty, but from among Americans. A Viceroy with a veto should reside in America. In addition to these bodies there should be a "National Parliament composed of the Lords and Commons of Great Britain, Ireland and America, with an authority to manage and regulate the general affairs and interests of the empire, leaving to the distinct legislature of each of these great component parts of the state, the power of taxation, and the regulation of its own internal polity." The whole was to be confirmed by articles of agreement between the two. *The Alarm, or a Plan of Pacification with America.* (New York: 178–), pp. 4–6, reprinted in the American History Leaflets, No. 14. This idea of solving the problem by articles of compact was natural enough in the day of the compact theory. See *A Few Political Reflections submitted to a Consideration of the British Colonies by a Citizen of Philadelphia,* (Philadelphia: 1774), which suggests that "matters are now become reduced to such a crisis that it becomes absolutely necessary to form a charter of connexions." See also John Day's *Remarks on American Affairs,* (London: 1774), "A compact and other necessary regulations to support it should be entered into as expeditiously as the importance of the subject could admit."

Franklin was right in his forecast that Britain would not bring herself officially to offer imperial federation until it was too late. Chatham's last effort was devoid of any suggestion of it, and as for Burke's last minute attempts at reconciliation, there is his recorded opinion that a "useful representation is impossible; I am sure it is not desired by them [i.e., the Americans] nor ought it, perhaps, by us, but I abstain from opinions."[58] Lord Howe's efforts at reconciliation just after the battle of Long Island were too patronizing to offer such a thing and were properly met with the American reply by Franklin, "Long did I endeavor, with unfeigned and unwearied zeal, to preserve from breaking that noble China vase, the British Empire, for I knew that once being broken, the separate parts could not retain even their share of the strength or value that existed in the whole and that a perfect reunion of those parts could scarce ever be hoped for."[59] From the time of the failure of this mission nothing more was done until the defeat and surrender of Burgoyne and the fact of the French alliance sobered the ministry into proposing in 1778 to a bewildered and dejected House of Commons a new scheme for reconciliation. In consequence, the Carlisle Commission went out to America authorized to concede every point in the dispute with the colonies except independence and to offer them a share in the government based upon imperial federation and a provision for "agents from the different states who shall have the privilege of a seat and voice in the Parliament of Great Britain."[60] But it was too late.

The idea, then, of solving the imperial problem by permitting the Americans to elect members to sit at Westminster and granting them a share in the management of the empire by their participation in its chief legislative body seems to have been presented in the

[58] Hansard, *Parliamentary History*, XVII. 519. That he was right, see resolution of First Continental Congress, October 14, 1774, in *Journals of the Continental Congress* (Ford Ed.), I. 63, 68.

[59] The Franklin-Howe Correspondence in 1776, reprinted in Sparks edition of Franklin's *Works*, V. 101 ff.

[60] The principal documents in this matter, together with the offer made by the commission are in the *Annual Register* for 1778, pp. 329, 336. But the instructions given the commission in this regard entitle us to question their sincerity and to state with a fair degree of certainty that no true scheme of Imperial Federation could ever have been based on such instructions. *MSS. of the Earl of Carlisle: Hist. MSS. Commission*, 15th Rept., *App. Pt. VI. pp.* 322–333.

years before the Revolution. No generally accepted term, such as the modern one of "imperial federation," seems to have been current at that time to express the idea for which the modern term has been coined. Nevertheless, it is fair to say that the ideas expressed were not merely similar in their aims to the more recent ones: they were the same. Hence, although one may not attribute to Thomas Pownall, for example, the expression "imperial federation," yet he should be accredited with a concept which only that expression will adequately describe. What in fact were these schemes described in the latter part of this chapter if they were not what the terminology of Britannic policies has since come to know as "imperial federation"?

3

THE COMMONWEALTH OF NATIONS

T HE TWENTIETH century has revived, rather than originated, the idea that the British Empire is not one state but a league of states, not one nation but a commonwealth of nations.[1] Our ordinary political vocabulary is a poor thing at best because of the different senses in which the same word is used by different, although fairly authoritative writers. In dealing with the British imperial problem as it emerged in the eighteenth century, current terms were inadequate, and the twentieth century finds conditions in that respect little improved. At the outset it is well to get rid of certain popular distinctions of German origin which seem to have a considerable grip upon English and American political scientists. The American aspect of the British imperial problem is only confused by references to the *Staatenstaat,* the *Bundestaat,* and the *Staatenbund.* Why indeed should those terms be used? The American Revolution was but a stage in the development of a politically-minded people toward

[1] "I think we are inclined to make mistakes in thinking about this group of nations to which we belong, because too often we think of it merely as one state. The British Empire is much more than a state. I think the expression 'empire' is misleading, because it makes people think we are one single entity, one unity, to which the term 'empire' can be applied. We are not an empire. Germany is an empire, so was Rome, and so is India, but we are a system of nations, a community of states, and nations, far greater than any empire which has ever existed; and by using this ancient expression, we really obscure the real fact that we are larger and that our whole position is different, and that we are not one nation, or state or empire, but a whole world by ourselves, consisting of many nations and states, and all sorts of communities under one flag." Gen. J. C. C. Smuts to both Houses of Parliament, May 15, 1917.

an ideal of self-government according to law, a development which began centuries ago in England. Is there not something a little incongruous about summoning to throw light on the story of the British Empire the nomenclature of a people who waited till the twentieth century before they sloughed off ideas which the English and Americans outgrew in 1688? Yet there are even better reasons for striking out for new terms. The *Staatenstaat* is confessedly only the "Holy Roman Empire," which will hardly serve as a prototype for a league of free nations.[2] Moreover, the *Staatenbund* and the *Bundestaat* are nothing but the "confederation" and "federal union" of our own vocabulary, and all four are alike inadequate to the subject with which we are dealing. There is no use trying to place the Britannic Commonwealth of Nations in a class with the Germanic Confederation of 1816–66, as would inevitably be the result of using the expressions *Staatenbund* or "confederation." As to the *Bundestaat* or "federal union," those terms express the kind of political union found in several of the component parts of the Britannic Commonwealth separately, and are inadequate to connote the whole.[3] That entity which history knows as the British Empire is the result of growth in which English work and English experience have certainly played a larger part than the work or experience of any other people. Then why not use English words to express the relationship? The Scotch-American James Wilson certainly did not have the latest stage of the evolution of the British Empire in view when he coined the expression "Commonwealth of Nations," but he did have in mind such a political concept as would justify the adoption of that term as adequate to describe the particular form which the more enlightened colonial statesmen of the empire were trying to visualize in the years between 1765 and 1775.

This, then, is the third of the concepts of the nature of the connection between Great Britain and her American colonies held in the eighteenth century. We find such men as John Adams, James Wilson, and Thomas Jefferson thinking toward this idea. Reserving the first named for a separate chapter, we shall in this one consider

---

[2] "Der eigentliche typische Charakter des Staatenstaates ist in dem alteren Deutschen Reich ausgeprägt." H. Schultze, *Lehrbuch des Deutschen Staatesrechtes (Leipzic:* 1886), p. 44. Cf. G. Jellinek *Von der Staatsverbindungen,* p. 137; J. W. Garner, *Intro. to Polit. Sci.,* p. 165; A. B. Hart, *Intro. to Study of Federal Government,* p. 19.

[3] Canada or Australia is a "federal union" or *Bundestaat* in itself.

the latter two, and it is believed that none will deny them a place among the more profound thinkers of the Revolutionary period. Before taking up their ideas in detail, let us consider some other and earlier figures, men who were wrestling with the problem of how a so-called "sovereign" state could be a member of such a league of states as would assure concerted action of people with common ideals in times of international crisis and yet, at the same time, retain its separate identity and individuality. The concept is not an easy one to grasp, and it has plagued the worshippers at the shrine of sovereignty both early and late. However, notwithstanding the distress to a logical and rational mentality caused by the contradictions and inconsistencies involved in working out this theory, the enlightened mind must needs bring into play other tools besides logic in the problems of law and politics. It was a poet of the Britannic Dominions, and not an Anglo-Saxon, who said, "A mind all logic, like a knife all blade, cuts the hand that uses it,"[4] and this thought should be ever present in an examination of the plans for what today we call British imperial partnership.

It requires a statesman who is at the same time a close student of government to express clearly the ideas of this group of thinkers. Perhaps by none were they more clearly set forth than by James Madison, one of the closest students of government who ever graced the Presidential chair. "The fundamental principle of the Revolution," said he, "was that the colonies were coördinate members with each other, and with Great Britain, of an empire united by a common executive sovereign, but not united by any common legislative sovereign."[5] This is, in short, the whole essence of the theory of "imperial partnership," of "the commonwealth of nations," or whatever other term one chooses to employ to express the relationship actually existing between Great Britain and the dominions at the beginning of the twentieth century. Although some members of this group were inclined to let Westminster continue to function as a "common legislative sovereign" or imperial parliament, yet it was

---

[4] Rabindranath Tagore.

[5] "The legislative power was maintained to be as complete in each American parliament, as in the British parliament, and the royal prerogative was in force in each colony by virtue of its acknowledging the king for its executive magistrate, as it was in Great Britain, by virtue of a like acknowledgement there. A denial of these principles by Great Britain and an assertion of them by America produced the revolution." *Madison's Works* (Hunt Ed.), VI. 373.

with the distinct understanding that this arrangement was a convenience, not a right, and that the powers of this parliament be strictly limited.[6]

It is, then, not entirely correct to say that the plans proposed and the task at which men have labored in an effort to solve the British imperial problem have been exclusively directed toward imperial federation, which, as we observed in the last chapter, involves sending members to parliament from the four corners of the earth.[7] "Imperial partnership" is an alternative with a new name, but it is not a new alternative.[8] Unfortunately for the empire, those men who had conceived the idea most clearly left off in the midst of their efforts to solve the British imperial problem and turned their attention to the allied task of constructing a government for what has since become the United States of America, thus depriving the British Empire of the benefit of their thought.

Among these men was Richard Bland of Virginia, who in 1766 published *An Inquiry into the Rights of the British Colonies,* which Jefferson lauded as the "first pamphlet on the nature of the connection with Great Britain which had any pretension to accuracy of view on that subject."[9] The main proposition was simple enough: "America is no part of the Kingdom of Great Britain." Here is the germ of what is now styled "imperial partnership." If America was

[6] Cf. John Adams, infra.

[7] E.g., G. B. Adams in his *British Empire and a League of Peace,* (1919), p. 5, says "the plans proposed have been exclusively along a single line. The task at which men have labored has been to find some means for the representation of the outlying dominions in a central parliament of the empire, either the then existing parliament of the British Isles, or in an imperial parliament." This author's essay is acute and stimulating, and his conclusions seem so entirely in accord with the imperial partnership idea that a recognition of the men who envisaged the imperial problem along those lines would really have strengthened his position and have confirmed his sound conclusions.

[8] A. B. Keith, *Imperial Unity and the Dominions,* (1916), pp. 530–88, are devoted to this term, as applied to the modern aspect of the situation.

[9] Jefferson went on to say of Bland: "He would set out with a set of sound principles, pursue them logically till he found them leading to the precipice which he had to leap, start back alarmed, then resume his ground, go over it in another direction, be led by the correctness of his reasoning to the same place and again back about and try other processes to reconcile right and wrong but finally left his reader and himself bewildered between the steady index of the compass in their hand, and the phantasm to which it seemed to point." Jefferson's *Works* (Washington Ed.), VI. 485.

no part of the kingdom of Great Britain then what possible jurisdiction could a legislature which was exclusively the legislature of Great Britain have over territory not a part of Great Britain? Bland lived at a time when the idea of the supremacy of Parliament was as common as the idea of private property in public utilities was in the nineteenth century, and he could not give up that preconception, although he stood on the verge of the new era. Nevertheless, his work, by its very inconsistencies, shows the emergence of the new idea. While admitting the supreme power of Parliament, he contended that the King had certain prerogatives, which he exercised independently of Parliamentary consent, and among them was the granting of permission to his subjects to remove to a new country upon certain stipulations, made by him and not by Parliament. Moreover, Bland made it clear that the supremacy of the British Parliament was a thing limited by the provision of the British constitution. Here are the roots of two ideas: first, that the King had other subjects than those represented at Westminster, and, second, that there are some things Parliament cannot do. Reserving the latter idea for a future chapter, we have to notice here that the former was a perfectly well known doctrine of British constitutional law.[10]

In England in 1765 it was perfectly well understood that there were at England's doorstep some dominions which, while appendages of the crown, were not subject to the jurisdiction of the Parliament at Westminster. The Channel Islands and the Isle of

[10] Richard Bland, *An Inquiry into the Rights of the British Colonies,* (1766: Williamsburg, Va.), pp. 17, 18, 20, 22, 26. That he considered Virginia an equal partner with England in the British Empire is seen from the following: "In January, 1659, *Sir William Berkeley* was replaced at the head of the government by the People, who unanimously renounced their Obedience to Parliament, and restored the Royal Authority by proclaiming Charles the 2nd King of *England, Scotland, France, Ireland* and *Virginia,* so that he was King in *Virginia* some time before he had any certain assurance of being restored to his throne in England." p. 20. See also Bland's *"The Colonel Dismounted, or, The Rector Vindicated in a Letter addressed to His Reverence containing a Dissertation on the Constitution of the Colony"* (Williamsburg, Va.: 1764), of which L. G. Tyler remarks that Bland believed at that time that "To all intents and purposes Virginia was a co-ordinate Kingdom with England." L. G. Tyler, *Leadership of Virginia in the War of the American Revolution, William and Mary Quarterly Historical Magazine,* XIX. 26. *The Colonel Dismounted etc.,* is reprinted in the *William and Mary Quarterly Historical Magazine,* XIX, 31–41.

Man are interesting objects in the museum of British constitutional politics. In the very year in which the Stamp Act was passed the status of these islands was laid before Parliament, and the counsel for the Proprietors of the Isle of Man explained that the island 'is part of the crown but not of the realm of England; it is under allegiance to the King, but it is ruled by its own laws and customs."[11] The distinction, therefore, which the colonials made so frequently between allegiance to the crown and allegiance to the realm was not a mere fiction of their own. In the debate on the repeal of the Stamp Act, Lord Camden had said, "Guernsey, Jersey and the Isle of Man are not yet parts of the Empire and have never yet been taxed."[12]

Closely related to the idea that the King had one realm in England, another in the Isle of Man, and others in America, was the thought that therefore the people of no one of the component parts of the empire should necessarily have any jurisdiction over those of any other part—i.e., in other words, "that the legislatures of Great Britain can have no more authority over them [the colonials] than the Parliament of Paris." Inconceivable as this notion was to the loyalist Galloway, yet it was the normal result of the general proposition, and early in the decade before the Revolution we see it emerge in the query of Stephen Hopkins, "can it possibly be shown that the people of Britain have a sovereign authority over their fellow subjects in America?"[13] For this governor of Rhode Island believed the Britannic dominions to constitute an "Imperial State" consisting of "many separate governments, in which no single part, though greater than any other part, is by that superiority, entitled to make laws for, or to tax such lesser part." This assertion of the doctrine that the empire was an empire of co-equal states makes one curious to see what more the Rhode Islander thought on the subject, and we are disappointed to find that Hopkins, like Bland, got to the verge of the new idea, and then "started back alarmed" at what he found, and admitted the "existence of things of a general nature, quite out of reach of these particular legislatures," which he assigns to the jurisdiction of the British Parliament. After all the logical result of the assertion that the legislature

---

[11] Hansard, *Parliamentary History,* XVI. 34. February 15, 1765.

[12] Hansard, *Parliamentary History,* XVI. 169.

[13] *Rights of the Colonies Examined:* (Providence: 1765), reprinted as *Grievances of the American Colonies Candidly Examined:* (London: 1766), and in *The Rhode Island Records,* VI. 418.

of one division of the empire could have no jurisdiction over that of another was to deny to Parliament the control even in strictly imperial concerns. But, as has been indicated, these men were not wholly logical. Moreover, even in the twentieth century, we find colonial and dominion statesmen proclaiming their dominions autonomous, yet vigorously denying that this fact takes them out of the circle of the Britannic Commonwealth. The latter statesmen are no more logical than their American predecessors, and in fact the Americans merely represent an earlier stage of the evolution of the view held by the latter. Neither Bland nor Hopkins, however, got as far as making the practical proposal which Samuel Johnson of New York made in 1760.

Johnson was no radical, nor, on the other hand, was he the arch conservative that his contemporary namesake, the great lexicographer, seems to have been. He was one of those profound thinkers to whose writings one naturally turns in seeking for the roots of any great philosophical formula, such as those whose development we are endeavoring to trace. Under the pseudonym of "Philanglus Americanus" this first president of what is now Columbia University suggested a colonial union with a viceroy and with a council composed of representatives from each colony in the union. This council was to meet annually in New York, under the presidency of the lord-lieutenant, or viceroy, "to represent and consult on whatever may contribute to the union and stability and good of the whole." In this assembly "the common affairs of war, trades, etc., might be considered, and the confirming and negativing the laws passed by each government, the result to be confirmed or negatived" not by Parliament, but by the King. Such a scheme implied that the colonies should decide even those matters of trade and foreign affairs which most of the early statesmen were willing to grant to Westminster, and its author, seeing clearly that this was a long step in the direction of total independence, hastened to make a pious qualification. Since the only danger was that of total separation, it would remain for the church to counteract this untoward event. This rather quaint and naïve way of covering his retreat, while not as practical as the suggestions of Bland and Hopkins, was thoroughly consistent with Johnson's position in colonial history.[14] A similar solution was proposed by Drayton of South Carolina, who wanted a "High

[14] *Documents Relating to the Colonial History of New York* (N. Y.: 1856), VII. 442–3. Cf. also Woodbridge Riley in *Camb. Hist. of Amer. Lit.,* I. 81–6.

Court of Assembly of North America" with powers similar to those subsequently held by the Continental Congress.[15]

But it was not in America alone that such ideas were current, for in 1766 John Almon in London published the proposal sometimes attributed to Joshua Steele[16] which entailed "leaving every part of the old system as it now is, that every kingdom or province should continue its parliament or assembly, or whatever form of internal government it is possessed of, and defray all its expenses within itself," showing at least the presence of the idea that the empire was an empire of separate political entities. In addition, it was proposed to "superadd for union and utility of the whole, a new sovereign council, consisting of deputies from each province of the *Great Commonwealth.*" An examination of this proposal suggests that here in embryo was the type of thing which a hundred years later developed into the Imperial Conference. The Great Council was strictly enjoined from meddling in the internal affairs of any constituent dominion of the "Great Commonwealth," and to those dominions was to be left the task of determining for themselves how they should raise their quotas of supplies and troops, much as was done in the World War in 1914. It would be difficult to contend that the council was not a legislative body (making the scheme one of "imperial federation"), but it would be equally difficult to contend that it was, and since the general spirit was to preserve the old system of separate kingdoms, it seems fairer to include it among the earlier suggestions of imperial partnership.[17]

But there is another reason for assuming that some persons in England must at least have been conversant with the ideas of more progressive Americans; during a large part of the time between 1765 and 1775 Benjamin Franklin was in London, expressing these views. Franklin successively held all three of the theories of the nature of the empire with which we are dealing, and he slipped from one to the other with the same ease that finally led him into an advocacy of total separation and independence. By 1769 he had apparently adopted the third theory, and the publication in England

---

[15] *Letter of a Freeman,* (Gibbes reprint), p. 18.

[16] An English reformer. Both Sabin and Rich, in his *Bib. Amer. Nova,* I. 154, attribute this to him. Cf. *Dict. Nat. Biog.,* LIV. 129.

[17] J. Steele, *An Account of a Late Conference on the Occurrences in America in a Letter to a Friend.* (London: 1766).

of some pamphlets which stated rather flatly the "our colonies" theory of colonial dependency provoked from him some delightfully explicit statements as to the nature of the empire. One pamphleteer, with a mental shudder, had complained, "If each assembly in this case were absolute, they would, it is evident, form not one only, but so many different governments, perfectly independent of one another." In this conclusion Franklin acquiesced with pleasure, saying, "This is the only clear idea of their real present condition. Their only bond of union is the King."[18] For the colonies were not within the realm of England, or Great Britain, and hence, "the British state is only the Island of Great Britain; the British legislature are undoubtedly the only proper judges of what concerns the welfare of that state; but the Irish legislature is the proper judge of what concerns the Irish state, and the American legislatures of what concerns the American states respectively. By the 'whole empire' does this writer [i.e., the author of the pamphlet to which Franklin is replying] mean all of the King's dominions? If so the British Parliament should also govern the islands of Jersey and Guernsey and Hanover; but this is not so."[19] Believing as he did that there could be a "dominion of the crown, not within the realm,"[20] Franklin held that the English were "bewildering themselves by supposing the colonies within the realm, which is not the case, or ever was," for in fact the "Americans are without the realm and not of the jurisdiction." Hence he was able to proclaim with perfect consistency, "I am a subject of the crown of Great Britain," while he denied the power of Parliament over the colonies, for, said he, "America is not part of the dominions of England, but of the King's dominions."[21] At this late date [1769] he still thought it practical to bring representatives from America to Westminster, but remarked, "the present mode of letting them govern themselves by their own assemblies is much preferable. They will be better gov-

[18] Franklin's *Works:* (Bigelow Ed.), IV. 309, Franklin comments on *"An Inquiry Into the Nature of and Causes of the Disputes Between the British Colonies in America and Their Mother Country,* (London: 1769).

[19] Franklin's *Works,* (Bigelow Ed.), IV. 317, 327. He wrote in reply to *The True Constitutional Means of Putting an End to the Disputes Between Great Britain and her American Colonies,* (London: 1769).

[20] Franklin's *Works,* (Bigelow Ed.), III. 490.

[21] Franklin's *Works,* (Bigelow Ed.), IV. 312.

erned, and Parliament has business enough here with its own internal concerns."[22]

Indeed Governor Bernard had not been very far wrong when early in the controversy he said, "it is my opinion that all the political evils in America arise from want of ascertaining the relations between Great Britain and the American colonies." Nor was he far wrong in explaining the American position as being a claim "to be perfect states, not otherwise dependent on Great Britain than by having the same King," because all the colonies had "compleat legislatures within themselves."[23] In such an empire it was evident a hundred and fifty years ago, as it is evident today, that the King was a fiction, albeit a very useful one. Consequently it is not surprising that we find plans which suggest "superadding a council for the union and utility of the whole" which would give the necessary popular sanction to fictitiously royal acts. One of the most detailed of these plans appeared after the Revolution was under way. It included "not only a reconciliation with the thirteen united provinces" but a "more firm union of Great Britain with the other colonies of Canada, the Floridas, Nova Scotia, etc." The connecting administrative link between the "independent nations" which composed the empire was to be a "great council of state" composed of delegates sent by the governments of the constituent nations, and their action was not to be final until confirmed by the "several parliaments" of the component nations. This fairly elaborate plan for better uniting the several kingdoms of the United Empire was substantially a league of states whose chief administrative organ was to be not a government but a conference.[24]

The year 1774 found the necessity for a solution of the imperial problem so acute that numerous plans appeared looking toward a reconciliation between America and Britain. Not the least important among them was the suggestion of Joseph Galloway, of Philadelphia, who shares with Thomas Hutchinson a leading place among American statesmen opposed to the Revolution. It would be unfair to

[22] Franklin's *Works*, (Bigelow Ed.), IV. 310. This idea was at least understood in England; Cf. *An Apology for the Late Conduct of America*, in the London *Gazetteer*, 7 April, 1774. Force, *Amer. Arch.*, 4th ser. I. 241–2.

[23] *Barrington–Bernard Correspondence*, 23 Nov., 1765, p. 96.

[24] *Proposal for a Plan toward Reconciliation and Reunion with the Thirteen Provinces in America, and for a Union with the Other Colonies by One of the Public*, (London: 1778), pp. 1, 3.

Galloway to class him with the adherents of the doctrine of British overlordship and the believers in the supremacy of Parliament. He had a plan of reconciliation predicated upon the existence of a power which limited Parliament. He never reached the thought that the empire was a commonwealth of nations, for he believed "the colonists are members of the British state, and owe obedience to its legislative authority." But neither was he an imperial federationist, for he could not but think that to divide the authority of Parliament between superior and subordinate jurisdictions would operate to "weaken and confound the operations of the system and to subvert the very end and purpose for which it was formed."[25] Perhaps Galloway has no claim to a place in this chapter. Nevertheless, he did present to the first Continental Congress a scheme for "Accommodation on Constitutional Principles," which rejected the possibility of colonial representation at Westminster and proposed a "Plan of union between Great Britain and the colonies" which merits examination as a scheme upon which "imperial partnership" might have been built, if not as a scheme of "imperial partnership." It is a matter of common knowledge that the fundamental acts upon which the political constitution of the great self-governing dominions of the Britannic Commonwealth now rest were originally passed by the Parliament at Westminster. But this theoretic admission of the overlordship of the Parliament of Great Britain has not prevented the normal development of the dominions to their present status in which Westminster could hardly take back what in theory it formerly granted. Galloway's plan called for a Grand Council chosen by "the representatives of the people of the several colonies in their respective assemblies," which together with a president-general appointed by the King should constitute a "government." This government should meet each year, and the Grand Council should exercise for America "all the rights, liberties and privileges as are held and exercised by and in the House of Commons of Great Britain."[26] The president-general was to be the chief executive, should possess a veto power, and, together with the Grand Council, was to "hold and exercise all the legislative rights, powers and

[25] Joseph Galloway, *A Candid Examination of the Mutual Claims of Great Britain and the Colonies, by the Author of Letters to a Nobleman on the Conduct of the American War,* (London: 1780, reprinted from New York: 1775), p. 35.

[26] *Journals of the Continental Congress,* (Ford Ed.), I. 43 ff.

authorities necessary for regulating and administering all the general police and internal affairs of the colonies, in which Great Britain or the colonies, or any of them" should be in any way concerned. The colonial union government should exercise this colonial jurisdiction jointly with Parliament, and, in the case of colonial affairs, each should have a veto on the acts of the other. Such a plan would have made possible the avoidance by the colonials of the obnoxious acts which precipitated the crisis and would have given room for the natural development of self-governing communities such as has taken place since 1850 elsewhere in the Britannic dominions.

The biographer of Thomas Hutchinson, the other great loyalist, has expressed the opinion that that statesman forecast the present colonial system of the British Empire. The implication—and not an unreasonable one—is that Hutchinson had an idea of the nature of the empire upon which it might have been possible to construct the present system.[27] The justification of this view is seen in Hutchinson's insistence that whatever the measures taken "to maintain the authority of Parliament," Parliament should accompany them with a "declaration that it is not the intention of Parliament to deprive the colonies of their subordinate power of legislation, nor to exercise the supreme legislative power, except in such cases and upon such occasions as an equitable regard to the interests of the whole empire shall make necessary."[28] All this is fair enough, but the trouble with Hutchinson, as with Galloway, is that he insisted upon being logical. The supremacy of Parliament was and, in the twentieth century, still is, logical in the absence of other imperial machinery, but it betrayed evidence of poor taste and indiscretion to say so. Hutchinson could not refrain from saying so, and even in his "Vindication" he insisted that "Britain and its colonies are alike dependent on the supreme authority of the whole empire," and to him that authority was "The King, the Lords and Commons."[29] We may observe that the expression "*its* colonies," like "*our* colonies," is hardly the mark of the Britannic statesman.[30]

The last year of the old British Empire's peaceful existence witnessed the publication of the works of John Adams, James Wilson,

---

[27] J. K. Hosmer, *Life of Thomas Hutchinson,* (1896), pp. 137, 261.

[28] *Mass. Arch. Hist.,* XXVI. 313, quoted in Hosmer, supra, p. 137.

[29] *Diary and Letters of Thomas Hutchinson,* (1884), I. 576; *Strictures upon the Declaration of the Congress at Philadelphia,* (London: 1776).

[30] Cf. Sir Richard Jebb, *Britannic Question,* p. 71.

and Thomas Jefferson on the nature of the empire, and all three seem to have come to the conclusion that the "commonwealth of nations" was the only tenable theory. Jefferson's work is well known, containing, as it does, much of the language which subsequently found its way into the Declaration of Independence. It is, however, questionable whether the works of the two prospective Presidents of the United States equal that of James Wilson in clearness of vision, accuracy of analysis, or consistency of presentation. The "Considerations on the Nature and Extent of the Legislative Authority of the British Parliament"[31] presents in its very title the core of the imperial problem at that time. The opening sentence repeats it: "No question can be more important to Great Britain and the colonies than this—does the legislative authority of the British Parliament extend over them?" Wilson answered in the negative, but, loyal to the idea of the Britannic Commonwealth, he hastens to add, "a denial of the legislative authority of the British Parliament over America is by no means inconsistent with that connection which ought to subsist between the mother country and her colonies."[32] That connection did not involve the ascendancy of the mother country; indeed, "the superiority of Great Britain over the colonies ought to be rejected"[33] for the "Commons of Great Britain have no dominion over their equals and fellow subjects in America." The distinction between allegiance to and dependency on the crown and allegiance to and dependency on the realm or Parliament receives at Wilson's hands a treatment which is certainly illuminating and paves the way relentlessly to the final conclusion "that all members of the British Empire are distinct states, independent of each other, but connected together under the same sovereign, in right of the same crown."[34] In reply to the argument that there must be some superior superintending power to regulate the trade of the British Empire, his answer is both keen and significant. First, "it has been the opinion of some politicians, of no inferior note, that all regulations of trade are useless; that the greatest part of them are hurtful; and that the stream of commerce never flows with so much beauty and advantage as when it is not diverted from its natural channels." But since he was a sufficiently practical man not to let the dream

---

[31] By James Wilson (Philadelphia: 1774).

[32] Wilson's *Works*, (Philadelphia Ed., 1804), III. 236.

[33] Ibid., III. 237.

[34] Ibid., III. 241.

of universal free trade carry him too far, he suggested that the power of regulating trade be entrusted "to the king, as part of his royal prerogative." One could wish for an elaboration of this point, as the colonials understood far too well the character of the British government as a limited monarchy to attribute despotic powers to George III. Wilson seems to have had in mind a distinction between the King in his imperial and in his royal capacities; in the latter capacity the King, he believed, was inextricably associated with the ministry of Great Britain. Whether such a distinction would have, if understood, led to the calling of an imperial conference of ministers from all parts of the empire, we cannot say, but we do know that six months after the publication of the "Considerations," Wilson delivered a public address in which he said, "We do not send members to the British Parliament: we have parliaments of our own,"[35] and "The distinction between him [the King] and his ministers has been lost: but they have not been raised to his situation: he has sunk to theirs."[36] Taken together, his utterances certainly indicate an unwillingness to concede that the American dominions were anything less than equal partners in the empire, with an equal unwillingness to break away from the allegiance to the Britannic idea. It has been said of James Wilson that he represents ideas far in advance of his own day, ideas which the world is only just beginning to understand. Perhaps his conception of the nature of the British Empire is another instance of this prevision.[37]

Jefferson's position, though not as carefully worked out as Wilson's, was quite similar. His "Summary View of the Rights of British America" took the ground which from the beginning he had thought "the only orthodox and tenable one, which was that the relation between Great Britain and these colonies was exactly the same as that of England and Scotland after the accession of James and until the union, and the same as her present relations with Hanover,

[35] *Speech delivered in the Convention for the Province of Pennsylvania,* (Phila: Jan: 1775), *Works,* III. 247, 259.

[36] *Works,* III. 269.

[37] Cf. L. H. Alexander in *N. Amer. Rev.,* CLXXXIII. 971. Cf. Wilson's view in 1790: "Two sovereign states may employ the same executive magistrate, or bear allegiance to the same prince without dependence on each other, and each may retain all its national rights free and undiminished. This last, also, as shall hereafter be shown, was the case of Great Britain and the American colonies before the political connexion between them was declared to be dissolved." Wilson's *Works,* I. 362.

having the chief executive, but no other necessary political connection."[38] Parliament was, in his way of thinking, "only the legislature of one part of the Empire."[39] What right "one free and independent legislature" had to "take upon itself to suspend the powers of another, free and independent as itself," Jefferson could not conceive.[40] The position accorded the King was substantially the same as that which Wilson gave him: he was the "common sovereign, who is thereby made the central link, connecting up the several parts of the Empire."[41] In this doctrine Jefferson apparently never got anyone in Virginia to agree with him except George Wythe, who "concurred in it from the first dawn of the question, 'What is the political relation between us and England?' Our other patriots, Randolph, the Lees, Nicholas and Pendleton stopped at the half-way house with John Dickinson, who admitted that England had a right to regulate our commerce and lay duties on it for the purpose of regulation, but not for raising revenue."[42]

What Jefferson was doing for the Virginians, what Adams did for the people of Massachusetts, and what Wilson did for Pennsylvanians, was done for the North Carolinians by James Iredell. In his address "To the Inhabitants of Great Britain" in 1774, he made clear his conception of the nature of the empire in which the King was the executive head of many co-equal legislatures in as many co-equal political communities. As it then existed, he believed the Empire lacked any one supreme power, such as Parliament aspired to be, but he insisted, "we are ready at any time to enter into fair negotiations by means of which to concert a plan of cementing the general interest of the Empire upon a broad basis, and securing *a proper union of counsel and authority,* and *the individual freedom* of each member of the Empire, so far as is con-

[38] The "Summary View" appears in Jefferson's *Works,* (Washington Ed.), I. 122. Cf. also his Autobiography: *Works* (Washington Ed.), I. 8.

[39] Jefferson's *Works,* (Washington Ed.), I. 125.

[40] Ibid., I. 131.

[41] Ibid., I. 127.

[42] Ibid., I. 8. Wythe believed "that we were co-ordinate 'nations' with Great Britain and Hanover." See Jefferson's *Works,* I. 113. Consequently Channing is not quite accurate when he says "Imperial Federation, not dependency or democracy was in Jefferson's mind." E. Channing, *Hist. of the United States,* III. 183. The fact was that neither imperial federation, nor independence, but what in this chapter has been called "imperial partnership" in a commonwealth of nations, was what Jefferson was thinking out.

sistent with general welfare." This is scarcely the language of one who believed that the Empire as it then existed was in fact any more than what the most advanced modern thinkers contend that it is.[43]

In this same year, 1774, two very interesting English liberals made suggestions which betoken the existence of a more enlightened sentiment in England than was manifested in Parliament. John Cartwright was one of the earliest agitators for Parliamentary reform, and so it is not surprising to find that he wrote a pamphlet which bore the interesting sub-title, "Arguments to prove that not only in taxation, but in trade and manufactures and government, the colonies are entitled to an entire independence of the British legislature, and that it can only be by a formal declaration of these rights, and forming thereupon a friendly league with them, that the true and lasting welfare of both countries can be promoted."[44] The idea of the Empire as a league was not born with the twentieth century. Cartwright's league took in all of the American states, including Quebec and the Floridas, and all were "held and declared to be free and independent states, each to be subject only to such law and government as now subsists, or shall hereafter be enacted by its own proper legislature." The King was to be separately the King of each of the constituent nations of the league and to be "the protector of the whole against foreign powers." This would not make the constituent nations separate units in international law, despite the declaration that they were "free and independent states," a fact which once more emphasizes the inadequacy of our political terminology, which finds it so difficult to admit the existence of an entity thus composed. Cartwright even admitted the right of each nation of the league to make treaties with the others "in order that a firm, brotherly and perpetual league may be concluded between Great Britain and them." However much such a proposition must have shocked the advocates of the Navigation Acts, it does not seem so impracticable in the light of later experience.[45]

The other "philanthropist, pamphleteer and scholar" was Granville Sharp, in whose work is to be found one of the earlier suggestions that the Britannic Commonwealth might become a prototype

[43] G. L. McRee, *Life and Correspondence of James Iredell,* (N. Y., 1858), I. 207, 209, 214, 218, 219.

[44] *American Independence: The Interest and Glory of Great Britain,* (London: 1774), p. 63.

[45] Cf. Edward Smith in *Dict. of Nat. Biog.,* IX. 224.

for a world-wide league of nations. In his "Declaration of the People's Natural Right to Share in the Legislature," Sharp enunciated the doctrine that as "the King and the people constituted the sovereign power in Great Britain," so the King and the people of America constitute the sovereign power in America. For "representation of the people in every part of the British Empire is absolutely necessary to constitute an effectual legislature according to the fundamental principles of the British Constitution."[46] Nevertheless, "however distinct these several parts and provinces may seem in point of situation, as well as in the exercise of a separate legislative power for each (which constitutional rights they have enjoyed beyond the memory of man), they are nevertheless firmly united in the circle of the British diadem, which will never be divided, if the safe and honest policy be adopted of maintaining the British constitution inviolate in all parts of the Empire." In pursuing this idea Sharp beheld his vision of an "empire of the world" based upon and exemplified by a union of all those communities with which expanding Britain has peopled the world.[47]

Efforts at reconciling the colonies upon this general basis of a league of equal states by no means ceased with the outbreak of the war. The effort made by the government in sending out the Carlisle Commission in 1778 was accompanied by a revival of these schemes, prominent among which was William Pulteney's proposal. Far from believing that the Declaration of Independence had made a union impossible, he thought it only more likely to be favorably considered. Events since 1775 must, he believed, have disillusioned the Tories as to the willingness and capacity of the Americans to defend their principles with their lives, and consequently the time had come to compromise, or even to consent to the reorganization of the Empire upon the terms which the Americans laid down. He urged that the old theory of colonial dependency be dispensed with, and that the status of the colonists as equal participants in the benefits of the British Constitution be acknowledged. The work was immensely popular and ran through five editions.[48]

[46] *Declaration*, etc., p. 17. See also *Memories of Granville Sharp, Esq.*, by Prince Hoare: (London: 1820), pp. 172, 181.

[47] Cf. A. F. Pollard in *Dict. Nat. Biog.*, LI, 421, Cf. also G. L. Beer's *English Speaking Peoples*, which is a recent revival of Cartwright's idea.

[48] William Pulteney, *Thoughts on the Present State of Affairs with America and the Means of Conciliation*, (London: 1778). The author was a Member of Parliament from Shrewsbury, and should not be confused with the other pamphleteer of the same name, the Earl of Bath.

Among the efforts to uncover a theory which would supply the compromise between dependency and independency, few are so penetrating as that which appeared in London in 1780 under the name of "A Plan, or Articles of Perpetual Union, Commerce and Friendship, Between Great Britain and Her American Colonies."[49] Here was an Englishman who urged that "From hence we should be taught to view the colonies, not as a few insignificant and petty states, but (what they soon will be) as a large, flourishing and powerful empire; not as children whom we may chastise at pleasure, but as friends, as equals, and as brethren."[50] His "medium between the claims of total independence and those of legal subjection" was drawn in the form of a treaty between Great Britain and Ireland and America. These three with the dependencies annexed to each were considered to form an "empire" which was a single political unit as far as defense from external aggression was concerned. In all other matters, British America was to be a free and independent nation; indeed, he had no objection to calling her such. In case of war the troops of any part of the empire could be used for the defense of the whole—but should "on no account be employed in conquests, or in foreign expeditions, without the formal consent and cheerful approbation of those engaged."[51] Each American province was to have a governor appointed by the crown, but this governor was to be practically at the mercy of the popularly elected legislative body, without whose consent he could do nothing, and by whom his salary was paid.[52] Colonial legislatures could override the laws of England, whenever they saw fit to do so for local purposes. All this seems extremely liberal, so much so that one is a little suspicious. Some justification of that suspicion is found in the commercial clauses of the proposed treaty. The preferential rates to be granted to British vessels and British products ensured the commercial supremacy of the mother country as far as her European competitors were concerned. The author fell in with things as they

[49] Subtitle: *Founded in the Solid Basis of Justice and Proposed as a Medium between the Claims of Total Independence on the one hand and those of Legal Subjection on the Other.*

[50] *A Plan, etc.*, p. 9.

[51] *A Plan, etc.*, p. 19.

[52] There were to be four provinces into which the colonies were grouped. p. 21. (1) Nova Scotia and the New England Colonies; (2) New York, New Jersey and Pennsylvania; (3) Maryland, Virginia and North Carolina, (4) South Carolina to Florida. Canada was suggested as a possible fifth.

were as far as to recognize the Continental Congress and provide for its continued existence as the "grand legislative, superintending and controlling power through all British America," and as possessing the sole power of taxing for imperial purposes. The executive of British America was to be a council of twelve to be elected by the people at the same time they chose their delegates for the legislature. This left practically no power to the representative of the crown, the Lord Commissioner, who was to be appointed by the King and "to whom all acts which shall be passed by Congress shall be formally presented, not for the purpose of his assent or approbation, but merely to be transmitted to Great Britain as a matter of information only."[53] It was admitted that the Lord Commissioner was in the nature of an ambassador rather than a governor. His position was similar to and quite as innocuous as that of the royal governors-general in the great self-governing dominions today. The whole plan was worked out with an apparently sincere desire to secure for the members of the empire such a "moderate dependence as may in no one instance be gallingly felt, thereby to save the expense of military and other establishments, and yet to secure a firm and lasting union" with Great Britain.[54] In the face of the failure of the Carlisle mission and the increasingly manifest inability of the British to subdue the colonies, such a scheme was necessarily fruitless, but it is fairly concrete evidence that the discussions incident to the American Revolution brought to light men who were attacking the problem of trying to mediate between states of "moderate sovereignty."

This chapter would be incomplete if it did not take notice of the latest application of the theories of Bland, Wilson, Jefferson, and John Adams. The treaty which promises to terminate the centuries of terror in Ireland gives Ireland just the place in the empire which the Americans demanded in 1774. The sole constitutional threat is allegiance to a common king, which apparently has worked in regard to the other dominions, Canada, New Zealand, Australia, South Africa, and the like. It is a far cry from James Wilson to Michael Collins, but Lloyd George is infinitely further from the group that dominated the British government in the time of George III.[55]

[53] *A Plan, etc.*, pp. 21, 46, 50.
[54] Ibid., p. 69.
[55] Treaty between Great Britain and Ireland creating the Irish Free State, Dec. 6, 1921. Articles I, II, and III. Reprinted in *Current History*, XV. 568–9.

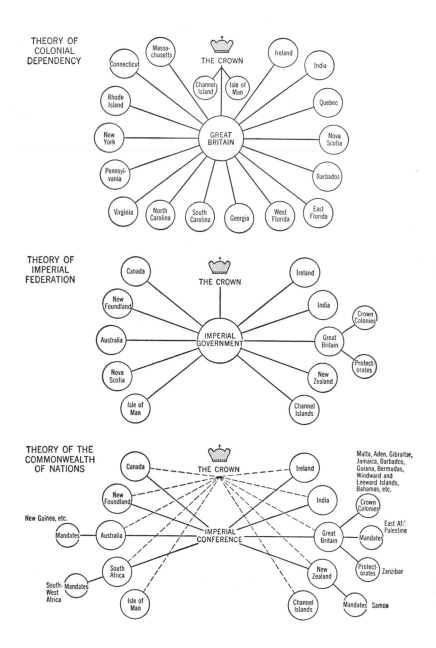

THEORIES OF BRITISH AND BRITANNIC IMPERIAL ORGANIZATION

No. 1. THE BRITISH EMPIRE, *The Theory of Colonial Dependency,* or the theory of a mother country and her children colonies. This was the theory current in the "Old British Empire" (before 1784). Great Britain and her Parliament are the head and center of the empire, and all the colonies are subject to her. The Channel Islands and the Isle of Man are not colonies, but are subject directly to the crown. This diagram illustrates the point of view of those who held to the theory of "parliamentary supremacy." Several colonies are omitted for the sake of brevity and clarity, for the diagram is intended only to indicate the theory and not to be a sketch of the constitution of the empire in detail. It ought to be observed that it is questionable whether India can be considered a part of the empire prior to 1784. Each circle represents a *government.*

No. 2. THE BRITISH IMPERIAL CONFEDERATION, *The Theory of Imperial Federation.* This represents an idea which has never been put into practice. It involves the subordination of the government of Great Britain to the level of the other governments in the empire and the erection of a central imperial government, with an imperial parliament to which all the dominions send representatives. This is what would have happened if the American cry of no taxation without representation had been heeded, for this shows how the "colonies" might have been represented. The diagram is constructed with the present dominions, as the question has seriously been debated in late years as a possible future model for imperial constitutional relations. It does not, however, seem practical. A circle represents a *government.*

No. 3. THE BRITANNIC COMMONWEALTH OF NATIONS, *The Theory of Britannic Partnership.* This diagram represents what the empire has actually become and what the more enlightened Americans were asking for in the eighteenth century. A circle represents a *government;* the Imperial Conference is not a government, but is more akin to an international conference. This diagram takes some liberty with the facts for the sake of simplifying the idea. There is no uniformity in the relationship of the various dominions to the commonwealth. It should be observed that many of the so-called crown colonies are moving in the direction of the dominion status as they are being granted rights of local self-government—e.g., Malta.

4

TAXATION AND REPRESENTATION:
SOME RECONSIDERATIONS

THE STORY OF THE taxation controversy forms an essential part of the American historical background for an association or league of nations. Yet, were one to sit down and read any one of the better known secondary accounts of that controversy, it is somewhat questionable whether he would associate it with modern problems in international law. Nevertheless, the more we try to understand the relationship which the United States must bear to whatever form of world organization eventuates from international conferences and practices, the more there seems to run through the ten years preceding the Revolution a tale that needs to be told. And it is a tale that is worth recounting if one has no other motive than historical curiosity. At the outset we should eliminate from our thought any antipathy or partiality toward Great Britain, insofar as the phrase "no taxation without representation" rouses either the one or the other in us. It would seem almost commonplace to suggest that that slogan should be viewed as a symptom of defective imperial machinery, but it is a commonplace not always observed. There is reason to say that the familiar "no-taxation-without-representation" battle-cry was but the final stage of a ten-year struggle to make the British Parliament understand that its chief task was to formulate a satisfactory league of nations.[1] It was bound

[1] In the year of the Stamp Act, Gov. Bernard of Massachusetts asserted that the political reorganization of the American governments was a condition precedent to settling the dispute between England and her colonies. Nine years later, on the eve of the Revolution, he published some letters which he

to be noticed by the statesmen of a little more than ordinary vision that "the degree of authority which might rightfully be exercised by the mother country over her colonies has never been accurately defined."[2]

What the people of the Revolutionary period thought and proposed about an improvement of the superintending machinery of the empire in the period when the necessity of such improvement came most critically before that part of the British Empire which became the United States of America is a story which one must look far to discover. Among the host of valuable commentaries on the American Revolution, there are several which lead us up to the very edge of the subject and then, digressing into some other field, leave the reader with a most unsatisfied feeling. Yet during that ten years between the passage of the Stamp Act and the outbreak of the war for independence, the statesmen of the thirteen overseas self-governing dominions of the British Empire in North America participated actively in an effort to solve the problem of the commonwealth of nations. By the American Revolution they evaded, for the time being, any further responsibility in the matter, as far as that particular commonwealth is concerned. Hence it is in the decade before that evasion of responsibility that one may hope to discern the roots of the movement to organize a league or commonwealth of semi-sovereign states.

One feels instantly challenged for not beginning his search earlier, for the Articles of Confederation of the United States of New Eng-

---

had written many years before when still governor, in which publication he remarked, in the preface, what an unfortunate blunder it was that at the time of the English Revolution of 1688 "the constitutions of the governments of America were not settled in Parliament and the rights of the Imperial state over them acknowledged, with such regulations and limitations as the several natures of them, upon constitutional principles and good policy should require." If only this had been done, then at the late date of 1774 Great Britain would not "be at a loss for the principles upon which the connection of its subordinate governments with the Imperial state may be best preserved and the union of the whole maintained and continued." *The Barrington–Bernard Correspondence: 1760–1770*, p. 93. *Select Letters on the Government of America and the Principles of Law and Polity Applied to the American Colonies.* (London: 1774), p. ii.

[2] John Marshall, *A History of the Colonies Planted by England on the Continent of North America, From Their Settlement to the Commencement of the War Which Terminated in their Independence,* (Philadelphia: 1824), p 352.

land bear the date of 1643.[3] It is indeed true that the so-called "Plans of Union" began to appear at the end of the seventeenth century. But it is submitted that these efforts to formulate a union of the provinces of America are better conceived as a part of the American historical background of the idea of a federal union, and they can be employed to little advantage for the purposes of this study. The New England Confederation of the seventeenth century forms a better prototype for the Dominion of Canada, or the Commonwealth of Australia, than it does for any commonwealth or league of nations. Historians have not neglected the story of these "Plans of Union" in the story of the United States as a federal union. Yet the other and larger question does not reach a critical point while there is as yet no Grenville to bother himself with colonial dispatches.[4] The plans of union were dictated to a very large extent by the motive of defense, either against the Indians or the French, while the other idea could not appear until there was some motive for asserting the status of the members of the empire-commonwealth. It was but natural that the earlier plans should present themselves as adaptable to the situation which called them forth, and that was not so much international coöperation as common defense. Hence when the

---

[3] See *Plymouth Colony Records*, IX. 3.

[4] Dr. A. C. McLaughlin has for many years been trying to impress his students and readers with the significance of the problem of imperial order in the preliminaries of the American Revolution. His chapter on the "Background of American Federalism" (*America and Britain:* 177–221: N. Y.: 1918) is an able interpretation of the decade before the Revolution as an unsuccessful attempt to solve the British Imperial Problem. Failing to find this solution, the decade becomes to him the "Background of American Federalism." Dr. H. C. Hockett has attacked the same problem and finds this story, "The American Background of Federalism" (vid. *Amer. Hist. Rev.*, XXVI, 427). He believes that the chief contributions to political thought were to the problem of Federalism wherever found, and particularly he believes that the American position in the pre-Revolutionary controversy fore-shadowed the modern British Imperial Organization. If I have interpreted these gentlemen correctly, it is my own belief that this story serves yet another purpose, and I believe I am justified in retelling it from the point of view of the "American Contribution to Sovereignty." Dr. Hockett has advanced the view that it was not the American Revolution which forced the British to abandon their old narrow colonial system, but the ideas of Adam Smith and Canadian demands for responsible government. If this be true, and it is my opinion that it is true, then the political thought of the American Revolution becomes a contribution to the philosophy of International Law, i.e., it forms a background for a league or association or nations.

early plans do take into consideration the relationship between the component parts of the empire, they are apt to emphasize the subordinate position of the proposed colonial union, as in Franklin's Albany Plan[5] (1754), where provision was made for the disallowance by the King in Council of the acts of the Grand Colonial Council. Such a plan as that prepared by the Lords of Trade in 1754 was one of "general coöperation of the American colonies," and is chiefly actuated by a desire to make the colonies undertake their own defense in case of war.[6] The other plans providing for "general coöperation between the component parts of the empire-commonwealth" begin to appear after the close of the Seven Years War, when other elements and motives enter the situation.

The close of that war (1763) ends an epoch in American history, for the motive of defense against the French has, to a large measure, vanished. Hence it is that in the plans of colonial coöperation which now appear there enters the element of imperial coöperation. For example, Galloway's plan, which has been classed among the plans of union, makes an advance over the earlier programs for a purely colonial union in that the colonies desire such union "not only among themselves, but with the mother state."[7] The taxation controversy, which arose after the end of the old epoch had fixed the minds of the colonists upon the defective imperial machinery of the Britannic Empire Commonwealth, and the ten years of taxation wranglings between 1765 and 1775 have yielded many stories for the chronicler. Yet among these stories one does not find frequent reference to direct efforts to solve the difficulty as one of quasi-international organization. The reason is not far to seek. The century which insisted upon telling the story of the Revolution in terms of red-coats and Hessians was no sooner in its grave than another century opened with an explanation of the American Revolution in terms of the struggle for commercial supremacy. "The primary cause of the American Revolution must be sought in the character of the old colonial system," those acts of trade and navigation, "which were based on political and economic theories generally accepted as valid in the seventeenth century, but which are, never-

[5] Franklin, *Works:* (Sparks Ed.), III. 36.

[6] *Documents Relating to the History of New York,* VI. 903.

[7] A. B. Hart and E. Channing in *Amer. Hist. Leaflets* No. 14, so class Galloway's Plan. For that plan see Peter Force, *Amer. Arch.,* 4th Series, Vol. I. 905.

theless, the fruit of ignorance and inexperience."[8] "Commercialism, the desire for advantage and profit in trade and industry, was at the bottom of the struggle of England and America; the immutable principles of human association were brought forward to justify colonial resistance to British selfishness."[9] There is no need to discuss the accuracy of these conclusions; they represent deductions based upon careful scientific investigation. But attention may profitably be directed to them in partial explanation of the insufficiency of our knowledge of the efforts made prior to the Revolution to settle the dispute between Britain and her colonies by the method of reforming the empire commonwealth. A recent writer has observed with a good deal of cogency that "the issue between England and America is therefore not to be resolved by commuting the burdens of the penny tax, or exposing the sordid motives of British merchants and Boston smugglers, still less by coming armed at all points with law cases and acts of Parliament, with a statute book doubled down in dog's ears, to defend the cause either of liberty or of authority."[10] Such warning has not prevented writers from approaching the subject of the American Revolution as a "problem of separation,"[11] but it does inspire one with a desire to see what reason there is to view the Revolution as an unsolved "problem of devolution."

The remark that the controversy over taxation fixed the thoughts of Americans on the nature of the imperial machinery and its defects may not pass unchallenged. Nevertheless, there is reason to say that this dispute had that deeper political significance not ordinarily attributed to it. Although one spectator historian of the Revolution called the taxation controversy the "very hinge upon which the Revolution turned,"[12] still historians, earlier and later, have conceded that "the Stamp Act and the insignificant duty on tea, precipitated, but did not alone produce the American Revolution,"[13] that "taxation was the excuse rather than the cause of the

[8] G. E. Howard, *Preliminaries of the American Revolution*, p. 47.

[9] E. Channing, *History of the United States*, III. i.

[10] C. Becker, *Beginnings of the American People*, p. 203.

[11] W. E. Foster, *"Stephen Hopkins, Statesman,"* supplies this apt expression which epitomizes the point of view of numerous writers.

[12] D. Ramsay, *History of the American Revolution*. (Phila.: 1789), I. 48.

[13] T. Pitkin, *Political and Civil History of the United States*, (1828), I. 4.

Revolution."[14] Hence we approach the subject as a symptom rather than as a disease itself.

For purposes of clarity and convenience, the story of the constitutional aspect of the taxation controversy may be understood to develop in three successive stages. In the first the colonies admitted the right of Parliament to levy customs duties (external taxes), but denied the right of Parliament to levy excise taxes (internal taxes) upon them. In the second, the colonies conceded the right of Parliament to regulate the trade of the Empire, and hence exercise a legislative authority over the unrepresented colonies, but denied the right of Parliament to levy taxes of any kind whatever, internal or external. In the third stage of the controversy, the colonies admitted the right of Parliament to act as a quasi-imperial superintending power over them and over all the dominions, but denied that Parliament had any legislative authority over the colonies as a general proposition, on the ground that the colonies were not represented in Parliament. Such a story illustrates how, throughout the controversy, the colonists were attempting to work out philosophically and politically some formula by which they could become free nations and yet at the same time continue their participation in the Britannic league of nations. To say that they were attempting an impossible task is simply to blind oneself to the history of the British Empire since the middle of the nineteenth century. To say that they were essaying the task at all entails the responsibility of demonstration.[15]

A literary history of the Stamp Act year would throw in high relief Daniel Dulany's "Considerations on the Propriety of Imposing Taxes on the British Colonies."[16] Representative of the stage which American thought had reached on the constitutional aspect of the taxation dispute, the work is doubly interesting as having had such

[14] M. Farrand, *Development of the United States,* (1918), p. 38.

[15] The testimony of Thomas Hutchinson who, previous to being Governor of Massachusetts, had been a citizen of that province, is significant: "The colonies, in general, during these disputes, had acquired a new set of ideas of the relation they stood in to the Parliament of Great Britain." "From admitting a principle of partial dependency, gradual advances were made until total independency was asserted." *History of the Province of Mass. Bay:* (London: 1838), III. 164, 165.

[16] *Considerations on the Propriety of Imposing Taxes on the British Colonies for the Purpose of Raising Revenue by an Act of Parliament:* [Daniel Dulany]. (Annapolis: 1765).

influence in shaping Chatham's opinions.[17] "By their constitutions of government, the colonies are empowered to impose internal taxes," reasoned Dulany, yet "this power is compatible with their dependence, and hath been expressly recognized by the British Ministers."[18] Fastening upon the expression "internal taxes," Chatham made the most of it in his celebrated speech in January, 1766, when he drew a distinction between what Parliament could and could not do in asserting its jurisdiction over the colonies. Somewhat scornfully he replied to Grenville, "if the gentleman does not understand the difference between internal and external taxes, I cannot help it,"[19] and laid down the proposition that Parliament could not impose the former but was permitted to impose the latter. The former as a trade regulation was permissible; the latter, as taking money from the pockets of the people without their consent, was utterly without warrant. Around this distinction is built the first phase of the constitutional argument. A line was drawn which was supposed to explain the nature of the imperial machine. The rights of local self government, including that of internal self-taxation, were asserted "without striking at, or impeaching in any respect, the superintendence of the British Parliament."[20] In consequence of the exercise of that "superintendence," revenue might be produced, and certainly the trade and manufacture of the colonies would be curtailed.

The Chatham-Dulany line of argument assumed the supremacy of Parliament over the colonies, while admitting them to be in the single case of internal administration, including taxation, free from Parliamentary interference.[21] It was a question of divided sovereignty, so familiar in federal unions. In the thought of these two, Westminster occupied the position of what, on first glance, appears to be a federal parliament in addition to its capacity as a local legislature for Great Britain. In consequence, might it not be fair to say that such a legislature had the right to impose federal trade

[17] M. C. Tyler, *Literary Hist. of the Amer. Revolution,* I. 111 q. v. for illustration, with parallel quotations from Chatham and Dulany.

[18] Dulany, *Considerations,* etc., p. 15.

[19] ". . . . there is a plain distinction between taxes levied for the purpose of raising revenue, and duties imposed for the regulation of trade, for the accommodation of the subject, although in consequence of the latter, some revenue might arise from the latter." Hansard, *Parliamentary History,* XVI. (1765–71), 100.

[20] Dulany, *Considerations,* etc., p. 15.

[21] Hansard, *Parl. Hist.,* XVI. 101; Dulany, *Considerations,* etc., p. 16.

regulations, and if, in consequence, some income was unintentionally produced, the treasury of the federation, if such it was, would be entitled thereto? The weakness of this position was observed by at least one spectator-historian, who commented with pertinence: "Mr. Pitt's declaration against Parliament's right to impose internal taxes, and his saying 'I am glad America has resisted', were seized upon by the popular leaders in the colonies. They praised and idolized him for the same, *without regarding* what he had declared in favor of the authority of Parliament in all cases of external taxation, and for the enforcing of all laws for that purpose; and notwithstanding his having said 'If obedience be refused, I would not suffer a horse nail to be made in the plantations'."[22] In this same group belongs Edmund Burke, much lauded as the friend of the colonies. Although his famous utterances came in 1774 and 1775, a decade after this controversy, yet he had, in fact, not progressed at all beyond the conception here outlined. To him, likewise, the Parliament of Great Britain sat as an imperial federal parliament, superior to the colonial legislatures in every way, retaining all the right of imposing taxes for imperial purposes. Indeed, it seems reasonable to say that Burke, far from representing an advance on Chatham, made a distinct step backward, for he would permit a reserve power in Parliament to coerce the subordinate legislatures even to the extent of imposing taxes upon them for imperial purposes. This position of Burke should be held in mind when examining the theories and doctrines presented by the more profound colonial thinkers, and also when studying the ultimate solution as worked out by the great self-governing dominions of the empire in the nineteenth century.[23]

[22] W. Gordon, *History of the Rise, Progress, and Establishment of the Independence of the United States of America*, (London: 1788), I. 206. An interesting illustration of the lack of contemporary attentiveness to what Chatham had really said may be found not only on the statues of him erected in America, but in the numerous medals struck off to William Pitt, Defender of Liberty. See C. W. Betts, *American Colonial History Illustrated by Contemporary Medals*, (1894), pp. 229–32.

[23] A year before his *Speech on Conciliation*, Burke had clearly given expression to his opinion of the nature of the British Empire, in language worth giving in full: "The Parliament of Great Britain sits at the head of her extensive empire in two capacities; one as the local legislature of this island . . . . the other . . . . is what I call her imperial character, in which she superintends all the several inferior legislatures, and controls them all without annihilating any. As all these provincial legislatures are only co-ordinate to

Chatham's appeal to the House of Commons to repeal the Stamp Act was followed in the next month by an event which should illuminate the constitutional aspect of the controversy. In attempting to portray the thought of a past age, a controversial document with give-and-take argument is often worth a dozen dogmatic utterances, for in such a document, in self defense, one must make his idea plain, if he have any clear idea at all. Ten years earlier Benjamin Franklin had commented on the limited understanding of his fellow colonials who would take no definite action on the problem of colonial union.[24] In his "Examination Before the House of Commons" we might fairly expect that he would throw some light on the nature of that British Empire in which he was wont to glory. He, too, employed the distinction between "internal" and "external" taxation, and when pressed for an elucidation of the distinction he dodged by turning his answer into that clever warning not to press the colonials too far, over which historians have been chuckling ever since. This quotation is one of those which assumes a different aspect on being put back in its context. Considerably earlier in the course of the "Examination," Franklin had come out flatly with the statement that the colonies would not object to an "external tax," a duty laid upon commodities imported, and thus passed on to the consumer by being added to the price of the goods. The "internal tax," as forcing money from the people without their consent, was what the colonials objected to.[25] "But the payment of duties laid by an act of Parliament, as regulations of commerce, was never disputed."[26] Upon this the questioner pressed on and inquired what would happen if Parliament were to lay such an external tax as

---

each other they ought all be subordinate to her; else they can neither preserve mutual peace nor hope for mutual justice, nor effectually afford mutual assistance. It is necessary to coerce the negligent and restrain the violent, to aid the weak and deficient, by the overruling plenitude of her power. But in order to enable parliament to answer all these ends of provident and beneficent superintendence . . . . the power must be boundless. The gentlemen who think the power of parliament limited may talk of requisitions, but suppose the requisition is not obeyed? . . . . I consider the power of taxing in Parliament as an instrument of empire, not as a means of supply. . . . Such is my idea of the constitution of the British Empire as distinct from the constitution of Great Britain." Hansard, *Parl. Hist.,* (1771–74), XVIII. 1266–7. Speech of April 19, 1774.

[24] Franklin's *Works,* (Bigelow Ed.), III. 410 ff.
[25] Franklin's *Works,* (Bigelow Ed.), III. 422.
[26] Ibid., III. 419–20.

would not leave the colonist the alternative of simply not buying the taxed goods, as, for example, if Parliament should lay a tax upon some necessity being imported into America. At this point, if Franklin had any clear idea, we might expect he would have given it. But he evaded the issue by saying that Parliament would be unable to do such a thing because there was no "single article imported into the northern colonies but what they can either do without or make themselves."[27] This diverted the questioner and relieved Franklin for the time being from the necessity of vindicating his impossible distinction. But such an answer could only leave the Commons under the impression that if they were to levy a customs duty and incidentally raise money, the colonists would have no constitutional objection.[28]

One would like to know who it was that pressed Franklin for information on this point.[29] It is extremely likely that Townshend was present if he did not actually ask the questions. Since his chief offense is that he took the Americans at their word, and levied "external taxes," it is a matter of some importance that Dulany and Franklin aided him to misinterpret the American opinions. Further efforts on the part of the inquisitors enabled Franklin to turn the laugh of history on his opponents by the shrewd forecast that the colonials would soon object to any taxation.[30] In its context the final clever evasion puts the Doctor in a little different light and classes him with Chatham, Dulany, and Burke, of all of whom it is probably proper to say, they did not object to the Stamp Act on the ground that Parliament had no general right to legislate for the

---

[27] Ibid., III. 423.

[28] Dulany had made his distinction between "an act imposing a tax for the single purpose of raising revenue, and those acts which have been made for the regulation of trade, and have produced some revenue in consequence of their operation as regulations of trade." p. 46.

[29] Walsh's *Life of Franklin* in Delaplaine's *Repository of the Lives and Portraits of Distinguished Americans,* (Phila. 1815), II. 74, notes "We have in our hands a document for which we are indebted to the Hon. Joseph Hopkinson, that discloses a part of the private history of this memorable transaction. It is a series of notes sent by Dr. Franklin to a friend who desired to know by whom the several questions were put." This document attributes the questions on internal and external taxation to members of Grenville's ministry, and particularly to Mr. Townshend. Another source, given in Bigelow, *Life of Franklin,* I. 510, attributes some of them to Lord North.

[30] Franklin's *Works,* (Bigelow Ed.), III. 447.

colonies.[31] They all admitted a general right in Parliament to legislate for the unrepresented colonies.[32] The final break found the two colonials, Dulany and Franklin, on different sides. Chatham and Burke struggled on for a restoration of good relations, but, in the light of the ultimate evolution of the imperial structure, they were on the wrong track in the position they had taken. The time had come for the surrender, not the assertion of the Parliamentary supremacy of Westminster.

For, although the American advocates at Westminster might draw fine distinctions in their behalf, the colonials soon realized that they must retreat from any such position as that entailed by a distinction between internal and external taxation. Charles Townshend had taken the Americans at the word of their defenders. According to the report of one of the colonial agents at London, "the Chancellor of the Exchequer [Townshend] declared in one of these meetings

[31] See Chatham in Hansard, XVI. 100–1; Burke, *supra;* see Franklin's remark: "The authority of Parliament [to make laws for America] was allowed to be valid in all laws except such as should lay internal taxes." *Works,* (Bigelow Ed.), III. 417. See Dulany: "The subordination of the colonies and the authority of parliament to preserve it have been fully acknowledged. Not only the welfare but probably the existence of the mother country as an independent kingdom may depend upon their trade and navigation." "From these considerations, the rights of the British Parliament to regulate the trade of the colonies may be justly deduced, ... it is a common and frequently most proper method of regulating trade by duties on imports and exports." *Considerations, etc.,* p. 46–7. And further the same author says "On the other hand the colonies acknowledge themselves subordinate to the mother country, and that authority vested in the supreme council of the nation, may be justly exercised to preserve that subordination." p. 37. And also "May not, then, a line be drawn between such acts as are necessary and proper for securing the dependence of the colonies, and such as are not necessary or proper for that purpose?" p. 17.

[32] In 1768 Franklin wrote to his son, "As to the farmers combating, as you say they intend to do, my opinion that parliament might lay duties, though not impose internal taxes, I shall not give myself the trouble to defend it," for since every nation had the right to impose an export tax and thus, by increasing the selling price, tax the ultimate consumer, he still considered the distinction legitimate. England, for instance, exported coal to Holland and charged such an export tax that the Dutch paid the tax, yet England would have no right to levy an internal tax in Holland. *Works* (Bigelow Ed.), VI. 131. Very properly then does the Tory chronicler, Lord Mahon, record "most strongly did he [Franklin] urge the distinction between internal and external taxation, the former, he said the colonists would always resist, the latter they had never questioned." *Hist. of England:* 1713–1783, ch. xlv.

[of the colonial agents] that although he had not the least doubt of the right of Parliament to tax the colonies internally, and he knew no difference between internal and external taxation (which, by the way, is a doctrine very generally adopted here), yet since the Americans were pleased to make such a distinction, he was willing to indulge them, and chose for that reason to confine himself to the regulation of trade by which a sufficient revenue might be raised in America."[33] The result was the "Townshend Acts" in which the external, or customs duties were laid on tea and certain other articles. Naturally enough, then, the Tory spectator-historian remarks, "the new ministry, laying hold of this distinction, and availing themselves of a supposed concession, procured an act of Parliament to be passed for imposing certain duties on glass, paper, tea, etc."[34] Another, a more sympathetic observer, reviewing the controversy twenty years later, remarked, "Before the Stamp Act the colonies admitted a distinction between internal and external taxation, between raising money for the regulation of trade and raising money for the purpose of revenue," but since Parliament did take them at their word and the colonists were "obliged to enter afresh the field of political controversy, great numbers began to think that there was no real, but only a nominal, difference between internal and external taxation, agreeable to what was insisted upon by the party opposing the repeal of the Stamp Act."[35]

[33] W. Johnson, colonial agent for the province of Connecticut, to Gov. W. Pitkin, May 16, 1767, in *Mass. Hist. Soc. Coll.,* Ser. 5, IX. 228.

[34] C. Stedman, *History of the Rise, Progress and Termination of the American War.* London (1794), I. 53. The author was on Sir Henry Clinton's staff.

[35] W. Gordon, *History of the Rise, Progress and Establishment of the Independence of the United States of America,* London (1788), I. 220. That his analysis was correct, see Stephen Hopkins, *Rights of the Colonies Examined,* (Providence: 1765.) (Reprinted in *Rhode Island Records,* VI. 416, 422). A sound comment was made to the effect that "the distinctions which have been made on this subject are not well grounded; that parliament has a right to impose external, not internal duties. . . . these sentiments have been delivered and received as maxims; but the difference between the right of imposing external and internal duties is merely imaginary, grounded on no principle of justice or policy, contradictory to the claims of the Americans, whose resolutions assert the exemption from all duties not imposed by themselves; and is treated as an idle distinction by Mr. Otis, the chosen champion of American privelege." From *The Conduct of the Late Administration Examined,* London (1767), p. 7. Otis had in fact done so. Vid. *Vindication of*

So after all the arch conservatives, Mansfield[36] and Grenville, had probably been right in their contention that the "constitution knows no difference between impost duties and internal taxation."[37] At this point colonial writers began to draw a new distinction. To this second stage of the controversy belongs John Dickinson. Seeing clearly that the earlier distinction had played too easily into the hands of the Grenville group, and that the triumphant Tories now argued that although the duties imposed by the Stamp Act might be internal taxes, yet the new taxes under the Townshend acts were external taxes, Dickinson rejoined, "To this I answer with a total denial of the power of Parliament to lay upon these colonies any 'tax' whatever."[38] With this statement we must couple his equally firm conviction: "Parliament unquestionably possesses a legal authority to regulate the trade of Great Britain and all her colonies . . . . he who considers these provinces as states distinct from the British Empire has very slender notions of justice or of their interests."[39] The new distinction between the right of Parliament to regulate trade and the right of Parliament to levy any tax at all necessarily involved the question: Suppose the trade regulation should produce revenue? Dulany had foreseen this when he commented, "the authority of the mother country to regulate trade being unquestionable, what regulations are the most proper are to

---

the British Colonies, etc., pp. 29 ff. A Tory finally summed the whole matter up thus, "Much has been said about internal and external taxation, I know but little difference between them." Isaac Hunt, *The Political Family*, (1775), p. ii. See also Lord Lyttleton in Hansard, *Parliamentary History*, XVI. 167.

[36] "I know no difference between laying internal and external taxes." Hansard, *Parliamentary History*, XVI. 176.

[37] Quoted from *Regulations Lately made Concerning the Colonies and Taxes imposed on them Considered*, London (1765), usually ascribed to Grenville, largely because Jared Sparks wrote that on his copy now in the Harvard Library. (Vid., M. C. Tyler, *Literary History of the American Revolution*, II. 472) If this constitutes historical evidence it should equally be noticed that what is probably President Joseph Reed's copy (now in the Historical Society of Pennsylvania) has written across the title page "Published previous to the Stamp Act and supposed to have been written by Charles Jenkinson." Jenkinson was later (1796) Earl of Liverpool.

[38] *Letters from a Farmer in Pennsylvania to the Inhabitants of the British Colonies in North America*, (Philadelphia 1768), p. 18. See also Ford's edition of John Dickinson's *Writings*, in the *Memoirs of the Historical Society of Pennsylvania*, XVI. 277.

[39] *Farmers Letters*, p. 7.

be, of course, submitted to the determination of Parliament, and if an incidental revenue should be produced by such regulation, these are not therefore unwarrantable."[40] The question then was: when does "incidental revenue" assume the character of a tax? Obviously, replied Dickinson, the intent governs; "the nature of any imposition laid by Parliament on these colonies, must determine the design in laying them."[41] "Impositions" for maintaining the integrity of the British Empire were entirely permissible, but "taxes" were under no consideration allowable.[42] Why this highly attenuated distinction between "taxes" and "impositions"? Because the "prosperity of these colonies is founded on their dependence on Great Britain," and some philosophical formula had to be worked out for securing freedom from Parliamentary interference, yet insuring the maintenance of the empire and America's participation in it.[43] Hence Dickinson admitted the right of Parliament to legislate for the unrepresented colonies, acknowledged that Parliament in England could forbid the erection of a steel mill in America,[44] called Chatham "our great advocate," and yet would not allow Parliament the single function of taxing the colonies.[45] To him Franklin's distinction, based on the legality of disguising a tax as a trade regulation, did not help solve the real problem, for that was a policy suitable only for "arbitrary and oppressive governments."[46]

Dickinson's new distinction was reflected elsewhere when the colonies began to appreciate that Dulany, Chatham, and Franklin had led them astray. They began to understand at the same time that the character of a legislative act should be determined by the

[40] Dulany, *"Considerations etc."* p. 34.

[41] John Dickinson, *Letters from a Farmer in Pennsylvania,* Philadelphia, (1768), p. 32.

[42] "The nature of any impositions she may lay upon us, may, in general, be known by considering how far they relate to preserving in due order, the connection between the several parts of the British Empire." Ibid., p. 33.

[43] "Every 'tax' being an imposition, though every 'imposition' is not a tax . . . . external impositions for the regulation of trade . . . only prevent the colonies from acquiring property in things not necessary in a manner judged to be injurious to the welfare of the whole empire." Ibid., p. 21.

[44] Ibid., 22n, citing 23 Geo. II, chap. 29, Sec. 9.

[45] Ibid., p. 12.

[46] ". . . . this policy did not escape the cruel and rapacious Nero," Ibid., p. 36.

intent.[47] However, the necessary requirements of the political organization of the British Empire demanded, if it was to continue to exist, that somewhere there exist a superior superintending agency empowered to order the mutual relations of the component parts of the empire. "Political necessity," concluded Gouverneur Morris, "therefore requires that this power be placed in one part of the empire," which should normally be that part which protects trade. "Internal taxation to be left to ourselves. The right to regulate trade to be vested in Great Britain, where alone is found the power of protecting it. I trust you to agree with me that this is the only possible mode of union. Not that Great Britain should lay imposts upon us for the support of the government, for its defense, nor should she regulate our internal police. These things effect us only. To these things we ourselves are competent. But can it be said that we are competent to regulate trade?" Such a suggestion is regarded as absurd, for what indeed would be the result if Ireland, the colonies, and Great Britain were all to regulate the trade of the empire? In fact, some who subsequently supported the Continental Congress clung to this distinction and acknowledged the superintending authority of Great Britain down to the break in 1775.[48]

But this new distinction was no sooner under way than it was attacked on both sides of the water. The pertinent question was asked whether, if Parliament imposed a trade regulation which was

[47] In January, 1768, Massachusetts Bay protested to Shelburne, "Your Lordship can judge whether any necessity can render it just and equitable that the supreme legislative of the empire should impose duties, subsidies, talliadges, taxes, *internal or external, for the sole purpose of raising revenue* on subjects that are not and cannot be represented." From *Petitions of the Assembly of Massachusetts Bay to the King, with Several Other Papers,* Boston (1768), p. 15. Similarly, when the Ministry demanded of Massachusetts that she rescind the circular letter in 1768, the General Court informed Lord Hillsborough that "the people of this province have attended with deep concern to the several acts of the British Parliament which impose duties and taxes, not for the purpose of regulating trade, but solely for the purpose of raising revenue." From *The American Gazette: Being a Collection of Authentical Addresses, Memorials, etc., on the Disputes Between Great Britain and Her Colonies,"* (London: 1768), 2nd edition, p. 9, No. I. See also *"Instructions to the Representatives of the City and County of Philadelphia, Signed by Freemen,"* July 30, 1768. "We observe that duties laid for the sole and express purpose of raising revenue have been lately imposed on several articles imported into these colonies" in *American Gazette,* No. II. 90.

[48] Morris to Penn, 20 May, 1774. Force, *Amer. Archives,* 4th Series, I. 343.

positively not intended to raise revenue but which did in fact produce revenue, that trade regulation thereby became unconstitutional
and void?[49] It was natural that most of the critics should concern
themselves more with picking technical flaws in the arguments than
essaying the constructive task of working out a system which would
solve the problem of empire-building, upon which subject there was,
of course, relatively little clear thinking. Franklin very properly
remarked that no plan for imperial reorganization was likely to be
successful "while the nature of our present relationship is so little
understood on both sides of the water, and the sentiments concerning it are so widely different."[50] Nevertheless, up to the time the
break came, the pro-colonial writers were struggling with this distinction between taxation and trade regulation. The denial of the
suggestion that the enactments of Parliament were in fact trade
regulations, with the insistence that the colonies would submit to
trade regulations, is a fact that ought never to be lost sight of in
British imperial history, for it manifests the essential loyalty of the
colonies to the idea of the empire, however antagonistic their economic interests to the policies of a particular ministry.[51] The distinction made by Dickinson was equally assailable by the partisans
of Great Britain on the ground that it was "only a pretense under
which to strip Parliament of all jurisdiction over the colonies."[52]

[49] "It is the purpose of parliament in laying the tax which it seems gives
the right of laying it. Curious reasoning this! Now, should it happen that
Parliament was at any time mistaken in its purpose, and that a tax which
is imposed with the intention that nobody should pay it, i.e., that it should
operate as a prohibition, should really turn out to be such a tax as the
commodity on which it was charged could bear, and the people of the
colonies were willing to purchase it at the price to which the tax had raised
it, what should we do then? On the other hand, suppose Parliament should
be mistaken in a tax laid for revenue, and it turned out to be a prohibition
would the tax then become a constitutional one?" From *The Controversy
between Great Britain and her Colonies Reviewed*, Boston (1769), pp. 16
and 17.

[50] Franklin's *Works*, (Bigelow Ed.), IV. 131.

[51] "The right of Great Britain to regulate the trade of the colonies shall
be admitted; but that the duty on tea is a regulation of trade, this is a
matter of controversy." From, "*The Other Side of the Question, or a Defence
of the Liberties of North America, in reply to a Late Friendly Address to all
Reasonable Americans*," by a *Citizen*, New York, (1774) p. 11.

[52] "The boasted distinction between taxes for the regulation of trade and
taxes for the purpose of raising revenue, we see therefor is a distinction
without a difference, and it will in no sort serve to protect the colonies from

Perhaps it might be so regarded, but the main point which so many seem to have missed is just that salient fact, that a clear-headed American was trying to think in terms of a political union based on liberty and mutual confidence. For Dickinson believed that "The happiness and prosperity both of the colonies and Great Britain depended upon an intimate union and connection,"[53] and his subsequent actions down to the actual Declaration of Independence are witness to how anxious he was to preserve the integrity of the empire.

Dickinson's reasoning certainly forced Franklin to abandon his position of drawing distinctions between the kinds of taxes Parliament could and could not impose and led him to that position which he was finally obliged to take of denying any power in Parliament over the colonies. But now Franklin in turn scouted Dickinson's finely drawn distinction and turned his face definitely in the direction of independence. Yet it was somewhere between these two theories that the problem of constructing a league of self-governing commonwealths must find its solution if at all. Being strictly logical was fatal at this stage of the controversy. No doubt there is much to be said for Franklin's conclusion, "the more I have thought and read on this subject, the more I find myself confirmed in the opinion that no middle ground can be maintained; I mean not clearly, with intelligible arguments. Something might be made of either of the extremes, that Parliament has the power to make all laws for us, or that it has the power to make no laws for us; and I think the arguments for the latter, more weighty and numerous than those for the former."[54] Moreover, there is cogency in his comment: "The sovereignty of the crown I understand; the sovereignty of the

parliamentary internal and external taxation, however much it may serve as a pretence under which to strip Parliament of all jurisdiction over the colonies." From *The Controversy, etc.,* p. 19.

[53] "*A Letter From the Country to a Gentleman in Philadelphia*" signed "*Rusticus,*" and published as a broadside. Reprinted in Life and Writings of John Dickinson, II. 461.

[54] Franklin had written in 1768 in a letter to his son: "I am not yet master of the idea these [the Farmer's Letters] and the New England colonies have of the relation between Britain and her colonies; it being difficult to draw lines between duties for the regulation of trade, and those for revenue; and if parliament is to be the judge, it seems to me that establishing such a principle of distinction will amount to little." Franklin's *Works,* (Bigelow Ed.), IV. 130.

British legislature outside of Britain, I do not understand."[55] But discussions which involve the term "sovereignty" are often more apt to be academic than illuminating. Hence it was that Dickinson attempted to take his stand on that untenable middle ground, and to understand that incomprehensive assertion of jurisdiction by the British legislature outside of Britain when such a thing was necessary to preserve the integrity of the British Empire Commonwealth. The question may then be fairly propounded, whether the history of the British Empire from 1783 to the present does not in fact vindicate the opinion of John Dickinson that "tacit acquiescence" in the "superintending authority of the British Parliament" would prove a practical way to solve the problem of the empire's organization.[56] Dickinson believed the empire worth keeping together, and the fact that, despite the action of the American colonies in 1775,

[55] *Notes* on replies to the House of Lords protest against the repeal of the Stamp Act. Ibid., III. 483. Franklin employed the expressions common at the time about the colonies being attached to the crown, and not to the realm; from which it followed that the King ruled Massachusetts through the General Court of Massachusetts, and Great Britain through the Parliament at Westminster, and that the two were co-ordinate legislative bodies. Ibid., III. 490.

[56] Dickinson, in his effort to find the suitable compromise ground, remarked, "As they were members of one great Empire, united under one head or crown, they tacitly acquiesced in the superintending authority of the Parliament of Great Britain and admitted power in it to make regulations to preserve the connection of the whole entire, though under color of this sundry regulations were made that bore hard on the colonies, yet with filial respect and regard for Great Britain, their Mother Country, the colonies submitted to them." This exercise of jurisdiction by the "British legislature outside of Britain," he, unlike Franklin, not only understood, but advocated. The trouble was that a "new party had lately arisen in England, who under color of the superintending authority of parliament, are laboring to erect a new sovereignty over the colonies inconsistent with liberty or freedom." From Dickinson's *Address Read at the Meeting of the Merchants in Philadelphia*, 1768. In his *Life and Writings*, II. 411–3. At least one Englishman had the vision to propose the solution: "First, that we should leave the Americans to tax themselves: secondly, we should retain to the British Parliament every power that is not inconsistent with our justice and their liberty; that a law should be passed immediately repealing every act that taxes the colonies. I do not propose that it should contain any counter-declarations, or that power will be in terms disclaimed. It will be sufficient that they be repealed and that we do not revive the claim." *The Case of Great Britain and America, Addressed to the King and Both Houses of Parliament*, (London; Philadelphia reprint, 1769), p. 14.

the empire has kept together, is again, in some measure, a vindication of his opinion.[57] Perhaps it is fair to say that, after all, Dickinson
was on the right track as far as reconciling the differences between
the two parts of the empire was concerned, and he differed from
the more radical New Englanders because he was sincere about it.

But within a year of the final break the two earlier distinctions
had been pretty well abandoned, and the constitutional phase of the
taxation controversy had taken on that appearance of "no-taxation-
without-representation" which is the outstanding feature of so many
of the utterances even from the beginning of the dispute. One contemporary critic noticed that the Americans had introduced "a new
distinction" to take the force off their former concessions, contending
that the duties laid upon the necessities of life such as paper, glass
and paint, were equivalent to an internal tax and therefore inad-
missible.[58] Surely this is exactly what the Americans had done, and
one of their number commented, "I could never be convinced by
their [the Americans'] arguments of the practicability of drawing a
line so near the border of taxation as not to encroach upon that
ground."[59] A Tory remarked with equal vigor, "Others, finding
that the claims of the colonists could not be supported on those
pillars [i.e., natural rights] have racked their inventions to find out
distinctions which never existed, nor can exist in reason or common
sense: a distinction between the right of Parliament to legislate for
the colonies and a right to tax them [i.e., Pitt's argument], between
internal and external taxation [i.e., Franklin's argument], between
taxes laid for the regulation of trade and for the purpose of raising
revenue [i.e., Dickinson's argument]."[60] "Shall we," asks the
"Virginian," "shall we, Proteus-like, perpetually change our ground,
assume every moment some new and strange shape, to defend, to

[57] See John Adams, *Diary, Works,* (C. F. Adams Ed.), II. 409, for Dickinson's strenuous efforts at reconciliation six months after the battle at Lexington had been fought.

[58] *The American Querist: or Some Questions Proposed Relative to the
Present Disputes between Great Britain and her American Colonies by a
North American,* (1774), p. 20.

[59] *A Few Political Reflections Submitted to the Consideration of the British
Colonies. By a Citizen of Philadelphia,* (Philadelphia: 1774), p. 17. Attributed
by M. C. Tyler to Richard Wells.

[60] Joseph Galloway, *A Candid Examination of the Mutual Claims of Great
Britain and her Colonies with a Plan of Accommodation on Constitutional
Principles,* New York (1775), p. 2.

evade? Shall we establish distinctions between internal and external taxation one year, and laugh at them the next? Shall we confound duties and taxes, and regulations of trade with revenue laws?"[61] The real issue which should be stated and adhered to was "that whatever taxation and representation might be, taxation and government were inseparable." Truly, the colonials had come a long way since Chatham's day, for what he lauded as "essential to liberty" was now a "protean monster." Drayton, the "Freeman of South Carolina," represents in 1774 as much of an advance over Dickinson, as Dickinson did over Dulany in 1768. For, said he, "any taxation or legislation by the British Parliament over America without her consent is no better than mere tyranny."[62]

By the year of the Revolution, the various forces of discord between Britain and America had combined, and the resultant did not take the direction which would have found a place for the thirteen colonies within the British Empire Commonwealth. John Locke's dictum that it was a fixed and unalterable principle in the nature of things, and a part of the very idea of property, that what a man hath honestly acquired—that cannot be taken from him without his consent, had become inextricably entangled with the disputed powers of Westminster. Their product was the slogan, "no taxation without representation," which, among other things, was certainly a criticism of and a protest against the defective imperial machinery. It might have been met either by a cessation of taxation or by a grant of representation. The Americans were not at all one on the desirability of sending members to Westminster, but in either case the prime requisite was a really coöperative spirit. The Americans had certainly shown a coöperative spirit, if by nothing else, by their willingness to pass through the stages of making concessions in the matter of "internal and external" taxes, taxation and trade regulation, and the like. Not all the Americans had manifested this spirit, for many a one had struck at the doctrine of no taxation without representation from the very beginning of the controversy. Yet enough, both in quantity and quality, of the

[61] "*A Letter from a Virginian to the Members of Congress to be held in Philadelphia*, 1st September 1774, Boston: (1774), pp. 22–3.

[62] William Henry Drayton, *A Letter from a Freeman of South Carolina, to the deputies of North-America, assembled in the High Court of Congress at Philadelphia.* (Charlestown, S. C., 1774), Reprinted in R. W. Gibbes, *Documentary History*, p. 29.

colonials did take other stands to enable us to conclude that the coöperative spirit was present in America. The colonists demanded a correct definition of their status as members of the empire-commonwealth. Before the outbreak of the Revolution there was no such overwhelming proportion of irreconcilables as to make the Revolution inevitable. True, America had been settled to a large extent by non-conformists; but non-conforming Quaker Pennsylvania was among those least inclined to an open break. True, the trade and navigation acts were extremely galling; but far from learning a lesson from the American Revolution, Great Britain did not give up those trade and navigation acts for the succeeding half century during which a new overseas empire was being built up. True, George III had a German mentality and was also an obstinate man; but are these efficient historical causes?[63] Yet the act of sitting on the safety valve is, politically speaking, often an efficient historical cause. That is what the refusal to grapple with the imperial problem really amounted to. Inflexible political machinery which attempted to define an empire commonwealth in terms of the Kingdom of Great Britain was just such a cause. America and Britain in the two centuries had grown apart very clearly and definitely, as the social and economic historians have demonstrated. The only hope of preserving the empire lay in reforming the political machinery so that it would conform to the requirements of the new situation. The foregoing pages are an effort to present what evidence there is in the taxation controversy for saying that some men were making efforts to fit the old machine to the new situation.

[63] My colleague, Dr. Laprade, insists that the real explanation of George's obstinacy was not his German ancestry, but the fact that he was educated by the Scotch Lord Bute into the political philosophy of the Jacobites.

5

JOHN ADAMS AS A BRITANNIC STATESMAN

WITH THE SINGLE exception of the United States, all of the English-speaking people are members of a common political organization. Yet in looking through the histories for a record of the efforts of far-seeing statesmen who tried to grapple with the problem of the British Empire as such, in the days before the American Revolution, we are apt to find the story eclipsed by the moving narrative of the thoughts and deeds of those who, without a vision of the commonwealth of nations, hastened on to effect that single break in the political union in which all other English-speaking nations participate. During the period in which it was customary to look upon the American Revolution as something intrinsically good, the deliverance of a freedom-loving race from the tyranny of Parliament blockheads, men like Samuel Adams, John Hancock, and Patrick Henry could hold the center of the stage. With the growing recognition of other elements in the struggle, more consideration has been accorded to another group, the Hutchinsons, the Galloways, and the Coopers, whom the last century branded as Tories but whom we are now more willing to style "loyalists." There was yet another group, less eloquent than the first, more practical than the second, to whom attention may be directed with the confidence that the twentieth century will have a more sympathetic understanding of their efforts than had either the eighteenth or nineteenth.

Many of the ringing voices that proclaimed liberty and the rights of man under government in Faneuil Hall and in the Virginia House of Burgesses before the war were strangely silent in Independence Hall when the war was won. Otis had passed away;

Patrick Henry and Richard Henry Lee were openly hostile to the Constitution,[1] while that instrument was accepted in Massachusetts rather with the silent consent than with the enthusiastic support of those fathers of the Revolution, Samuel Adams and John Hancock.[2] There was another group, less tumultuous as orators, more thoughtful as statesmen, who lived through the struggles from the Stamp Act to the formation of the government under the Federal Constitution, whose voices were heard loyal to the British Empire up to the very end when the break came in 1775, and who lived to construct the new political union of semi-sovereign states in 1787. John Adams is not selected as representative of this group because he was necessarily its most brilliant member, for the most brilliant man of any period is seldom representative in any historical sense. He is selected rather because he was consciously a political scientist in a sense in which very few of his contemporaries were. His was a day of political philosophy; perhaps there never has been a period in which men so delighted to speculate in general terms upon the abstract propositions of human government. Yet of political scientists in the modern sense, there were few. A man willing and able to study government experimentally and by observation had need of a more profound mental equipment than he who could content himself with making the rafters of the town hall ring with his denunciations of whatever object of his wrath.

Political historians have told us in these later days what the Revolution was all about, but there is some advantage in knowing what a political scientist of that day conceived the central issue to be. John Adams contended that the problem was primarily political, that the dispute hinged upon a problem of state organization, that "the fundamentals of government" were at stake.[3] A man is apt to interpret events in terms of his specialty, so to a man of his type we must go to discover whether there was a contemporaneous appre-

---

[1] William Wirt, *Patrick Henry*, (15th Ed.) p. 287; R. H. Lee, *Observations Leading to a Fair Examination of the System of Government, and Several Essential and Necessary Alterations in it: In a Number of Letters from The Federal Farmer to the Republican*, (New York: 1787).

[2] J. K. Hosmer, *Samuel Adams*, pp. 392–401. See Col. Jos. May's interesting estimate of the attitude of Adams and Hancock, reprinted in Wells' *Life of Samuel Adams*, III. 258. A recent biographer of Hancock is disposed to be more lenient with him. L. Sears, *John Hancock, the Picturesque Patriot* (1912), pp. 286–7.

[3] *The Works of John Adams* (C. F. Adams Ed. 1856), cited herein, IV. 33.

ciation of the political problem to which in one sense the passage and repeal of Stamp and Navigation Acts were only incidental, the problem of the relations between the various dominions of the British Empire.

In the decade before the Revolution, John Adams was among those who tried persistently to attack the question as a constitutional one and to make his fellows understand it as a problem of government or political science. Yet, strange as it may seem, this is a distinctly neglected period of his life. A recent historian of the political science of John Adams hurries on to that later period of the Constitution and the Presidency, neglecting almost entirely the period before the Revolution. That same author is obliged to begin work with the remark, "the theory reviewed in this work is obsolete." But the period neglected is full of ideas which are only just now beginning to come into vogue.[4] So, too, the historian of the literature of the Revolution assures us that one of the chief sources for this period is "a vast morass of technical discussion, into which no living reader will ever follow the writer, and from which the writer himself never emerges alive."[5] This period of Adams' political writing furnishes the material for that neglected field which it is proposed here to examine. The "vast morass of technical discussion" might have been jargon at a time when the expression "league of nations" had not come into our vocabulary, but today it yields some interesting data for an unwritten chapter of British imperial history.[6]

It is essential to an understanding of John Adams that we keep in mind his temperate mental processes. Your radical is not infrequently found today advocating extreme political and legal measures for the amelioration of human ills, and tomorrow is heard to express his disgust with all purely human and rational methods of solving human difficulties. Today he may advise political reform, and tomorrow throw overboard all politics, economics and law, taking refuge in religion or spiritual philosophy. Without passing any judgment upon the merits of such procedure, it is fair to say that

[4] C. M. Walsh, *Political Science of John Adams*, (1915), in which but 7 of 361 pages are devoted to the period from 1765–87.

[5] M. C. Tyler, *Literary History of the American Revolution,* I. 392.

[6] A. D. Morse, *The Politics of John Adams, Amer. Hist. Rev.,* IV. 292, considers 1775 the starting point for a study of John Adams' politics. C. E. Merriam, *History of American Political Theories,* also emphasizes the later rather than the earlier period of John Adams' career. pp. 125–41. Both writers seem to me to ignore the most important things John Adams ever wrote.

a more abstemious thinker is likely to make a more solid contribution to the discussions incident to the task of improvising governmental machinery. It may not be unprofitable then to explore the field of thought of one who, while he acknowledged human limitation, believed in doing the best possible with what was at hand and tinkered with current institutions in an effort to leave them at least a little better than he found them. Of such a sort is the contrast between John and Samuel Adams. In an interesting exchange of letters between the two cousins in 1790 we discover the erstwhile political radical rather despairing of the usefulness of politics, disillusioned and fearful lest after all the Revolution had been but the substitution of one set of tyrants for another.[7] He felt that the true solvent of human ills lay in "impressing the minds of men with the importance of educating the little boys and girls," and training them in those spiritual values by which alone any progress can be made.[8] The rejoinder of the political scientist cousin, John Adams, leads us to believe that the President of the United States was a little more sincere, patient, and profound politician than the Governor of Massachusetts. For he admitted without question the value which the other attached to benevolence and enlightenment as the ultimate solution, but, he inquired, was not this asking people to demonstrate something which they did not yet understand? Could one solve problems in calculus before he had graduated from simple arithmetic? It was not right to advise the people to "depend for their safety, liberty and security on hopes and blessings which we know will not fall to their lot."[9] Rather should they be advised not to cleave to "the love of liberty in the soul of man for its preservation," but to understand that it were well that "some political institutions be prepared"[10] upon which man could lean during the period of his spiritual apprenticeship.

Abundant is the evidence of the love of John Adams for the subject of government as an object of intellectual curiosity and activity.[11]

---

[7] Four Letters: Being an Interesting Correspondence between those eminently Distinguished Characters, John Adams and Samuel Adams; (Boston: 1802), Works, VI. 405.

[8] Ibid., VI. 414.   [9] Ibid., VI. 415–6.

[10] Almost any few pages of the diary will convince the reader that John Adams fully understood his cousin's point of view; e.g., III. 423.

[11] A familiar one, "I know not how it is that mankind has an aversion to the study of the science of government. Is it because the subject is dry? To me no romance is more entertaining." IX. 567.

But in addition he possessed a political imagination which transcended the bounds of merely colonial concerns. Eulogized as the "first statesman of the Revolution" because he had "a sublime intuition of nationality" which he had seen through all the ages in the victorious van, his imagination kindled by the historic review that "led him in later years to head the movement that realized the prophetic vision of his youth," he was also a great deal more than this.[12] For the world is beginning to understand that "the intuition of nationality" is not an unmixed blessing, and to look deeper for really statesmanlike qualities.[13]

Focusing our attention, then, upon the earlier period of Adams' life, which the nineteenth century might well neglect, but which the twentieth reveals as concerned with a political problem which will no longer brook delay or evasion, we discover something more than a zealous advocate of American independence. The problem of the political constitution of the British Empire reached a critical stage with the passage of the Stamp Act of song and story, "an enormous engine fabricated by the British Parliament for battering down all the rights and liberties of America," whereat "our presses have groaned and our pulpits have thundered, our legislatures have resolved and our towns have voted."[14] Four years earlier, when James Otis' speech on the writs of assistance had stirred him so deeply, John Adams knew where he stood in "the contest that opened at that time, of which he could foresee no end."[15] Upon hearing of the passage of the Stamp Act in 1765 he did what was characteristic of the law-loving and academically inclined among the Puritans: he called a town meeting in his native village of Braintree. Equally characteristically went he to that meeting with his ideas already on paper in his pocket.[16] Knowing what he wanted,

[12] Mellen Chamberlain, *John Adams and Other Essays:* (1898). The theme of this essay is that John Adams saw the United States as a separate nation very early, and that his subsequent elevations were a triumphant vindication. This leads away from the subject of efforts to solve the British Imperial problem and to preserve the empire. Chamberlain does not do justice to John Adams, but does about as well as a nineteenth century writer could be expected to do.

[13] E.g., H. Morse Stephens, *Nationality and History, Amer. Hist. Rev.*, XXI. 225.

[14] *Diary*, II. 154.

[15] *Diary*, II. 125.

[16] *Diary*, II. 152–3.

he was appointed on the inevitable Committee on Resolutions, which, upon "withdrawing to Mr. Niles' house," opened up to him the opportunity to produce the paper which he had prepared. Such was the character of its contents that it was promptly and "unanimously adopted without amendment, reported to the town, and accepted without a dissenting voice."[17] So accurately did his ideas represent the thoughts of the inhabitants of Massachusetts that his resolutions were widely employed throughout the colony for similar purposes, and their author records that even Samuel Adams, commissioned to do a similar task for Boston, "took into his some paragraphs from mine."[18]

In this document, and in another which appeared about the same time, are found some salient points on the constitution of a league of self-governing states. The other document, intended as a legal study, made the pertinent inquiry, "is there not something extremely fallacious in the commonplace images of a mother country and children colonies? Are we the children of Great Britain any more than the cities of London, Exeter and Bath?"[19] To the statesman of the overseas dominions the British Empire must be an empire of equals. The town-meeting resolutions yield an equally basic rule of constitutional law. Otis had said, "An act against the constitution is void."[20] John Adams now elaborated this idea that there could be such a thing as an unconstitutional act. Among the provisions of the British constitution was this, that no man could be deprived of his property save by due process of law or by his consent. These principles, taken with another which he confided to his diary at the time, outline his conception of the function of constitutional law in the political union of the empire.[21] The other principle was contained in his comment, "The courts have not yet dared to adjudge the Stamp Act void."[22] Picking our way through the discussion of natural law, natural rights, compacts, and contracts, which were

[17] *Instructions of the Town of Braintree to their Representatives* (1765), Boston Gazette, 14 Oct., 1765. *Works,* III. 465.

[18] *Diary,* II. 154.

[19] *Dissertation on the Canon and Feudal Law, Works,* III. 445; Cf. John Andrews, *History of the Late War:* (London: 1783), p. 61.

[20] Appendix, J. Adams, *Works,* II. 525.

[21] "We further apprehend that this tax is unconstitutional, etc." *Instructions to the Representatives of Braintree,* III. 466.

[22] *Diary,* II. 155. "The Stamp Act ought to be waived by the judges as against natural equity and the constitution." Diary, II. 15.

part of every eighteenth century philosopher's stock in trade, we discover a virtual identification of these rights with the provision of the British constitution.[23] Insofar as this is a mere confusion of intellectual and political philosophy, we can profitably dispense with it. But insofar as it foreshadows a political union based on legal relationships, we have in embryonic form the conceptions of imperial relationships which the later writings of this period make clear. Three ideas thus emerge: first, that the empire was an association of equals; second, that the British constitution was a superior law, whereby the relationships of the constituent parts of the empire could be made clear, and third, that it was the function of the judiciary to disallow as unconstitutional an act of one of the legislative organs of the empire which did not comport with the superior law under which all existed or which attempted to impose the will of one of the partners upon another in violation of the fundamental understanding and its guarantees.[24] Evidences of this conception of the nature of the empire are vague at first, but as this was and is a concept which is not to be grasped in a short time, one may observe with interest that now frequently recurring entry in his diary: "At home today; thinking."

But John Adams was not yet done with the Stamp Act. Since the lawyers would not use stamped legal paper, the Governor of Massachusetts had closed the law courts. In December of 1765 came the argument before Governor Bernard in which Gridley, Otis, and John Adams tried to convince his excellency that the courts should be reopened. The parts played by the three are instructive. Had historians made less of the fact that the Stamp Act deprived John Adams of a lucrative law practice[25] and more of the fact that it gave him opportunity to state and to study the imperial problem, we might sooner have had our attention directed to the latter question. Gridley, as crown counsel, apparently dared not,[26] and Otis, if we may judge from his previous writings, could not, touch the underlying issue which the junior counsel on this occasion presented.[27] Perhaps they, too, saw it, but if we may believe the record

[23] J. Adams, Works, III. 453.
[24] "Clarendon" to the Boston Gazette, 27 Jan., 1766, III. 480; cf. IV. 99.
[25] Diary, II. 155.
[26] C. F. Adams, Life of John Adams, I. 78.
[27] James Otis, Vindication of the Conduct of the House of Representatives of Massachusetts Bay, (Boston: 1762). ". . . 'tis admitted that the Parliament

they failed to urge the point.[28] Adams pondered upon the course he was to pursue. Conscious of his obligations of "interest and ambition, as well as of honor, gratitude and duty, to exert the utmost of his abilities" in this important cause, he reflected on whether he should adopt the constitutional argument, or "shall we ground ourselves in necessity only?" Apparently he left the latter course to his colleagues.[29] For himself he argued that "Parliament has no legal authority to impose internal taxes on us, because we are not represented there," and grounded his argument "on the invalidity of the Stamp Act, it not being in any sense our act, having never consented to it."[30] His notes on this case are illuminating. Pursuing the "right, wrong and remedy argument," he took the position that a wrong had been done for which law must supply a remedy. Since a statute might be construed so that no wrong be done, then in law the Stamp Act was no act, was not law, and should be so regarded by the courts. The Governor evaded the issue by a significant admission that these were arguments which should be laid before a judicial and not before an executive officer.[31]

The next time the curtain rises, John Adams is discovered trying to keep one of his patriot friends out of well deserved trouble. The story of how in the autumn of 1768 John Hancock's sloop, *Liberty,* put into Boston with a cargo of wines and how the customs officer was enticed on board and, when he refused to wink at the proceedings, how he was locked up in the cabin while most of the wine was unloaded by the captain and crew who worked so hard that the captain died of heart failure the next day, shows how much respect some good citizens had for those trade regulations which they admitted Britain had a right to make. The upshot of this act

---

have the same right to levy internal taxes on the colonies as to regulate their trade; and that the right of levying both is undoubtedly in Parliament" p. 29. Also his *Rights of the British Colonies Asserted and proved* (Boston: 1764), of which his friend and biographer, William Tudor, has to admit, "There is a degree of incoherence in the reasoning, which grew out of contradictory principles, that were irreconcilable, the entire rights of the colonies and the absolute supremacy of Parliament." *Life of Otis* (Boston: 1823), p. 501. Hutchinson also noticed this: cf. Thomas Hutchinson, *History of the Province of Massachusetts Bay,* (London: 1838), III. 133.

[28] *Diary,* II. 159.
[29] *Diary,* II. 157.
[30] *Diary,* II. 158.
[31] *Diary,* II. 159.

of smuggling was that "a great uproar was raised in Boston," and John Adams was retained to appear in defense of Hancock.[32] This case gave opportunity for a general assault on the navigation acts as being unwarranted from the standpoint of constitutional law, as was any other law imposing taxes which might be made without consent. "My client, Mr. Hancock, never consented to it, he never voted for it himself, and he never voted for any man to make such a law for him."[33] Constructive consent and virtual representation were but "cries to deceive the mob," and such a conception of the nature of the organization of the empire would lead to that region "where arbitrary power sits upon her brazen throne and governs with an iron sceptre."

The constitutional argument was continued in 1773 when there occurred an exchange of addresses between the Governor, Hutchinson, and the two houses of the Massachusetts General Court, in which the differing views of the nature of the construction of the empire were clearly revealed.[34] The dispute, historically of intrinsic value, provided John Adams with yet another opportunity to descant on the relationship between the self-governing states of the imperial union. The Governor opened with a speech to both houses in which he stated positively, though perhaps not profoundly, "when our predecessors first took possession of this plantation it was their license and the sense of the Kingdom that they were to remain subject to the supreme authority of Parliament,"[35] and "I know of no line that can be drawn between the supreme authority of Parliament and the total independence of the colonies."[36] Since many a wiser man than Thomas Hutchinson has gone on the rocks of sovereignty in trying to steer his ship between the independence of a state and the jurisdiction which regulates its mutual relations with other states, this pronouncement of the Governor is of more immediate interest as discovering the existence of a political problem than

---

[32] Cf. William Gordon, *History of the Rise, Progress and Establishment of the Independence of the United States of America,* (London: 1788), I. 231 ff., and Hutchinson, *History,* III. 189.

[33] *Diary,* II. 215, and note.

[34] Papers in this controversy appear in *The Speeches of the Governors of Massachusetts from 1765–1775 and the Answers of The House of Representatives to the Same etc.,* (Boston: 1818), usually cited as Bradford's *Mass. State Papers.*

[35] Ibid., p. 339.

[36] Ibid., p. 340.

it is of revealing the wisdom or ignorance of that official. Both houses of the General Court appointed committees to draft replies to the Governor. The reply of the Council (the upper house), discussed the question of superior and subordinate jurisdictions from the standpoint of the subordinate.[37] But the reply of the House of Representatives attacked directly the question of the organization of the imperial union. The committee of the House consisted of the inevitable Samuel Adams-John Hancock group, but inasmuch as it was the wish of Major Hawley (who was an influential political boss), that the "committee take the opinion and advice of John Adams upon every question," that gentleman, although not a member of the committee, or even of the legislature at the time, was "very civilly requested and urged to meet the committee, which he did every evening till their report was finished."[38] Upon the first meeting of the committee he found one report already drawn up, probably by Samuel Adams and Warren.[39] It was "very prettily drawn" and "full of very popular talk and those democratical principles which have done so much mischief in this country."[40] John Adams "objected to all of them" and "got them expunged," whereupon he furnished the committee with "the law authorities, and legal and constitutional reasonings which are to be seen on the part of the house in that controversy." A report such as the committee had at first proposed was no answer nor attempt to answer the Governor's legal and constitutional arguments, such as they were. Full as it might be of the high-sounding principles of liberty, equality, and fraternity, John Adams believed that those arguments "based on nature and eternal and unchangeable truth" ought to be "well understood and cautiously applied," since it was not safe at all times and in all places "to resort to club law and the force of arms." Approaching the subject in a more scientific spirit, John Adams' contributions had "an effect on public opinion which was quite beyond expectation," and forty years later the author was still exulting in his triumph. "Mr. Hutchinson made a meagre figure in that dispute. He had waded in beyond his depth. He had wholly misunderstood the doctrine of allegiance."[41]

<hr />

[37] Ibid., p. 383.   [38] Diary, II. 311.

[39] So at least Adams says, Diary, II. 312; but his judgment in these matters was not infallible, as cf. his mistake about "Massachusettensis."

[40] Autobiography, II. 310; cf. Tudor's Life of Otis, p. 411n.

[41] J. Adams to William Tudor, II. 313.

Indeed Adams' doctrine of the nature of the empire hinged very largely upon the doctrine of allegiance. The distinction between allegiance to the crown and allegiance to the realm of Great Britain was a common one in the thought of the colonial politicians of the more conservative group.[42] The acquisition of the colonies of America, so the House informed the Governor, "was an acquisition of foreign territory, not annexed to the realm of England, and therefore at the absolute disposal of the crown." For that reason, "James I created the two Virginia Companies to be governed each by the laws transmitted by them to his Majesty, and not to Parliament," and "a declaration similar to this is contained in the first charter of this colony, and in those of the other American colonies, which shows that the colonies were not intended or considered to be within the realm of England though within the allegiance of the English crown."[43] The danger of translating these expressions into modern parlance is no excuse for neglecting or ignoring this popular idea in colonial politics. In essence the colonies were held to be part of the empire, but not an appendage of the Kingdom, so that the Parliament at Westminster had no more right in law to legislate for Massachusetts than had the provincial legislature of New York.

The Governor's argument had elaborated the theory that the clause in the various colonial charters which vested in the colonial assemblies the power and authority to make such laws as were not repugnant to the laws of England, should be interpreted to mean that no colony could make a law contrary to the law of Parliament. "This was a reserve of power and authority to Parliament, to bind us by such laws at least as are made expressly to refer to us, and consequently is a limitation upon the power of the General Court."[44] But the colonial statesmen attached a different significance to these words. The charter was a grant of the King and vested the authority to make laws "so always that the same be not contrary to the laws and statutes of this our realm of England." But this meant that the laws of the colonies should be as much as possible conformable to the principles and the fundamental laws of the English constitution,

---

[42] E.g., John Dickinson's Draft of Resolutions for the Stamp Act Congress, in his Works, (*Memoirs of the Penna. Hist. Soc.* XIV), p. 184; and James Wilson's *Considerations on the Nature and Extent of the Legislative Authority of the British Parliament,* (Phila. 1774).

[43] *Mass. State Papers,* p. 353.

[44] *Mass. State Papers,* p. 339.

its rights and statutes, then existing, (i.e., at the time the charter was granted), and by no means was meant to bind the colonies to a subjection to the supreme authority of the English Parliament."[45] And that this is the true intention of such provision in the charters is evidenced by the fact that "no acts of any colony legislature are ever brought into Parliament," although "they are laid before the King."[46] In further support of this view came John Adams' array of constitutional precedents which made Mr. Hutchinson cut such a sorry figure. Charles I had refused assent to a certain Parliamentary enactment, declaring as a reason that "the colonies were without the realm and jurisdiction of Parliament," and James I had asserted that "America was not annexed to the realm and it is not fitting that Parliament should make laws for these countries."[47] If then the colonies were not annexed to the realm, they are not "part of the Kingdom of Great Britain and consequently are not subject to the legislative authority of that kingdom."[48] Within the understanding of the colonials the charters had conveyed all the power necessary for the constitution of free and distinct states, and such they were as far as their relation with the British Parliament was concerned. All this was bolstered up with the legal authorities which "no man in Massachusetts at that time had ever read." Hutchinson and his supporters dared not deny the argument, "lest the book be produced to their confusion," and hence the Governor could but wriggle to evade what he had neither wit nor wisdom to confute.[49]

In his insistence on the distinction between allegiance to the realm and allegiance to the crown, John Adams had commented: "No ·country by the common law was subject to the laws of Parliament, but the realm of England."[50] Hutchinson had ventured to attack this, whereupon Samuel Adams wrote post-haste to the real author of the House's reply, saying, "the assertion is *mine,* but upon your authority," and he asked his cousin for the ammunition with which to combat the Governor.[51] That the latter's position was "vindicable" is made clear in the next act of the drama, which reveals John

[45] Ibid., p. 354.
[46] Ibid., p. 355.
[47] Ibid., p. 355.
[48] *Mass. State Papers,* p. 339.
[49] Letter to William Tudor: John Adams' *Works,* II. 313.
[50] *Mass. State Papers,* p. 354.
[51] *Diary,* II. 310–11, where this letter is reprinted in facsimile.

Adams the pamphleteer. In that year in which, apparently for the first time, His Majesty heard of a new unruly Adams across the seas,[52] the Boston *Gazette* printed the series of papers that have come down to us above the signature of "Novanglus." Written in reply to two Tory utterances, the pamphlet of "Veteran"[53] and the articles of "Massachusettensis,"[54] the "Novanglus" papers are literally a "History of the Dispute With America, from its Origin in 1754 to the Present Time, 1774." It is difficult to read the early numbers without feeling that the substitution of the term "loyalist" for the term "Tory" has lost us something. It is unfortunate that the latter term has acquired an opprobrious connotation, for "Tories" are exactly what the "Veteran" and "Massachusettensis" were to the Whigs of their day. The first instalment of "Novanglus" runs the whole gamut of the age-long liberal-conservative, Whig-Tory, radical-reactionary arguments. The Tories insisted that the political principles of the colonial Whigs might be "all right in theory but wouldn't work in practice." Novanglus replied that this was a most unscientific remark; if a thing didn't work out in practice it was because it wasn't all right in theory, and that as far as his observation of the English political laboratory was concerned, the theories for which he stood had been successfully practiced since the days of Magna Carta. The Whig principles were nothing new, they were simply the old and tried precepts of English legal and constitutional experience, and to say that in certain instances they were not applicable was like saying that in certain instances the law of gravity did not operate.[55] The argument then moved along the usual channels; to the allegation that the colonies should be more patient, that "a small mistake in policy has often furnished a pretense to libel the government, and persuade the whole people that their rulers are tyrants, and the whole government a system of oppression,"

---

[52] *Diary and Letters of Thomas Hutchinson* (1884), I. 163.

[53] *A Letter from a Veteran to the Officers of the Army encamped at Boston.* (Boston: 1774), which has a good deal more merit than Adams allowed to it.

[54] *Novanglus and Massachusettensis,* (Boston: 1818), in which edition the papers of "Novanglus" are very inappropriately printed first. *Works,* IV. 3. As late as 1819 John Adams was still attributing "Massachusettensis" to Jonathan Sewall, but in 1821 there is evidence that he had come to understand that Daniel Leonard was its author. On this point see J. Winsor's *Critical and Narrative History,* M. C. Tyler's *Literary History of the Revolution,* and Adams' *Works,* IV. 10.

[55] Novanglus, IV. 15.

"Novanglus" counters that "on the contrary, there never was a government yet in which thousands of mistakes were not overlooked. The most sensible and jealous people are so little attentive to government that there is no instance of resistance until repeated and multiplied oppressions have placed it beyond a doubt that their rulers have formed settled plans to deprive them of their liberty," for indeed "Machiavelli himself allows that not ingratitude but much love is the constant fault of the people."[56] To the contention of his adversaries that resistance will net the people nothing in the long run, he replied that he regarded that as equally wrong as to say that "the people are the sure losers in the end." "They can hardly be losers if unsuccessful, for if they live they will be but slaves, and if they die, they cannot be said to lose, since death is preferable to slavery."[57] Resistance was a well known political weapon in the history of English politics, and indeed the opening papers are full of watering the tree of liberty with the blood of patriots and tyrants.

With these preliminaries he plunged into that vital theme of the whole series, the nature of the relationship between the parts of the old British Empire. In this discussion his terminology is not always clear, but neither is our terminology clear after a hundred and forty additional years of experience. From the beginning, let it be understood, he believed the Parliament at Westminster had power to act as an imperial parliament in matters pertaining to the whole British Empire, such as the regulation of commerce or the conduct of war. But, simultaneously, we should bear in mind that he considered this a makeshift which was due to the absence of other and more suitable imperial machinery. Parliament had a double capacity, and when it acted as a Parliament of Great Britain it had no relation to the colonies. When acting in its imperial capacity it had only such relation to the colonies as they by their consent accorded to it. It was indeed true that the colonies were connected with Great Britain, "but we never thought Parliament the supreme legislator over us. We never generally supposed it to have any authority over us, but from necessity, and necessity we thought confined to the regulation of trade and to such matters as concerned the colonies altogether."[58] "The truth is, the general authority of Parliament was never gen-

[56] Novanglus, IV. 17.
[57] Novanglus, IV. 18.
[58] Novanglus, IV. 49.

erally acknowledged in America."[59] "Parliament has no authority over the colonies except to regulate their trade, and this not by any principle of common law, but merely by the consent of the colonies, founded on the obvious necessities of the case."[60] The significant aspect of the Acts of Trade and Navigation were to this colonial statesman no question of the "old colonial system," or the mercantilist school of economics. "Great Britain has confined all our trade to herself. We are willing that she should, so far as it can be for the good of the empire. We are obliged to take from Great Britain commodities that we could purchase cheaper elsewhere. This difference is a tax upon us for the good of the empire. We submit to this cheerfully."[61] A curious mixture indeed was all this, but it needs no genius to detect the strenuous efforts to secure autonomy while at the same time remaining within the circle of the British Empire. This indeed was the real task as many men saw, and this determination enabled him to repel as "malicious and injurious" the insinuation of "Massachusettensis" that what the colonies really desired was independence.[62] What the Americans wanted was a formula that would mediate between absolute dependence and absolute independence. "The Whigs allow from the necessity of the case, not provided by common law, and to supply a defect in the British Constitution which there undoubtedly is, if they are to be governed by that law, America has all along consented, still consents and ever will consent, that Parliament, being the most powerful legislative in the dominions, should regulate the trade of the dominions."[63]

The colonial statesmen frankly admitted that it was not necessarily strictly consistent to allow this single exception of trade regulation, to the general rule that Parliament had no authority over the colonies. But there is nothing new in the Anglo-Saxon habit of doing what is practical rather than what is consistent in politics. Such a conception of the rights and duties of the overseas dominions was "founding the authority to regulate our trade upon the compact and consent of the colonies, not upon any principle of common or statute law, not upon any original principle of the British Constitu-

---

[59] Novanglus, IV. 47.
[60] Novanglus, IV. 33.
[61] Novanglus, IV. 46.
[62] Novanglus, IV. 52.
[63] Novanglus, IV. 99.

tion; not upon the principle that Parliament is the supreme sovereign legislature over us in all cases whatsoever."[64] This pronouncement illustrates the essential and basic difference between the statesman of the kingdom, like Chatham, and the statesman of the dominions, like John Adams. To Chatham, Parliament had every legislative right over the colonies, except that of taxation.[65] To John Adams, Parliament had no legislative right over the colonies except that of trade regulation.[66] To Chatham, "the distinction between legislation and taxation is essentially necessary to liberty."[67] To John Adams, "the distinction between taxation and legislation has been found to be a distinction without a difference."[68] Without passing any judgment on the two men, it is worth noticing that the practice of the empire has followed the vision of the colonial rather than that of the English statesman, and it is no small tribute to John Adams that he saw more clearly than Chatham in a matter of British imperial concern.

The eighteenth century mentality grasped the possibilities of the twentieth century realization. "Massachusettensis" had mourned that the constitution was gone, since the spirit of the colonies had become truly republican. To this sturdy "Novanglus" replied, "The constitution is not gone"; moreover the spirit of the colonies is not any more republican than the "spirit of the British constitution itself was republican." Why cannot the overseas dominions be republican? What is a republic? From Aristotle to Harrington the philosophers agree that a republic is a government of laws and not of men, and the dominions might indeed be republican without impairing the stability of the empire.[69] The real question was whether the colonies were a part of the "kingdom of Great Britain? We are certainly not a part of the British Kingdom, realm or state, and therefore the supreme power in the kingdom is not upon these principles supreme over us." Yet in this there was nothing incon-

---

[64] Novanglus, IV. 99, and cf. James Madison's comment that this was "a practice without a right, and contrary to the true theory of the constitution" but nevertheless convenient and necessary, and hence permissible as a measure insuring imperial unity. James Madison's *Works,* (Hunt Ed.), VI. 374.

[65] Hansard, *Parliamentary History,* XVI. 100.

[66] Nos. 3 & 4 of Novanglus.

[67] Hansard, *Parliamentary History,* XVI. 100–1.

[68] Novanglus, IV. 113.

[69] Novanglus, IV. 68.

sistent with the admission that the colonies were "within the dominion, rule or government of the King of Great Britain."[70] It is easy to see how this might have seemed like hair-splitting in the eighteenth century, but the existence of the great self-governing dominions of the British Empire-Commonwealth of the twentieth century is an eloquent commentary on the distinctions made by the colonial statesman of the eighteenth.

As to an immediate solution, John Adams remarked: "No other plan of governing the colonies will ever restore harmony between the two countries, but desisting from the plan of taxing them, and interfering in their internal concerns, and return to that system of colony administration which nature dictated and which experience for one hundred and fifty years found useful."[71] So he conceived the empire: different countries united in the person of one king. "Massachusettensis" could not comprehend this. "If the colonies are not subject to the authority of Parliament, Great Britain and her colonies must be distinct states, as completely as England and Scotland before the union, or as Great Britain and Hanover now." To which the colonial lawyer replied, "there is no need of being startled at this consequence. It is very harmless. There is no absurdity in it at all. Distinct states may be united under one king; and those states may be further cemented and united together by treaties of commerce. This is the case. We have by our own express consent contracted to observe the Navigation Act, and by our implied consent and by long usage and uninterrupted acquiescence, have submitted to the other acts of trade, however grievous some of them may be. This may be compared to a treaty of commerce by which those distinct states have been cemented together in perpetual league and amity. And if any further ratifications of the pact or treaty are necessary, the colonies would readily enter into them provided their other liberties were inviolate."[72] By such analysis the King was the chief tie which bound the empire together in form, and he was "King of Massachusetts, King of Rhode Island, and King of Connecticut" as well as King of Great Britain and Ireland,[73] and John Adams expressed the pious wish that his Majesty might be graciously pleased to assume these titles. Of course, the colonists had no illu-

[70] Novanglus, IV. 107.
[71] Novanglus, IV. 98–9.
[72] Novanglus, IV. 113.
[73] Novanglus, IV. 114. Cf. also Bland's *Enquiry*, p. 20.

sions about the personal authority of the King, as they, too, remembered 1688.[74]

Throughout the controversy on both sides of the Atlantic there had been an appreciation of the fact that "it was necessary there should be some superintending power, to draw together all the will, and to unite all the strength of the subjects of all the dominions in case of war and in the case of trade."[75] The trade question was settled; let it remain as it was. The administration of war was the only outstanding difficulty which demanded any degree of centralized control, but John Adams did not believe that this alone would necessitate a highly centralized empire. Perhaps at the outbreak of a war, it might be an "inconvenience" that there was no general military authority, particularly if the colonies couldn't be coerced into supplying their quotas, but that should not entail a complete surrender of the rights of the dominions. The sentiment and pride of British subjects had been sufficient incentive in the past and would be in the future to insure the loyalty of the overseas dominions.[76] Experience in recent years seems to have vindicated the faith of this colonial statesman in the moral and spiritual unity of the empire.[77]

In defining the precise constitutional relationship between the various dominions, John Adams was confronted with the same difficulties that beset one who undertakes a similar task today. Yet within the limits of the materials of study at his disposal, he certainly made the most of his knowledge of English constitutional history. He called attention to the nature of the relationship between Edward I and Henry VIII. In the thirteenth century Wales was annexed to the dominions of the crown of England (12 Edw. I) by the Statute of Wales (Rhudlan), which was a royal, not a Parliamentary act. In this condition, Wales had no representation in Parliament, and according to John Adams' reasoning was not subject to the will of Parliament, but to that of the King. Wales was not attached to the realm of England until a distinct act of

[74] "This fierce spirit of Liberty is stronger in the English colonies probably than in any other people on earth." "They are therefore devoted to liberty according to English ideas and on English principles." Edmund Burke, in Hansard, *Parliamentary History*, XVIII. 491–5.

[75] Novanglus, IV. 115.

[76] Novanglus, IV. 116.

[77] G. M. Wrong, *Nationalism in the British Empire*, *Amer. Hist. Rev.*, XXII. 45.

Parliament (27 Hen. VIII), provided for its amalgamation with England. Could anyone show any such act of amalgamation for the colonies in America?[78] So, too, with Scotland: between the accession of the Scotch King James to the English throne and the Act of Union a hundred years elapsed during which the Parliament had no authority in Scotland. Ireland was another case in point; for although it was first conquered by Henry II, and at that time annexed to the realm of England, yet it was not until the passage of Poynings Law under Henry VII that Ireland was subjected to the authority of the English Parliament. Where was the Poynings Law for America?[79] Surely if such a condition of independence of Parliament was accorded the conquered nations of Wales and Ireland, it ought to be granted to unconquered America.[80] "The fact is that Massachusetts is a realm, and New York is a realm," and "The King of Great Britain is the sovereign of all these realms."[81]

As to the nature of the kingship to which the colonial statesman seemed to accord so much power and authority, the attack by "Novanglus" upon a pamphlet by the loyalist Galloway[82] clears up this point. Back among his favorites, he tells us that Lord Coke had made a distinction between allegiance due the King in his personal and in his political capacity. Allegiance was held in a famous case to be due to the "natural person of the King,"[83] and hence John Adams built up the distinction between allegiance due to the crown and allegiance due to the realm of England. With Coke he agreed that the King "in his political capacity did rule the divers nations and kingdoms of his empire," but had "to govern them by their distinct laws," thus preserving the separate identity of the component nations in the empire-commonwealth.[84] Perhaps in law there is much to be said on both sides of such an historical argument, but in that we are not so much interested here. It makes little difference now whether John Adams was right or wrong. What matters is that he could think in terms of a commonwealth of nations.

The "Novanglus" series, like the crown's case against Hancock

[78] Novanglus, IV. 134; Cf. J. F. Trout, *Edward the First,* (1893), p. 119.

[79] Novanglus, IV. 156.

[80] Novanglus, IV. 158.

[81] Novanglus, IV. 123; Cf. J. J. Zubly, *Stamp Act Sermon,* p. 6–7.

[82] *A Candid Examination of the Mutual Claims of Great Britain and the Colonies,* (New York: 1774).

[83] 7 Coke Rep. 19. Cf. Blankard v. Galdy; 2 Salk. 411.

[84] Novanglus, IV. 145.

in the case of the sloop *Liberty,* came to an abrupt end with the battle at Lexington. With that event the story of John Adams as a Britannic statesman must cease. The last number of "Novanglus" "was prevented from impression by the commencement of hostilities, and Mr. Gill gave it to Judge Cushing, who now has the manuscript."[85] The *Pennsylvania Gazette* for May 10, but three weeks after Lexington, announces the arrival of John Adams among the Massachusetts delegates at Philadelphia for the second Continental Congress. If, as his adversary had contended, "there is no possible medium between absolute independence and subjection to the authority of Parliament," if British statesmen would not understand the idea which for ten years he and his fellows had been trying to work out, then the colonists were going to be "absolutely independent."[86] He believed to the end that "an absolute independence of Parliament in all internal concerns and taxation is very compatible with absolute dependence in all cases of external commerce." But if the British would not try to work out any formula along this line, then the conversation could only be continued when as first American Minister at the Court of St. James, he was able to assure George III, "I have no attachment but for my own country."[87]

Any review of John Adams' political writings would be incomplete without mention of the sources of his ideas. Especially is this true when one assigns him a position in Britannic history, since English thinkers supplied him so largely with the inspiration and information upon which he built his own ideas. The sound of "Sydney, Harrington and Locke" re-echoes in the thoughts of any reader long after he has put a volume of John Adams' works aside. These with Hobbes, Milton, Hume, Nedham, Bacon, and the beloved legal lights like Coke, make him even more truly a product of the British Empire. Who seeks the influence of French or continental thought on the American Revolution must look elsewhere for his evidence. Needless to say, there is mention of Rousseau and Montesquieu, as there is of Grotius, Puffendorf, and Machiavelli, but we have his own word for it as well as the evidence of his writings that it is his English intellectual inheritance of which he is most proud.[88]

[85] *Diary,* II. 405.
[86] Novanglus, IV. 130.
[87] *Life,* I. 419.
[88] *Diary,* III. 22, 462; *Novanglus,* IV. 194; VI. 492. Cf. Dunning, *Hist. of*

Although it may be true that John Adams belongs to that reactionary period of American political thought to which history seems to have consigned him, he has nevertheless a claim to a position among the pioneers of a new class of Britannic thinkers, who are in the twentieth century still at work on the same task.

Pol. Theories from Luther to Montesquieu, p. 254n. Cf. Theodore Dwight, *Harrington and His Influence upon American Political Institutions and Political Thought* in the *Pol. Sci. Quar.*, II. 1–44. Harrington it was from whom Adams got his "commonwealth is an empire of laws, and not of men." James Harrington, *Oceana* (Morley Ed.; Lond. 1887), pp. 25–9.

6

SOME THINGS WHICH PARLIAMENT COULD NOT DO

L EST IT BE INFERRED from the preceding chapters that after all the American Revolution was little more than an accident, there now appears in our story the figure of one whose crashing sentences shook Americans from their belief that their problems might be solved within the British Empire. It was perhaps a little presumptuous to imagine that anything new can be said of Thomas Paine, for later investigation has now rescued him from the obloquy to which the orthodox conscience condemned him.[1] At last he has been given the place in American history[2] and in the history of American politics to which he is entitled.[3] That as a writer he helped to cut the Gordian knot of the British imperial problem for thousands of Americans is now a fairly well established fact.[4] But there is still room for doubt as to whether he has been given that place in political science to which he belongs. One discovers on examining a standard American treatise on political science that the index contains no mention of the name of Thomas Paine,[5] yet a recent source book on political philosophy classes with Aristotle and Plato, Hobbes and Locke, Montesquieu and Rousseau, the name of Paine, who is, incidentally,

---

[1] See the preface to the *Life of Thomas Paine* (1892) by his chief rescuer, M. D. Conway.

[2] E. Channing, *History of the United States,* III. 189–90.

[3] C. E. Merriam, *History of American Political Theories,* pp. 70–74.

[4] Cf. J. B. McMaster, *History of the People of the United States,* I. 152–4; and R. Frothingham, *Rise of the Republic,* pp. 476–80 and notes, where this has been worked out.

[5] Cf. e.g., J. W. Garner, *Introduction to Political Science,* or J. W. Burgess, *Political Science and Constitutional Law.*

the only writer in that volume who can in any way pretend to be an American.[6]

A close student of Paine's political theories has assured us that he cannot be classed as a great political thinker, that he was an agitator rather than a philosopher, and that everything he thought had been marked out before and better by others.[7] Into that question it is not our function to enter. But the eagerness of some writers to fit Paine's thought into certain already defined categories, to pigeonhole his work intellectually, has perhaps led to the neglect of some phases of his thought which may be worth a good deal more consideration than the aspects of his thinking to which most time and paper seem to have been devoted. Paine's contributions to the higher criticism of the Bible are not very important in this day of careful textual criticism and archæological research. And insofar as his theories of politics are merely copied from Locke or Rousseau, we have access to both of those writers. But this is not all of Paine, and perhaps ultimately it may be recognized that these things were the least of Paine, as far as his position in the history of thought is concerned. The criticism which he passed upon Rousseau ought long ago to have given the key to what he was trying to do. "We find," he writes, "in the writings of Rousseau and the Abbe Raynal a loveliness of sentiment in favor of liberty, that excites respect and elevates the human faculties; but having raised this animation they do not direct its operation, and leave the mind in love with an object without describing the means of possessing it."[8] The challenge instantly arises that Paine offer some thought of a practical nature. It is not within our province to discuss the validity of his answer, but the popularity of all his writings bears witness to their representative character in America, and with that we are concerned.

Paine's most sympathetic, if somewhat uncritical, biographer closes his work, after many years of study, by calling his subject the "Founder of the Republic of the World."[9] Whatever claims Paine

[6] F. W. Coker, *Readings in Political Philosophy.*

[7] C. E. Merriam, *Pol. Sci. Quar.,* XIV. 389, 402.

[8] *The Rights of Man:* (1791), in Conway's Ed. of Paine's *Collected Works,* II. 334. Citations unless otherwise noted are to this edition.

[9] Conway closes his work thus: "Here then close my labors on the history and writings of the Great Commoner of mankind, founder of the republic of the World, emancipator of the human mind and thought." *Works,* IV. xxiii. This is certainly a revaluation of Paine and if true, makes him deserving of a good deal more attention than has been given him.

may have to such a title are based on two things: his doctrinaire
efforts, which include most of his religious writings, and his practical contributions to the science of politics. The former do not fall
within the sphere or scope of this work, but the latter are a part of
our story. For Thomas Paine was an internationalist, though not
exactly in the sense in which that term is used today. He was no
acutely class conscious proletarian, with a specific economic program
for the amelioration of all human ills. He was an English Quaker
who saw the leaven of liberty at work in America, and so he went
to America. After very active participation in the realization of
American liberty, he saw the same leaven at work in France, and
so he went to France and participated with equal activity in the
liberation of that nation. Like many men of his day, he had a
great confidence in the power of abstract ideas, and the sense in
which he was an internationalist is that he went from one country
to another to spread and write about those ideas. It is, indeed, true
that he often divided mankind into the oppressors and the op-
pressed, but he thought of them not in terms of economic "haves"
and "have nots," rather in terms of their condition or state of
liberty, which in the last analysis depended upon the freeing of man
from ignorance and superstition rather than upon any scheme for
more equal distribution of the products of industry. He lived in a
day when the economic factors were only beginning to be recognized
by social reformers, and he naturally placed little stress on them.
Instead he had an almost unlimited confidence in the self-governing
capacity of the great mass of the people, a thought which one
usually associates rather with the period of Jeffersonian democracy.
It is, however, a part of the whole Revolutionary theory of politics,
which seems to have held that a political reform must precede every
other, and to have regarded political liberty as a *summum bonum*
in itself.

As to Paine's representative character, the evidence is pretty con-
vincing that he had that knack of expressing what people in general
were thinking, better than most of his contemporaries. It is possible
that a good deal of the talk about the influence of certain writers
is a little misleading. Doubtless writers do influence, but isn't it
possible that the nature of that influence lies less in the presentation
of a brand new idea than in the fact that the writer is the mouth-
piece of his day and time, and the more popular any given writer is,
the more faithful reproducer he is? We have a current illustration

of the point in the readiness of superficial writers to blame a certain
Central European historian for leading the mentalities of his people
astray. After all, did Treitschke really teach Germans the gospel of
might? If the German mentality had not reached that thought
anyway, is it likely that the efforts of a single historian could have
effected it? Conceivably it might have been so, with that author one
of a great number. But is it not equally fair to translate such a
vogue, when it exists, in terms of the readiness of people to read
the writings in question? It is not the number or profundity of
learned scholars that makes a country civilized so much as the
enlightenment of the mass of the people. Consequently the vogue
or popularity of a writer may be a very convenient index to the
thought of a people, even though scholars frown upon that writer.
Treitschke was rather the spokesman than the instigator of Deutsch-
tum. Similarly with Paine. Were we to believe some of our histories,
it would seem that up to a certain point no one thought of independence in America, then suddenly a single pamphlet converted
thousands to that idea. But may it not be that Paine's oft-attested
tremendous popularity in his own time is simply a register of the
stage which the thought of America had reached?

One of the chief difficulties which beset the path of the modern
political thinker appears to be his inability to get above or beyond
the state. Political scientists may disagree endlessly, but the one topic
upon which there seems to be any degree of unanimity is that their
subject deals primarily with the state. One of Woodrow Wilson's
principal works adopts that word as a title, and hardly a German
book but has the word "Staat" on its front page in some combination
or other. Thomas Paine, as a true child of the eighteenth century,
finds his subject not in the state, but in man. Belonging to that
school of thought of which Locke is the classic English and Rousseau
the classic French example, he predicates the equality of men as
his starting point. Both of his famous predecessors seem to have
been willing that the idea of man collectively should come into the
titles of their writings,[10] but Paine selected for the title of one of
his chief works what he seems to have considered the dominant note
in the philosophy which he represents, and rightly or wrongly builds
his edifice on the "Rights of Man." His conception of man seems
so fundamental to his whole thought that only an incomplete picture

[10] Locke, *Two Treatises on Government* and Rousseau, *Le Contrat Social.*

would omit it. The equality of man is based upon what he calls "the unity of man," by which he means "that men are all of one degree."[11] He would have this equality understood spiritually. It was as manifestly absurd to Paine as it is today, to say all men are equal and then to think of man in physical terms.[12] Neither was he thinking in terms of any "economic man."[13] He pointed out that the only possible basis for the equality of men was the creation of man in the likeness and image of his creator.[14] One is tempted to think that of all political thinkers Paine is one of a very few who could make a remark like that and not raise against himself the charge of superstition. Ordinarily such language tempts the historian of politics to hand his subject over to the theologian and be done with him. But the theologians have lost any claim they may conceivably have had to Paine, for when he was first handed over to them they made short work of him. Perhaps the stone which the theologians have rejected may yet become the corner of another temple.

It is rather difficult as yet to say whether there is any distinctively American theory of history or politics. But if Paine's works are not sufficiently consistent to make clear to us what his theory was, they certainly aid us materially in saying what it was not, and that is something. John Dewey's chapter on the Germanic philosophy of history leaves one under the impression that the German God was the state;[15] Kuno Francke[16] admits it, and Friedrich Meinecke[17]

[11] Webster's definition of "degree" is "rank or station in life."

[12] "In a state of nature, all men are equal in rights, but they are not all equal in powers, the weak cannot defend themselves against the strong." *Dissertation on the First Principles of Government*, III. 272.

[13] "That Property will ever be unequal is certain: Industry, superiority of talents, dexterity of management, extreme frugality, fortunate opportunities, or the opposite, or the means of those things, will ever produce that effect without having recourse to the harsh ill sounding names of avarice and oppression." Ibid., III. 268.

[14] *Rights of Man*, Paine's *Works*, II. 303–308.

[15] Dewey epitomizes the Hegelian idea thus: "The march of God in history is the cause of the existence of states; their foundation is the power of reason realizing itself as will. Every state, whatever it be, participates in the divine essence; the state is not the work of human art; only reason could produce it. The State is God on Earth." *German Philosophy and Politics*, p. 111.

[16] "To the German it [the state] is a spiritual collective personality leading a life of its own, beyond and above the life of individuals, and its aim is not the protection of the happiness of individuals, but their elevation to a nobler type of manhood and their training for achievement in all the higher con-

alleges it. Be this as it may, it is now writ large in letters that all may read that the German God was something other than love. Thomas Paine's doctrine differed very widely from the deification of the state with which the world is now familiar. His emphasis was not upon the nature of the state but upon the nature of man; he was not interested in the living state, but he was interested in living man; he did not endow the state with a metaphysical nature, but he did try to understand the metaphysical aspect of man.[18] Man, to whom in Paine's thought no higher title could be given, man was the basis of that "society" wherein the compact was made to form a government. Men being equal only in the quasi-spiritual sense of having equal rights, government was necessary to restrain the weaknesses of men, to prevent them from encroaching on the rights of less powerful neighbors. The aggregate of men was "society," "the nation," "the people," and a heavy line of demarcation was drawn between them and their tool, *government*. From this train of thought, Paine could never lose sight of the fact that government was merely the instrument, the creature of society. This idea forms the groundwork for the concept of the "state" as a portion of society, which seems to be the sense in which Englishmen and Americans use that word. But under no circumstances can it form the groundwork for the idea "Staat," which seems to have demonstated itself as a thing existing of and for itself.[19]

---

cerns of life—in popular education, in scientific inquiry, in artistic culture, in communal and industrial education." *A German-American's Confession of Faith,* p. 26.

[17] "It was Ranke who taught us to honor truth and regard states as living personalities, animated with vital impulses and desire for power; they are all proud, covetous of honor and egotistical, but no one of them is like the other." *Deutschland und der Weltkrieg,* (tr.) p. 577.

[18] The verification of this cannot be ascertained by mere hunting up of foot note references. The whole of the first part of the *Rights of Man* as well as *Common Sense* are illuminating; but one should see also the later works wherein this thought seems to be mature. While perhaps it may not be correct to go as far as Paine's admiring biographer and call him "the spiritual successor of George Fox," yet it is apparent that in thinking of man Paine was frequently in the realm of "the real as opposed to the phenomenal being," (Webster's definition of metaphysics.) Cf. John Adams' *Dissertation,* Etc., *Works,* III. 462–3.

[19] The contrast with the German thought is not brought out for the purpose of stating what the German thought is on this point. Perhaps there is no dominant "German thought," in the same sense that there is no "average

The distinction between "society" and "government" is, then, the opening thought of that famous "Common Sense," which even the hostile critic was compelled to praise as "speaking the language the American colonists had felt, but had not thought, its popularity, terrible in its consequences to the parent country, was unexampled in the history of the press."[20] The distinction upon which the modern political scientist insists is between the *state* and the *government*. Paine's distinction was between *society* and *government*. That this is no matter of words can be seen from a simple illustration: a Louis XIV might have called himself the state, but even he would hardly be so egotistical as to confuse himself with society. Of course, we have no Louis XIV today, but in the Teutonic *Staat* idolator we have a confusion of state and government which is probably even less scientific than that of Louis and has demonstrated itself as more dangerous to society. It is here that Paine's thought seems to be a contribution which political science has overlooked; beginning with society he does not erect an idol which ultimately shows itself the enemy of society; he would have society instruct an agent, which must obey the mandate of its principal. In other words, instead of constructing a Frankenstein monster which destroys it, society gives orders to its servant. It is quite immaterial to this analysis whether the modern, and especially the German theory of the state is as it has been presented here or whether it is something else. If the contrast brings out the thought of Paine it serves the purpose for which it was introduced.

Paine's concept appears and reappears constantly throughout his works, particularly in his doctrine of constitutional law. In commenting on this distinction between society and government, he observes: "How often is the natural propensity of society disturbed or destroyed by the operations of government; when the latter, instead of being engrafted on the principles of the former, assumes to exist for itself, and acts by partialities of favor and oppression, and it becomes the cause of the mischiefs it ought to prevent."[21]

---

man." Rather is the analysis in the nature of a convenient fiction which clarifies Paine's thought by contrast. On the interesting subject of the later stages of this, attention is directed to Ralph Barton Perry's thoughtful discussion of *The Present Conflict of Ideals,* p. 263 passim; although distinctly a war-book this volume brings out vividly the opposing points of view.

[20] Cheetham, *Life of Paine* (1819), quoted by Conway, *Life,* Preface.

[21] *Rights of Man,* Paine's *Works,* II. 409.

Thus government occupies not only a subordinate position, but it holds that position only during good behavior. This was the philosophy of the Revolutionary period, in which Jefferson could talk about watering the tree of liberty with the blood of patriots and tyrants. But Paine drew from this the principle that "the strength and permanent security of a government is in proportion to the number of people supporting it."[22] In other words, government is a thing which depends upon the consent of the governed; governments are not unlimited and above law, but are limited by instructions from their principals, by the orders from their masters.

Paine's doctrine of the nature of a constitution and constitutional law is that they were the instructions which the principal gave its agent, the orders which the master gave his servant. "A constitution," he says, "is a thing antecedent to government and a government is only the creature of the constitution." On this point the Revolutionary thought split with the traditional English conception of a constitution. "From a want of understanding the difference between a constitution and a government, Dr. Johnson and all the writers of his description have always bewildered themselves. They could not but perceive that there must necessarily be a controlling power existing somewhere, and they placed this in the discretion of the persons exercising the government, instead of in the constitution formed by a nation. The laws which are enacted by governments control men only as individuals, but the nation, through its constitution, controls the whole government."[23] Here is the meeting place of the eighteenth century philosophy and the American doctrine of constitutional law which subordinates the government to the higher law, the constitution. The American doctrine is the logical resultant of the philosophy of the Revolution. If men are all equal in the sense that they have equal rights, if they form governments to protect those rights, then there must be somewhere a fundamental set of rules which delineates those rights and lays down the terms on which the protection is granted. If the protecting agent destroys what he is created to protect, then the process is simple enough; society simply appoints another agent who will observe its instructions and abide by the fundamental law. From this assumption develops normally the American doctrine that a law against the constitution is void, and no government can put it

<hr>

22 *First Principles of Government*, III. 267.
23 *Rights of Man*, Paine's *Works*, II. 436.

into effect, because as no fountain can rise above its source, no government can be above the law of the constitution.

Paine's discussion with Condorcet illustrates how fundamental he believed this doctrine was. The latter asked him a number of questions on the construction of government and administration. Paine answered by leading Condorcet back to the fundamental principle which has been outlined above. In answer to the question as to how the balance should be preserved between the legislative and executive branches of the government and in answer to the question how a unicameral legislature can be prevented from running away with itself, he gave virtually the same answer: "A constitution, in defining the limits of power, together with the principles which the legislature is bound to obey, has already provided a most powerful and trustworthy check upon any abuses of power."[24] This kind of political thinking, which resulted in the theory that the sovereign will of the people was to be found in and expressed through the constitution, represents the whole line of development from the revolutionary thought of the seventeenth century through the revolutionary thought of the eighteenth down to the American doctrine of the supremacy of the law of the constitution. For Americans this law which is above the government has become such a real thing that it is enforceable in the courts, and the American does not hesitate to appeal to that law over the head of the legislature which has enacted something that he conceives to be contrary to it. Let us now observe the emergence of that idea in the era of the American Revolution.

When an Englishman of the time of Burke, or even in our own day, said that such and such an act of Parliament was "unconstitutional," he merely meant that in his opinion the act was opposed to the spirit of the British constitution, but that it was thereby either void or a breach of a higher law would not have entered his head. On the other hand, when a John Adams or James Wilson said that an act of Parliament was unconstitutional he meant something entirely different. The supremacy of Parliament was, as we have observed, a thought which obsessed Westminster at this time. As Parliament was the body which made British constitutional law, naturally its members could not conceive of a constitution which was contrary to their will. But in America another idea appeared. What did the colonists mean by their constant harping on the point

[24] *Four Questions on Government,* II. 238, 239, 241.

that they were entitled to the rights and liberties of Englishmen? Did they mean that they enjoyed the benefits and owed the duties which British constitutional law secured for the British people? Did they really mean that they carried with them upon emigration from England all of the laws of England, as being bound by them and entitled to their protection wherever they should settle? Manifestly they did not, for as Franklin very properly pointed out "they left the realm in order to avoid the inconveniences and hardships they were under, where some of those laws were enforced, particularly the ecclesiastical laws for the payment of tithes and others."[25] If they had carried those laws with them they might just as well have stayed at home. What then was the nature of the laws which secured to them the rights which they claimed as Englishmen, laws which they claimed to have brought over with them; laws which during the pre-Revolutionary period they so frequently and eloquently invoked in justification of their position, and where were those laws to be found? The answer is found in such documents as the letter of the House of Representatives of Massachusetts Bay in January of 1768 to Lord Shelburne, in which it solemnly warned that official that neither the supreme legislature nor the supreme executive could alter the fundamental rules of the Constitution.[26]

In the next month the doctrine is repeated: "This House is at all times ready to recognize his Majesty's high court of Parliament as the supreme legislative power over the whole empire, its super-intending power *in all cases consistent with the fundamental rules of the constitution.*"[27] If Parliament was sovereign, who were the members of the Massachusetts legislature that they could lay down rules under which that sovereignty was to be exercised? The answer is that they were Americans and that Americans were at that time putting into operation the idea that there is no government above the law. Such a doctrine was all but unthinkable in England, for had not Blackstone declared that "no court has power to defeat the intent of the legislature"?[28] In Massachusetts at this time the word "court" was used in two senses. There were the General Court (legislative), and the Executive Courts (judicial). The former,

[25] *Works,* (Bigelow Ed.), IV. 300.

[26] Reprinted in *The True Sentiments of America,* (London: 1768), p. 15. This is an interesting and valuable collection of various documents in the controversy from 1765–68.

[27] *True Sentiments,* etc., p. 22.

[28] Bl. Com. Intr. 91, (Chitty Ed.).

which Blackstone did not have in view, now undertook deliberately to do what Blackstone said could not be done. Samuel Adams, author of the above-quoted letters of the House of Representatives of Massachusetts, wrote a series of letters in behalf of that body to various members of the ministry and other prominent English statesmen in which he reiterates time and again that it is the American sense of the word "constitution" that "the constitution is fixed; it is from thence that the supreme legislative as well as the supreme executive derives its authority. Neither, then, can break through the fundamental rules without destroying their own foundation."[29] He had three years earlier made clear what he meant by appealing to what he called the rights of Englishmen to which the colonists were entitled. He meant the fundamental principles of that British constitution to which he was now appealing over the heads of the government.[30] If it be inquired where those principles were to be found, Samuel Adams is quite representative of his age in discovering them not only in the great monuments of English constitutional law, but in what that generation knew as "natural law," of which they seemed to conceive the constitution as the expression.[31]

But was such a law really law in the sense that it was enforceable in the courts? We have observed that there was another kind of courts in Massachusetts, the Executive Courts (judicial),[32] and certainly they were the courts which Blackstone had in view. Yet we have seen that Otis and John Adams had demanded that even these courts question the validity of an act of Parliament which was contrary to the constitution.[33] Apparently in the thought of these colonials, the law of nature was a thing that could be "adopted into the Constitution"[34] or "engrafted into the British Constitution,"[35]

---

[29] To Rockingham, 22 Jan., 1768: *Mass. State Papers*, p. 142.

[30] To John Smith, 19 Dec., 1765: Samuel Adams *Works*, (Cushing Ed.), I. 46.

[31] To Conway: Feb. 13, 1786: Almon, *Prior Documents*, pp. 181, 182.

[32] John Adams, Supra; and Hutchinson, *History of Mass.*, III. 505. Cf. also Josiah Quincy, *Memoir of Josiah Quincy, Jr.*, p. 68.

[33] Otis in his speech on the Writs of Assistance. See J. Adams *Works*, II 522, 525; John Adams on the Stamp Act, supra.

[34] House of Reps. of Mass. to Dennys DeBerdt, 12 Jan., 1768; S. Adams *Works*, I. 135.

[35] House of Representatives of Mass. to Shelburne, 15 Jan., 1768, *Mass State Papers*, p. 137.

and having thus been made a part of English law by the great constitutional documents, Magna Carta and the like, it was so very real that the colonists might appeal to it over the head of Parliament.[36] Although it probably would not be correct to say that all the Americans of this time were looking forward to the time when a court was to decide upon the constitutionality of an act, certainly many Americans who were not great lawyers were thinking in terms which formed the background of the idea that governments existed under the law of the constitution. For instance, Samuel Adams did not enunciate the doctrine of judicial control with the clearness with which historians have pointed out that Otis and John Adams foreshadowed that idea,[37] but he did make this pronouncement: "When a question arises on public administration, the nation will judge and determine it in conformity with its political constitution."[38] Samuel Adams, like Paine, we may perhaps regard from his personal popularity as somewhat more representative of the mass of the people than the more intellectual men and profound thinkers of the type of John Adams or James Wilson.

Moreover, this kind of talk went on not merely among the radicals. Even such an advocate of parliamentary supremacy as Daniel Dulany believed that the right of Parliament to legislate for the colonies was qualified by the constitutional compact between the colonies and Great Britain. He admitted that Parliament was the superior legislature and that the colonial assemblies were inferior legislatures, but he averred that there were certain matters reserved to the colonies into which the authority of Parliament could not properly interpose "for by the power vested in the inferior is the superior limited."[39] Another and even more critical commentator on British constitutional law, who also acknowledges the

[36] "It is the glory of the British Prince and the happiness of all his subjects that their constitution hath its foundation in the immutable laws of nature; and as the supreme legislature, as well as the supreme executive derives its authority from that constitution, it should seem that no laws can be made or executed which are repugnant to any essential law of nature." House of Reps. of Mass. to Conway, Feb. 13, 1768, Almon, *Prior Documents*, pp. 181–2.

[37] E.g., A. C. McLaughlin in his chapter on the "Power of a Court to declare a law unconstitutional" in his *The Courts, the Constitution, and Parties*, pp. 75–94.

[38] House of Reps. of Mass. to Camden, 29 Jan., 1768, Almon, *Prior Documents*, p. 187.

[39] Dulany, *Considerations*, etc., p. 16.

supremacy of Parliament, observed that that body was "grasping at a power altogether foreign and inconsistent with the principles of their own Constitution," in arrogating to themselves the right to tax the colonies.[40] Even the prospective Tory, Joseph Galloway, who advocated the theory of Parliamentary supremacy to the last, inquired pertinently "what are the modifications" of this supremacy?[41] When Blackstone had said that Parliament was supreme, he meant exactly that, and he proceeded to illustrate it by saying that even if Parliament passed an act making a man judge in his own case, he knew of no power that could defeat the intent of Parliament. Certainly it would be difficult to put the British theory any more clearly. But apparently Americans did know of such a power, and particularly objected to Parliament acting as judge in its own case. Governor Pitkin of Connecticut instructed the colonial agent of that province "on the sense of his people, admitting, therefore, that there is a supreme power in the British Parliament to regulate and direct the general affairs of the empire, it cannot surely be inferred from thence, that the British Parliament can by any act agreeable to the Constitution, deprive the subject of the essential privileges of it. The supposition is absurd, it involves a contradiction,"[42] i.e., that a creature of the constitution can change the constitution. It has already been observed that Richard Bland suggested a similar thought in his statement that "great as are the powers of Parliament, yet it cannot constitutionally deprive the people of their civil rights, which are founded on compact, without their consent."[43]

We now begin to see that an American of Burke's day did not mean the same thing as an Englishman when he called a law "unconstitutional." In England the Vinerian professors from Sir William Blackstone to Mr. A. V. Dicey have taught that Parliament is absolutely sovereign.[44] From this preachment it follows that what

---

[40] *Considerations on the Rights of the Colonies to the Privileges of British Subjects,* (New York: 1766), p. 21.

[41] Galloway, *Candid Examination,* etc., p. 6.

[42] *Mass. Hist. Soc. Coll.,* 5th ser., IX. 280.

[43] Bland, *Enquiry,* etc., p. 20.

[44] The former rules that "there is and must be in every state a supreme irresistible, absolute and uncontrolled authority, in which the *jura summi imperii,* or rights of sovereignty reside." 4 Bl. Com., 48–9; and further "That this supreme power is by the constitution of Great Britain vested in the King, Lords and Commons." 4 Bl. Com. 50–1. The latter lays down "Parliament means, in the mouth of the lawyer, the King, the House of Lords and the

Parliament wills is law, and the highest law cognizable by the English courts. Hence in the period we have elected to study it was a settled rule in England that no judicial court could decide that an act of Parliament was contrary to any superior rule of binding power; the Revolution of 1688 had fixed the supremacy of Parliament. But the legal historian would have us understand that this had not always been so, and there does indeed seem to be ground for the assertion that before the revolution of 1688, in the century in which the English common law was being translated from England to America, Coke had tried to establish the doctrine that "the common law will control the acts of Parliament and some times adjudge them to be utterly void."[45] This doctrine, planted in the new soil, seems to have grown strangely away from the law of England. It is interesting to reflect that the legal education of the lawyers in America prior to the Revolution was gained not from the celebrated "Commentaries" of Blackstone, which afterward became the nucleus of a lawyer's training. The books available in the colonies were not numerous; the volumes of colonial reports which we have today, scant and meagre at best, were most of them not printed until years after the cases were decided, and Blackstone's work did not appear in print until the Stamp Act year. What then did they study? The answer seems to be that in a very large degree they got what they knew from the writings of that celebrated Sir Edward Coke, who did not scruple to inform James, of Divine Right fame, that even the King was under the law, from Coke's Reports, Coke's Institutes, Coke on Littleton. The doctrine of Parliamentary supremacy was not so firmly fixed in the day when Coke wrote as it later came to be, and Coke believed he had ample precedent for imposing the limitations of law upon both King and Parliament. Moreover, American lawyers had read their Vattel as well as their Coke, and had not Vattel said, "It is from the Constitution that those legislators derive their power, how then can

---

House of Commons. The principle of Parliamentary sovereignty means neither more nor less than this, that Parliament thus defined has, under the English constitution the right to make or unmake any law whatever, and furthermore, that no person or body is recognized by the law of England as having a right to override or set aside the legislation of Parliament." A. V. Dicey, *Introduction to the Study of the Law of the Constitution.* (8th Ed. 1915), p. 38.

[45] Coke's Doctrine is in Dr. Bonham's Case, 8 Rep. 118a. Brinton Coxe in his *Judiciary and Unconstitutional Legislation,* (1892), has called attention to this matter and blazed the way for other modern studies.

they change it without destroying the foundation of their own authority?"[46] From these authorities it was an easy step to the pronouncement of Otis: "An act against the Constitution is void."[47]

It seems now to be fairly well established by the research of numerous scholars that the American doctrine of judicial supremacy,[48] far from being a figment of John Marshall's imagination, is one of the earliest contributions of Anglo-American thought in the field of political science. Finding its origin in that period of English history before the judicial and legislative functions of the High Court of Parliament were clearly separated, in the period when law was "declared rather than made," it was reinforced by the "natural rights" philosophy of the seventeenth and eighteenth centuries and emerged in the period under our observation as the doctrine of constitutional law of which Paine and Samuel Adams are such clear exponents.[49] I take that doctrine to be that in every state there exists a body of fundamental law, which is society's mandate and instruction to its agent, government; that that government has no right to violate or exceed these instructions, and that if it does so, its act is void. This is the doctrine which the American colonial thinkers, statesmen, and politicians were, as has been illustrated above, constantly stating as true, but any very effective means of putting it into practice was lacking. As soon as America became free from the English doctrine of Parliamentary supremacy, the doctrine of the supremacy of the fundamental law found immediate expression in that series of cases at the end of the eighteenth century in which the courts of the new nation took upon themselves the task of securing the dominance of constitutional over statutory law, thus enforcing the will of society rather than the will of government. It has been

[46] Vattel, *Law of Nations,* (Chitty ed.), p. 11; this matter has been amply worked out by A. C. McLaughlin, *Courts, Constitution and Parties,* (1912), pp. 63 ff.

[47] John Adams, *Works,* II. 522–25.

[48] This expression is the name given this doctrine by one of the latest and most comprehensive reviews of the whole American history of the doctrine; it supersedes now the earlier works of Brinton Coxe and J. B. Thayer, and so amply covers the field that to say anything again on the subject would indeed be in the nature of a twice-told tale. See C. G. Haines, *The American Doctrine of Judicial Supremacy* (1914).

[49] C. H. McIlwain in *The High Court of Parliament and its Supremacy* (1910), traced the English constitutional history of this doctrine and left little to be desired in the way of information to illustrate what is summarized above.

amply and ably demonstrated that the famous case of Marbury vs. Madison, which fixed the power of the courts to declare a law unconstitutional in the American political system, was not the introduction of a new legal principle, but rather the culmination of a whole series of decisions which began to find place in the books almost as soon as the Declaration of Independence cut America loose from the doctrine of the supremacy of Parliament.[50]

One of these cases peculiarly deserves our attention, as in it James Iredell appeared as counsel and so convinced the court that Justice Ashe ruled, "it was clear that no act of legislature could by any means repeal or alter the constitution, because if they could do this, they would at the same instant destroy their own existence as a legislature, and dissolve the government thereby established." Having secured this decision, Iredell then proceeded to explain to the people of his state that in the formation of a constitution, the people had deliberately rejected the idea of legislative sovereignty or supremacy and had thereby provided for the defense of the minority against the whims of "a fluctuating majority." Law was above the majority. There was no doubt in his mind that the legislature was a "creature of the Constitution," and that if that legislature undertook to pass an act inconsistent with the constitution, the redress must come from the courts, because the constitution is law, and the courts are the bodies which administer law; naturally they must decide which of two conflicting laws, statute or constitution, is to prevail, and as the constitution is admittedly the superior, they must administer the limitations upon the power of the legislature.[51]

Constitutionally speaking, the American Revolution meant the rejection by America of what was and is the theory of the British constitution. The British Empire has survived by doing in practice what the Americans asked Parliament to do openly in the period under observation, that is, it has quietly dropped overboard the

---

[50] The tale of these cases has been rehearsed by Brinton Coxe, McLaughlin, and Haines, supra, so that any review that might be made here would be quite superfluous, and the merest repetition of what has already been established. It ought not, however, to be overlooked that much of the ground breaking in this field was done in a very able dissertation by Horace Gray, which rather unfortunately has been somewhat buried as Appendix I to the volume of *Quincy's* (Mass.) *Colonial Reports.*

[51] Bayard V. Singleton, (1 Martin, N. C., 42: 1787), Iredell's address *"To the Public,"* in G. L. McRee, *Life and Correspondence of James Iredell,* (N. Y., 1858), II. 145–8, and 173–4.

theory of Parliamentary sovereignty as far as the empire is concerned.[52] The doctrine of Parliamentary supremacy was, as numerous historians have indicated,[53] of comparatively late growth in English constitutional development, and the American Revolution demonstrated that it had no place at all in Britannic constitutional development. The statesmen at Westminster see that today; was there not one statesman at Westminster in the era of the American Revolution who saw that the doctrine of Parliamentary sovereignty could not be maintained if the Empire was to survive? One naturally thinks of Burke and Chatham and of their futile efforts to show Parliament that in the matter of colonial taxation they could not do everything and anything that they desired to do. Yet when all was said and done, both of those men were among the group who held that the British Parliament was an imperial parliament.

There was one Englishman, however, who had read his Locke, who understood his constitutional law, and who seems almost like a voice crying in the wilderness of parliamentary sovereignty and supremacy. He was Charles Pratt, first Baron Camden, Lord Chief Justice of the Common Pleas (1762–66) and Lord Chancellor of England (1766–70). He seems to have been singularly overlooked by posterity, and one cannot forbear expressing the hope that when his life is written it will be written either by an American or by an Englishman who understands the American view.[54] To Americans, Camden must always be of peculiar interest. He introduced into English law the principle of the common law, that fifty years earlier Andrew Hamilton, of Philadelphia, had fixed in the structure of colonial law by the celebrated Zenger trial at New York.[55] Camden it was whose decision invalidating the use of "general warrants"

[52] The accuracy of this statement may be questioned. I content myself with trying to establish that Americans in the period under observation were asking Great Britain to let that theory go by the board; the chapters supra on the "British Imperial Problem in the XVIIIth Century" and "The Commonwealth of Nations" suggest the type of work that can be done to prove the conclusion which I draw here.

[53] C. H. McIlwain, prominent among these, supra.

[54] McIlwain, into whose province this might have come, dismisses Camden in a footnote as the "last whisper of an old theory." p. 309n.

[55] The rule which was overthrown concerned the law of libel, permitting the judge to decide whether the publication complained of was in fact libellous. The new rule of Hamilton and Camden permitted the jury to decide whether the publication complained of was libellous, and took from the bench its power to curb the freedom of the press.

would have gladdened the heart of James Otis, had the colonial courts had the courage to take a like stand in the matter of the writs of assistance.[56] And it was Camden who released John Wilkes on *habeas corpus* after that firebrand had been arrested for his No. XLV of the *North Briton,* an act which caused the solemn reporter of the Common Pleas so far to digress from his function as to note at the end of his report, "caused a loud huzza in Westminster Hall."[57] Even old Dr. Johnson was obliged somewhat begrudgingly to admit the popularity of this idol of the Whigs.[58]

Camden's maiden speech in the House of Lords was an attack on the unsportsmanlike Declaratory Act with which the Rockingham ministry accompanied its repeal of the obnoxious Stamp Act. It deserves careful consideration, and, indeed, it supplies the title for this chapter, that there are some things which Parliament cannot do. "My Lords," he began, "he who disputes the authority of any supreme legislature, treads on very tender ground. In my opinion, the legislature has no right to make this law. The sovereign authority, the omnipotence of the legislature, is a favorite doctrine, but there are some things which you cannot do. You cannot enact anything against divine law. You cannot take away any man's private property without making him compensation. You have no right to condemn any man by bill of attainder without hearing him."[59] Of those things which Parliament cannot do, the first goes off into that question of natural, i.e., divine, law, which is a story in itself. But the last two are purely questions of human law, in which the speaker was trying to put a rule above Parliament. He went on to argue from the case of Wales, just as John Adams had done, and to discuss that analogy of the Channel Islands which, as we have pointed out, so clearly delineates the nature of the empire as a Commonwealth of Nations. But the doctrine this new peer brought into the "hospital of incurables"[60] in his first speech aroused the wrath of that ponderous body. One of its most important inmates, the Lord Chancellor Northington, bestirred himself from the wool-

[56] See Hutchinson, *History of Mass.,* III. 93–5.

[57] 2 *Wilson's Reports,* 166.

[58] Boswell's *Johnson:* (G. B. Hill Ed.), II. 404. For anecdote as to his far-sighted vision on the American question, vid. Josiah Quincy, *Memoir of Josiah Quincy, Jun.,* (Boston: 1825), pp. 269–70.

[59] Hansard, *Parliamentary History,* XVI. 161 ff. Feb. 10, 1766.

[60] Chesterfield's sobriquet for the House of Lords.

sack to rebuke the impertinence of the fledgling peer. With meas-
ured discourse he solemnly reiterated the old story about the
summum imperium of Great Britain and the sovereignty of Parliament in a manner insulting not only to Camden but to the American,
Franklin, who was a listener below the bar. His Lordship assured
his colleagues that "With great submission to the noble and learned
lord [Camden], I believe that all except himself will admit that
every government can arbitrarily impose laws on all its subjects."[61]
This was far, indeed, from Paine's doctrine that the "subjects" are
the masters of the "government." But Northington gave evidence
that he understood America and the Americans even less when he
went on to make clear to the Lords that since America showed
herself so refractory, Great Britain had only to withdraw her protection, "and then the little state of Genoa or San Marino may soon
overrun them." A body in which the Lord Chancellor himself could
utter such stuff as this was no place for a constitutional lawyer like
Camden to try to interpret the newly emerging American contribution to political science, that government exists for the people and
under the law of the constitution, not above the people and the law.

Camden's second effort in behalf of America exhibited an understanding of American thought far in advance of most Englishmen
of his day. Lord Campbell's chief defect as a biographer of the
Lord Chancellors lies in his excessive Whig bias, but even he cannot
understand what Camden, whom he ardently admired, was driving
at in this speech.[62] The part of Camden's remarks which is such
an enigma to Campbell refers to the Declaratory Act in which Parliament asserted its sovereignty and supremacy over the colonies in
all cases whatsoever. Camden calls it a "bill, the very existence of
which is illegal, absolutely illegal, contrary to the fundamental laws
of nature, contrary to the fundamental laws of this Constitution."[63]
How a law which was enacted by the only body qualified to enact
laws could at the same time be "illegal" was quite beyond the comprehension of the noble lords. Even the admiring Campbell throws
up his hands at this point and acknowledges that it seems to him
to exhibit false reasoning and false taste. Says he, "I confess I do not
understand the reasoning by which, admitting that the British
Parliament had the supreme power to legislate for the colonies, a

[61] Hansard, *Parliamentary History,* XVI. 177.
[62] John, Lord Campbell, *Lives of the Lord Chancellors of England.*
[63] Hansard, *Parliamentary History*, XVI. 177 ff.

law passed to lay a tax on them, though it may be unjust or impolitic, is a nullity."[64] Neither could most of the peers of Camden's day understand it; neither could Mansfield nor Blackstone. Yet Campbell's confession gives the key to the situation. To an Englishman, an "unconstitutional" law was merely "unjust" or "impolitic," while to an American it was a "nullity." And this was not merely the technical talk of the lawyers, Otis and John Adams. Mansfield and Northington might have received some illumination had they been parishioners of Jonathan Mayhew of Boston, a preacher and patriot-politician, who occupies a prominent place in the pulpit of the American Revolution. Mayhew took it for granted that Magna Carta was a part of the British Constitution, "all acts contrary to which are said to be, ipso facto, null and void."[65] Not that an act contrary to the Constitution was merely mischievous, as Northington would say, but that it was "ipso facto, null and void," which is the language of Coke. But then, after all, Northington admitted, "I seek for the liberty and the Constitution of this Kingdom no further back than the revolution [i.e., of 1688]," and Coke lived before that day.[66] Even Junius, whom no one could accuse of being a Tory, and who, sparing as he was in compliments of a favorable nature, yet admitted that Camden was a character "fertile in every great and good qualification,"[67] could not follow this doctrine that "the authority of the British legislature is not supreme over the colonies in the same sense in which it is supreme over Great Britain."[68]

[64] Campbell, *Lives,* Ch. cxlii, on Lord Camden.

[65] Jonathan Mayhew, *The Snare broken: A thanksgiving Discourse preached on May 23, 1766.* (Boston: 1766.) p. 12 (*The Stamp Act Sermon*). Cf. the language of James Wilson, "That the act of the British Parliament for altering the charter and constitution of the colony of Massachusetts Bay and those for the impartial administration of justice in that colony for shutting the port of Boston, for quartering soldiers on the inhabitants of the colonies, are *unconstitutional* and *void;* and can confer no authority upon those who act under the colour of them." Speech to the Convention of the Province of Pennsylvania, January, 1775, *Works,* (Ed. 1804). III. 258. In other words, an "unconstitutional" act was not merely an unwise law which would have to be put into effect anyway, but it was not law at all; it had neither existence nor power. Cf. also the Sullivan Draft of the non-Importation Agreement, before it was modified by the First Continental Congress, *Journal of the Continental Congress,* (Ford Ed.), 1774, I. 67, 68, 69, 70.

[66] Hansard, *Parliamentary History,* XVI. 161.

[67] *The Letters of Junius,* (London, 1786), Letter LIX.

[68] *Junius,* Letter LXIX.

For the rest, Camden's disapproval of the whole ministerial policy was and is well known, yet he was one of a minority which numbered also Burke and Chatham. He kept on calling insistently for the rescission of the Declaratory Act, just because therein lay the crux of the whole question from a constitutional standpoint.[69] It is most interesting to compare the letters which Samuel Adams wrote to Chatham and to Camden when in 1768 he was inditing those epistles which have been mentioned above. The letter to the former commends Chatham for the attention he has devoted to the American cause and expresses appreciation of that statesman's efforts as a zealous advocate of the colonial cause.[70] But the letter to Camden commends him for the accuracy with which he has envisaged the constitutional question, for his "great knowledge of the Constitution and the law of nature, of the just extent of parliamentary authority and the rights of British subjects."[71] Camden had serious doubts about the sovereignty of Parliament, and that is primarily what it took to make what we are calling a Britannic, as contrasted with a British statesman.[72]

The phase of the thought of the American Revolutionary period discussed in this chapter is certainly one of the most noteworthy aspects of the whole question. Discussions which rest with the compact theory and presume that no further digging need be done would seem to miss the whole point of the thought of that period. The analytical political scientist too often dissects the philosophy of the eighteenth century and reduces it to its elements, each of which goes into a pigeonhole, this one labelled "compact," that one labelled "natural rights," and so on. This process is somewhat like trying to understand human beings by the sole method of conducting a post-

[69] Hansard, *Parliamentary History,* XVIII. 164, and Ibid., XVIII. 208.

[70] 2 Feb. 1768, Almon, *Prior Documents,* p. 187.

[71] 29 Jan. 1768, Almon, *Prior Documents,* pp. 173–4. In Virginia, R. H. Lee got up a subscription of £96 10s. to have Camden's portrait painted (by either Reynolds or Benjamin West), and have that portrait brought to Virginia to memorialize "the inestimable benefit derived to British-America from your Lordship's protection."—J. C. Ballagh, *Letters of R. H. Lee:* (N. Y. 1912), I. 22–26, 38.

[72] Camden said he "would not enter the large field of discussion, or collateral reasonings, applicable to the abstruse and metaphysical distinctions necessary to the investigation of the omnipotence of parliament, but this he would venture to assert, that the natural law of mankind and the immutable laws of justice were clearly in favor of the Americans." Hansard, *Parliamentary History,* XVIII. 164.

mortem. Doubtless the post-mortem has its place, but it is apt to deal solely with flesh and bones and to miss completely the spirit, which is, after all, the important thing. As to whether the thinkers who have been here discussed did actually make what is known as a "contribution," a good deal depends on what is meant by that word. It is very easy to say that such and such a man can or cannot be classed as a great thinker, but I know of no expression so totally devoid of meaning. A contribution is a thing given or granted in common with others. In this sense, the men discussed here each made a contribution. As to the originality of that contribution, in the sense of whether it was new with them or copied from an earlier age, there are few useful canons of criticism. But even if these canons were well known, clearly defined, and universally accepted, it is questionable whether there is a great deal of value in ascertaining facts under them. There are indeed few fields of thought in which it is so true that the would-contributor finds that his "contribution" has already been made by someone else, and almost certainly by Aristotle, as it is in the field of politics. My point, therefore, is not that certain ideas were now uttered for the first time, rather that they were the ideas enunciated in the Revolutionary discussions. The era of the American Revolution was preëminently an era of putting theories and doctrines into practice.

It may perhaps be objected that there has been a confusion of Parliament with government in England. But we ought not to forget that it was Blackstone who placed the supreme power in Parliament, in King, Lords, and Commons. Moreover, we ought not to forget that when Charles II was welcomed back to England it was with the express understanding that the "government is and ought to be by King, Lords, and Commons." If King, Lords, and Commons constitute Parliament and also constitute the government, drawing a distinction between the last two is not very useful for the purposes of this discussion. Objection, then, will probably not be made to the general conclusion which we draw from this chapter, that the Americans, in establishing the fact that there were some things which Parliament could not do, were establishing in part an idea of politics native with them, namely, that there was no government above the law. This conclusion involves two additional questions. If they limited Parliament, what did they do about sovereignty, and what did they mean by law? To those questions we now devote ourselves.

7

THE LEGAL THEORIES OF JAMES WILSON

"WITHOUT DETRACTING, therefore, from the real merits which abound in the imperial law, I hope I may have leave to assert that if an Englishman must be ignorant of either the one or the other, he had better be a stranger to the Roman than to English institutions." Such was the spirit in which Blackstone approached his task, not with the enthusiasm of a narrow nationalism, but with the mild suggestion that that which is the fruit of English experience is of more immediate significance in dealing with English problems than the experience of Rome or Byzantium. This is the spirit in which the essay is made to call attention to the legal theories of an American jurist who seems to epitomize the spirit of American legal institutions in the time when they were first emerging as distinct from the institutions of England. James Wilson emigrated from his birthplace in Scotland to America in the days when John Dickinson was one of the leaders of the Philadelphia bar. Wilson studied law in Dickinson's office prior to the outbreak of the Revolution; he was one of those pre-Revolutionary pamphleteers who tried to make clear the nature of the British Empire as a commonwealth of nations rather than as a centralized and consolidated state. When those efforts proved of no avail he threw in his fortunes with the patriot party. The outbreak of the war found him a member of the Second Continental Congress. He has the remarkable record of being one of six men who signed both the Declaration of Independence and the Constitution of the United States, and he has the unique distinction of being the only member of Pennsylvania's rather large delegation to the Federal Convention who was also elected a member of the Pennsylvania State Convention which ratified the Federal Constitution. The part he played in those meetings is evidenced by the historical and legal comments which have been made upon him, "that he was the most learned lawyer of his time," "one of the deepest thinkers and most exact reasoners among the members of the convention," "the real founder of what is distinctive in our American jurisprudence," "recognized as the most learned member of the Constitutional Convention," "ablest and most learned of the associates" on the Supreme Court, of which he was a member.[1]

James Wilson's notable services in the period after the Revolution have secured his place in the political history of the United States,[2] but it seems extremely questionable whether what we may call the science of jurisprudence has accorded to him the place to which he is probably entitled. That question becomes even stronger when one hears some of the professors of international law proclaiming from their chairs either that there is no such thing as international law, or hears them define law in terms that deny international law a place. In the presence of such writers and lecturers one is tempted to paraphrase Blackstone, and, as he advised Englishmen not to sacrifice Alfred and Edward to Theodosius and Justinian, to suggest to them that perhaps they might find it of practical value not to sacrifice James Wilson to John Austin and his school. The difference between the sense and definition of law upon which the era of the American Revolution depended for its politico-juridical ideas and that which has produced a great deal of recent ante- and post-bellum chaotic thinking, can, it would seem, be nowhere better illustrated than by an examination of the legal theories of Wilson.

Following his own advice, that "law should be studied and taught as a historical science,"[3] let us regard his legal theories as part of the history of that science. In the opening lecture before the students of the Law School of the University of Pennsylvania, where Wilson was the first professor of law in 1790, the lecturer remarked: "Were I called upon for my reasons why I deem so highly of the American character, I would assign them in a very few words—that character

---

[1] The comments of McMaster, Bryce, S. F. Baldwin, J. M. Harlan, and Cooley; for appreciation see L. H. Alexander in the *North American Review*, CLXXXIII. 971.

[2] A. C. McLaughlin, *Political Science Quarterly*, XII. 1.

[3] James Wilson's *Works* (Bird Wilson Ed.), (Phila: 1804), I. 5. Citations throughout are to this, the first, edition of Wilson's works.

has been eminently distinguished by the love of liberty and the love of law."[4] Quite different was Blackstone's opening in his first lectures as Vinerian professor at Oxford wherein he specifies the laws and constitution of England as being a species of knowledge, "in which the gentlemen of England have been more remarkably deficient than those of all Europe besides."[5] Was Blackstone merely the more modest and Wilson merely the more boastful of the two, or were they talking about two different things when they used the term "law"? But let that story tell itself. If it be true that the "men of the Revolution saw only two alternatives: freedom or slavery,"[6] it is equally true that the men of the Revolution understood with a clearness which history cannot too frequently emphasize that freedom without the limitations of law was worse than slavery. "Without liberty, law loses its nature and its name and becomes licentiousness." This was the permanently valuable political philosophy of the American Revolution. Carefully documented historical explanations of the American Revolution in terms of taxation, the Acts of Navigation, or the competition for commerce tend to eclipse the element of sound political thinking in which the founders of the republic delighted. Yet in a true picture of the early republic, political thinking in the abstract occupied a much larger place than it does in the political science of the twentieth century. This is a fact which cannot be neglected, however much it be minimized.

James Wilson and other men who had the same intellectual ancestry, understood the interrelationship of law and liberty and conceived of liberty as freedom according to law. They threw off the yoke of England not as lawbreakers but as preservers of the law. It is well known that independence was far from the minds of the bulk of the citizens of American colonies when the first Continental Congress met.[7] What they wanted was liberty under the limitations prescribed by the British constitution. They felt that they were being

---

[4] Wilson *Works*, I. 5.

[5] Bl. Com. Intro. 4.

[6] C. E. Merriam, *American Political Theories*, p. 53.

[7] "As our proceedings during the existence and operation of the Stamp Act prove fully and incontestably the painful sensations that tortured our breasts from the prospect of disunion with Britain; the peals of joy which burst forth universally upon the repeal of that odious statute loudly proclaim the heartfelt delight produced in us by a reconciliation with her." Wilson's *Speech In the Convention of the Province of Pennsylvania,* January 1775, Wilson, *Works,* III. 251.

persecuted by the real law breakers, the Parliament that had violated the constitution. "Have not British subjects, then, a right to resist force employed to destroy the very existence of law and of liberty? They have, sir, and this right is secured to them both by the letter and the spirit of the British Constitution, by which the measures and the conditions of their obedience are appointed. The British liberties, sir, and the means and right of defending them, are not the grants of princes; and of what our princes never granted they surely can never deprive us."[8] It seems to be a peculiarity of the Anglo-American Revolution that it was conducted, not so much for completely overturning the old order and making a new lot of laws, as for the purpose of securing the benefit of the rights which the old laws assured but which a particular government was withholding. This fact should be kept in mind in trying to ascertain the conception of law in the period of the American Revolution. Law was not merely a convenient rule, which might be adopted one day and rejected the next at the whim of some Assemblée Nationale or Soviet; it was something a good more fundamental than that.[9]

To James Wilson, there were two totally distinct bodies of law: natural laws and human laws. The political thinkers of the eighteenth century frequently confused these categories elaborately. Wilson separated them, clearly, distinctly, and serviceably. The natural law was the immutable, universal, moral law, the will of God. It would be indeed valuable to know more about it. But it is hardly a subject to be treated in this effort and in this day when men are less confident than they were formerly of their ability easily to penetrate into the counsels of the Almighty. Hence we turn to the more modest task of trying to explain what James Wilson called human laws, and in that field there is much to be done. It was this second body of law that Wilson saw with such vividness when he set himself to attack the views of many of the publicists of his day on the nature of law. Those views presented just the same confusion of ideas and lack of clear thought that is manifested today in connection with that department of law which is known as international law. The stumbling block lay in the question of the definition of law, for upon that depended the question of obligation. Is it law if it is not observed? This question springs from a con-

---

[8] Ibid., III. 262–3.

[9] That this conception antedates the idea of Law as a Command, vide E. Jenks, *Law and Politics in the Middle Ages*, pp. 7–62.

ception of law quite familiar in the writings of publicists from Puffendorf to Blackstone and from Blackstone to Austin. The view that law is a command given by a superior to an inferior which the inferior must obey upon the pain of some sanction is an easy and a simple thing to understand. But, as has been observed, this definition leaves no room for such branches of law as international law. And the contributions which America has made to international law, both of letter and spirit, are of a character which naturally turns our inquiries toward some more representative American conception of law than that given by Blackstone or Austin. Such a conception formed a part of that political philosophy of the American Revolution in which so many of our national ideals took form, and there are few jurists who stated it so clearly as did Justice Wilson.

"Law is a rule of action," said Blackstone, "and it is that rule of action which is prescribed by some superior and which the inferior is bound to obey."[10] At this point the new professor of law in the new American university took issue with the Vinerian professor. "A superior! Can there be no law without a superior? Is it essential to law that inferiority should be involved in the obligation to obey it?"[11] Here Blackstone exhibited just that confusion of natural and human laws which Wilson was at pains to differentiate. Certainly, there were natural laws which presumed the existence of a superior —God—but to confuse these with human laws was to presume that God had some temporal deputy on earth to whom he had confided the power of enunciating his law. This was in essence the divine rights of kings which the Revolutionary thought of both England and America had overthrown. The conception of law that Blackstone prescribed was the essential element of "a prerogative impiously attempted to be established—of princes arbitrary to rule; and of a corresponding obligation—a servitude tyrannically attempted to be imposed—on the people implicitly to obey."[12] It was to the introduction of superiority as a necessary part of the definition of law that Wilson objected. The idea itself is as old as Rome and as tyrannous as Cæsar. "Indeed on the principle of superiority, Caligula's reasoning was concise and conclusive, 'If I am only a man, my subjects are

[10] Bl. Com.: Intro. 38.
[11] Wilson, *Works,* I. 65.
[12] Wilson, *Works,* I. 66.

something less; if they are men, then I am something more'."[13] Such would be the logical and necessary conclusion of attributing to a superior the authorship of human laws. Could such a conclusion ever be brought into line with the American political principles as set forth in the American constitutional documents? It is difficult to see how it could. For these were human laws, and once the element of superiority and inferiority was introduced, the element of the equality of man was lost.

Such a proposition arouses at once the question: what about the state? Did not, or would not, he admit that the state was superior to the individual? The question is a difficult one to answer, for Wilson's utterances do not, at first glance, seem to be altogether consistent in this matter. But a little reflective reading seems to make the matter not such a difficult one after all. In the first place, the eighteenth century thinker never lost sight of the fact that political machinery existed for men, and not men for political machinery. Hence, when he personified the state, it was as a figure of speech rather than as an act of awesome deification. Its dependence on the people which composed it was an essential element of the state. "In free states," says Wilson, "the people form an artificial person or body politic, the highest and noblest that can be known." In that definition, the eighteenth century would have emphasized the words "people" and "artificial" in a way in which one might not emphasize them today unless his attention was especially directed to it. The "moral person" which was thus constituted was described "as a complete body of free natural persons, united together for their common benefit; as having an understanding, and a will; as deliberating, resolving and acting; as possessed of interests which it ought to manage; as enjoying rights which it ought to maintain; as lying under obligations which it ought to perform. To this moral person, we assign by way of eminence the dignified appellation of 'state'."[14] In discussing the state, he observed "that it is its right and generally its duty, to form a constitution, and to institute civil government and to establish laws." From this the hasty reader might conclude that after all the state was the "superior" which made the laws, and hence Blackstone was quite right after all. But this conclusion would miss the whole spirit of the Revolutionary philosophy.

[13] Wilson, *Works*, I. 92.
[14] Wilson, *Works*, II. 120–1.

There is nothing quite like a debate to make a man show his whole hand, and hence we may look for Wilson's own interpretation of his idea of the state in the great debate with which the United States began.

In the Federal Convention of 1787 the idea of a "state" was a thing very much more clear-cut than ordinarily comes to mind when that word is used today in connection with one of the component members of the Federal Union. There were small-states men and large-states men, and there were states'-rights men, and they were a great deal more "state-conscious" than one would imagine who lives in the twentieth century, when the word "state," in connection with one of the United States, has become a relatively less important and less thought about entity. Yet, it was probably with just some such idea of the nature of the state as Wilson defines it above that the state-rights men and the small-states men urged the claims of their states. There was a "state-sensitiveness" in that day which has been distinctly on the wane since the War between the States. Consequently, if we would get ourselves in the proper mental attitude to understand the thought of a past era, we must understand what they meant by words which today have acquired a different connotation. When on that memorable thirtieth of June, the Federal Convention seemed deadlocked because the small-states men insisted upon equal rather than proportionate representation, the rights of the "states" were urged in a language which betokens the existence in the minds of the states-rights men of an idea of "state" much like in content the technical sense in which that word is used today, i.e., as an individual member of the family of nations. Delegates talked of their right to join some foreign power in case their wishes were not granted.[15] Under these circumstances James Wilson uttered words which more clearly delineate his conception of the relationship between the people, the law of the Constitution, and the state than we can glean from his more didactic utterances from the lecture platform. "If the minority withhold their consent to the new plan, if they will have their own way and go out of the Union, then let them go. Shall three-fourths be ruled by one-fourth? Shall three-fourths give up their right for the support of an artificial being called state-interest? For whom do we make a Constitution? Is it for men, or is it for imaginary beings called states; a mere

---

[15] Max Farrand, *Records of the Federal Convention,* I. 501.

metaphysical distinction?"[16] What Wilson was trying to help build was a national state and not a confederacy, hence when those spoke who had the confederacy idea in mind his chief argument lay in showing his colleagues that the state existed for the people and not the people for the state. If the people wanted one national unit, they were entitled to have it and not to be blocked by acutely-state-conscious delegates who, regarding the state as a thing in itself, wanted a confederacy of states.[17]

Had one asked James Wilson whether he regarded the state as superior to the individual, he would probably have said that such a question betrayed an unfamiliarity with the true nature of law. A state was merely an aggregate of people which expressed its will in the law of the constitution, which in turn formed a government. To endow a state with a metaphysical or a spiritual nature, to grant it an existence above or apart from the people was totally to misunderstand the thought of the Revolutionary period in America. Nowhere does this come out more clearly than in Wilson's discussion of sovereignty: the sovereignty of the state was not a term in which he thought; the sovereignty of the people was all he understood.[18]

Now if the element of superiority were permitted to remain in the definition of human law, mankind would be compelled to answer the question as to whether it was a superiority of force or of excellence by which the superior claimed his right to impose his will upon the inferior. The former is exactly what Anglo-American revolutions were fought to avoid, and it is easily disposed of. "For us, as men, as citizens, as states," it is sufficient to say that power is nothing more than the right of the strongest, and may be opposed by the same right, the same means and the same principles which are employed to establish it. Bare force, far from producing any obligation to obey, produces an obligation to resist."[19] On the other hand, if the superiority be based upon excellence, if the superior claim any superiority by virtue of his being more wise, who will take upon himself to make such judgment? To speak of superiors involves the implication that there are inferiors; is government con-

---

[16] Farrand, *Records of the Federal Convention,* I. 494.

[17] See also Wilson, *Works,* I. 360, where he uses "state" and "society" interchangeably.

[18] Wilson, *Works,* I. 25.

[19] Wilson, *Works,* I. 71.

sciously to take cognizance of the inequalities of men? If so, what is the standard? "Is this a foundation sufficient for supporting the solid and durable superstructure of law?"[20]

Wilson's knowledge of comparative governments was necessarily more limited than would be the case today, yet it is remarkable how carefully he selects the illustrations with which his points are elucidated. The classic references abound, of course; he would not have been a true representative of the eighteenth century if they did not. But his reading in the political scientists of all nations was extensive, not merely among the English writers, but among the Continental writers of his day as well. Yet he never forgets the essential distinction which makes his work of such practical value, namely, the separation of the idea of the law which God makes and the idea of the law which man makes. In the case of the former he would not deny the existence of a superior, but in the case of man-made laws he does make this denial, and manifests therein the germ of what is distinctively American in political science, government by the consent of the governed. "Let it be remembered all along, that I am examining the doctrine of superiority as applied to human laws, the proper and immediate object of investigation in these lectures. Of the law that is divine, we shall have occasion at another time to speak with the reverence and gratitude that becomes us."[21] In the light of this clear distinction, since the alleged superior cannot rest his title on any inherent qualities such as goodness or force, from what source can such superiority be derived? Divine source being ruled out, both by reason of the fact that it involves not human, but divine laws; or, if the two be confused, it is even more ruled out because it involves the divine right of kings, what source remains? "How is this superior constituted by human authority?"[22]

Is the superior constituted by law? If he is, then the power which constituted that law is his superior, and we are confronted by the same question as before.[23] So the will of a superior is discarded as an improper principle of obligation in human laws. It will stand the test of neither reason nor experience; it contains the germ of tyranny, and it provokes the alleged inferiors to resistance and revolt.

[20] Wilson, *Works*, I. 74.
[21] Wilson, *Works*, I. 71.
[22] Wilson, *Works*, I. 83.
[23] Wilson, *Works*, I. 85.

The idea of law as a policeman's club is just the idea which Wilson would have his students avoid. However much it might represent the law and the idea of law in foreign lands, it was not the Anglo-American idea as he understood it. Not that he was an advocate of pure moral suasion; far from it. He maintained, rather, that the force which is the sanction of law is not the exclusive property of an alleged superior to do with as he chooses. The superior which exists for the sake of convenience in administration exercises whatever force he does only at the bidding of the alleged inferior, by whose consent he exercises also his temporary superiority.

Thus it is, that when asked what in his view was the essential element of law which he would substitute for the idea of a superior with a sanction, Wilson states unequivocally, "In its place I introduce the consent of those whose obedience the law requires. This I conceive to be the true origin of the obligation of human laws."[24] Customs were the first laws known to men, certain conventional habits of actions which mankind observed simply by reason of the necessary requirements of peaceful human intercourse. Customary law was rudimentary law, and when the conventional types of action crystallized into rules enforceable in the courts of law, the evolution of law might be said to have reached its latest stage. Customary law was not the dictate of a superior to an inferior. It was introduced by voluntary adoption and became general by the simple process of instances of that voluntary adoption being multiplied. It became lasting by satisfactory experience, which ratified and confirmed what voluntary action had adopted and introduced. "In the introduction, in the extension, in the continuance of customary law, we find the operations of consent universally predominant." In the regulations of justice and of government, customs have been more effectual than the best of written laws. This view was in his estimation the only view that could be held by an eighteenth century lawyer. "Let me mention, in one word, everything that can enforce my sentiments: the common law of England is customary law."[25] One need go no further to understand what Wilson conceived to be the essential nature, origin, and source of the obligation of law. Here was not necessarily any elaborate fiction of social con-

---

[24] Wilson, *Works*, I. 99. Cf. "Finally the State submits itself to an objective law, based on the subjective right of the individual."—L. Duguit, *Law in the Modern State*, XXXIX. (Laski, tr.)

[25] Wilson, *Works*, I. 100.

tract or any discussion of the rights which mankind retained over and above what the limitations of the law took away from him. The simple distinction here made between common and statute law was not an ultimate distinction in origin or obligation. The law which was produced by the enactment of legislative assemblies derived its obligatory force only from that same consent, given less formally, but none the less effectively in the formation of the customary, common law. "Where is the difference whether the people declare their will by their suffrage or by their conduct."[26] For "customs for a long time were the only laws known among men," and "custom is, of itself, intrinsic evidence of consent."[27] In the Anglo-American legal system, Wilson could not regard statutory enactment as the only, or even the principal, species of law. The English common law, "founded on long and general custom" which in turn can be founded on nothing but free and general consent, is the principal connotation which the word "law" had for him.[28] To him the eighteenth century nomenclature was not his master, but his servant. Certainly, he would admit of "compact," "contract," "covenant," "bargain," and whatnot; "let them be called covenants, or bargains, or stipulations and anything similar to any of those, still I am satisfied, for still everything mentioned, and everything similar to everything mentioned, imports consent. Here history and law combine their evidence in support of consent."[29] This theory of the nature of law, Wilson regarded as quite different from that of Blackstone, whom he thought followed rather after Hobbes and Puffendorf. His own, though, he traces back rather through Vattel and Locke. This, moreover, was typical of the political philosophy of the Revolutionary period in America.[30]

If one would understand James Wilson's place in the history of jurisprudence, it is not so much the comparison with Blackstone which elucidates his theories as a comparison with another English legal writer of whom he probably never heard; John Austin was born in the year in which Wilson began to lecture. James Wilson's legal theories were the product of many years' study of the writers of many nations; but that studying was done in the intellectual

---

[26] Wilson, *Works*, I. 64.
[27] Wilson, *Works*, I. 99, 100. Cf. Jenks, *Law and Politics*, p. 57.
[28] Wilson, *Works*, I. 206.
[29] Wilson, *Works*, I. 101.
[30] Wilson, *Works*, I. 69, 82, 84.

atmosphere of the American Revolution, and chiefly in Philadelphia, where Wilson lived for many years. John Austin studied at the Inns, yet one cannot but feel that his jurisprudence was colored by those years spent studying in Germany in the intellectual atmosphere of the reaction after the Napoleonic wars. At any rate, his doctrines furnish an antithesis which brings out the Wilson doctrine by contrast. To Austin, as to Blackstone, a law was a command "which proceeds from superiors and obliges inferiors." Yet he is more explicit and emphatic than Sir William. "The term superiority signifies might; the power of affecting others with evil or pain, of forcing them through fear of that evil to fashion their conduct to one's wishes." "In short, whoever can oblige another to comply with his wishes is the superior of that other, so far as his ability reaches; the party who is obnoxious to the impending evil being, to that same extent, the inferior."[31] Such was Austin's theory of positive law. Of course international law has no place by this definition, for international law is customary law, *par excellence*. Austin's idea was of a law from above, the obligation to obey which comes from the fear of a superior force, rather than the idea of a set of rules which men have agreed to observe and which derive their obligation from the consent of those men. As to which is the higher sense of law, this is a question of demonstration.[32]

But if Wilson's legal theories be held to give us a formula by which international law can be elevated to a more respectable place in the science of jurisprudence, that was quite an incidental con-

---

[31] John Austin, *Lectures on Jurisprudence,* 3d Ed., (1869), I. The first lecture contains some interesting definitions, especially pp. 88–99. One of the clearest criticisms of Austin in more recent thought can be found in Paul Vinogradoff's little book *Common Sense in Law*—Chapter II.—Cf. also Duguit, *Law in the Modern State,* Ch. II.

[32] We are, perhaps, now, as never before, in a position to take historical cognizance of the effect of this distinction. The German has been accustomed to regard the American as a rather lawless person, a conclusion only heightened by the American's disregard for a sign bearing the magic word "Verboten." The American has learned to regard the German as an unfair player, one who disregards the rules of the game, who hits below the belt. The one obeys commands; the other observes rules. The one derives his sense of obligation through a sense of fear; the other through a sense of fair-play. The one is the product of discipline, the other of sportsmanship. Possibly, one may even go so far as to say that the one is concerned with the letter, and the other with the spirit of the law. At any rate it is easy to see which is the product of the Austinian and which of the Wilsonian point of view.

sideration on his part. When he comes to that subject itself, there is another contribution of a different sort. The course of lectures, which includes everything from legal philosophy to torts and crimes, brings the eighteenth century law students, in the fourth session, to the "Law of Nations." Once more we find the clear-cut distinction between those laws of nations which take their origin in the law of nature, in divine law, and those laws of nations which find their origin in consent. Any thorough study of Wilson must take account of the former, but since we have assigned ourselves the less pretentious task of setting forth his views on human laws, we must come at once to that investigation. Wilson's contributions to what he would call "the voluntary law of nations," or what we know as "international law" as opposed to "international morality," are scant indeed. He criticized Grotius freely for applying so rigorously that rule of consent which he himself emphasized when dealing with law in the abstract. He was frankly more interested in international morality and expressed opinions which take the form of pious expressions of hope, rather than statements of practice.[33] Should any of his students have dropped out of the course at the close of this lecture, he would have got little from his professor's exposition of the subject of international law. It is true that Wilson did touch upon the deeper questions of this field, for to say "he who has made a promise to another man has given that other a perfect right to demand the performance of the promise," is a statement which is hardly Machiavellian. On the obligations of treaties he is as explicit as any writer before or since: "Nations and the representatives of nations ought, therefore, to preserve inviolably their treaties and engagements: by not preserving them, they subject themselves to all the consequences of violating the perfect right of those to whom they were made. . . . In public as in private life, among sovereigns as among individuals, honesty is the best policy, as well as the soundest morality. Among merchants, credit is wealth; among states and princes good faith is both respectability and power."[34] But the trouble with such pronouncements then, as now, was that such principles are rarely denied in theory, while flagrantly violated in practice, a fact which makes Wilson's conception of the nature of law the more important.

But fortunately he does not stop here. The ninth lecture of the

[33] Wilson, *Works*, I. 149 ff.
[34] Wilson, *Works*, I. 176.

series bears the interesting title "Of Man as a Member of the Great Commonwealth of Nations." Herein he conceives the nations of the world as dwelling together in that natural society, that "state of nature," which the compact theorist assured him had existed prior to government. Yet even in this natural society, states existed under the law. For a state to make a figure in the great society of nations, it is sufficient that it be independent, i.e., "that it govern itself by its own authority."[35] But to secure justice in "the great society, equality is the basis and the rule. To this equality, the inferiority of subjection and the superiority of command are, alike, repugnant. This equality of nations is the great and general foundation of national rights. In this matter no regard is had for names, "all were alike before the law of nations, whether empires, kingdoms, commonwealths, or free towns."[36] The abstract admission as such of this legal principle is of little value unless some machinery be provided for its administration, and consequently one inquires how this right is to be secured in a world where war still exists, where "among nations, as well as among individuals, differences and causes of differences will sometimes unavoidably arise." "Since above independent nations no coercive authority exists to which recourse may be had for a decision of the controversies, there are several successive steps which should be taken. Controversies often happen in which neither party is intentionally wrong, where mere misapprehensions and mistakes are the cause of the friction. In such cases nothing more is necessary for amicable accommodation than candid conferences and mutual explanation."[37] Such is the simple method of bilateral diplomatic negotiations.

But "if the parties themselves, notwithstanding their peaceful and proper inclinations, cannot finally agree upon terms, according to which the differences may be adjusted, those terms may in many instances be arranged and settled by the kind and benevolent mediation of a common friend" who should remember that his office is to conciliate and not to judge.[38] But if neither friendly negotiation nor the benevolent mediation of a third power will avail, there is

---

[35] Wilson, *Works*, I. 360.
[36] Wilson, *Works*, I. 362. Cf. John Marshall's "No principle of general law is more universally acknowledged than the perfect equality of nations. Russia and Geneva have equal rights." *The Antelope*, 10 Wheaton, 66, 122, (1825).
[37] Wilson, *Works*, I. 364.
[38] Wilson, *Works*, I. 365.

yet another method "by which mutual irritation and much more dreadful extremities may be prevented between those who have no common judge on earth to whom they can appeal. This method is to refer the matter in dispute to an award of arbitrators."[39] If arbitration fail the next alternative is the summoning of an international congress "in which the differences of contending parties might be determined by those altogether disinterested in them; and in which, likewise, some effectual means might be devised and carried into execution for compelling nations at war to conclude peace upon fair and equitable conditions." But as Wilson wrote this twenty-five years before even the very deficient Congress of Vienna, he had little historical data with which to elaborate this point. The congresses of the eighteenth century called for such purpose "were nothing more than pompous farces, acted with great parade, by those who wished to appear solicitous for accommodation, but who in fact were little solicitous to promote it."[40] Beyond these methods of international conciliation, he knew of nothing which legal practice would suggest other than reprisals which would in most cases merely be the stepping stone to war. So much for the law of nations as he knew it. It will be observed that all these methods depend for solution on the existence of rules of law to which the negotiators and arbitrators may appeal, yet which are not rules or commands given by a superior to an inferior, because in international affairs there is no superior.[41]

But Wilson was too good a political scientist to stop there. "All the modes of adjustment which have hitherto been mentioned presuppose the reconciliation of irritated minds," is the way in which he introduced his own theory of solving the problems of war. "But must the peaceful adjustment of controversies between states, an adjustment so salutary and so necessary to the human race, depend on events so precarious or so very improbable? Must the alternatives in disputes and differences between dignified assemblages of men, known by the name of nations, be the same which are the prerogative of savages in the rudest and most deformed state of society— voluntary accommodation or open war, or violent reprisals, inferior in odium only to war? Individuals unite in civil society and institute

---

[39] Wilson, *Works*, I. 365.

[40] Wilson, *Works*, I. 367.

[41] Cf. Jenks' comment on "Law as a truth to be discovered and not as a command to be imposed." *Law and Politics*, p. 9.

judges with authority to decide, and with authority also to carry their decisions into full and adequate execution that justice may be done and war may be prevented. Are states too wise or too proud to receive a lesson from individuals? Is the idea of a common judge between nations less admissible than that of a common judge between men? If admissible in idea, would it not be desirable to try whether the idea may not be reduced to practice? To return to the original question—has or has not our national constitution given us an opportunity of making this great and interesting trial?"[42]

In a word, Wilson was struck with the idea which has occurred to many men since his day, that the United States Supreme Court was in effect an international tribunal for the settlement of disputes between states. As a matter of fact, that is just the function the Supreme Court has frequently exercised, administering international law, and being guided in its decisions by the principles of that law.[43] It was obvious to Wilson in the second year of the Supreme Court's existence that, being authorized to take jurisdiction in cases between states claiming to be sovereign, it would form an interesting object of study for comparative jurisprudence as an example of an international court. As a product of the English common law system, Wilson could not but be impressed with the latent possibilities of such a court, proceeding along lines analogous to those of the English common law courts administering a customary international law, which was akin to the customary common law, and in a certain sense even a part of it. Hitherto international law "has been applied and administered by the force or at the pleasure of the parties to the controversy; in the United States it can now be applied and administered by impartial, independent and efficient, though peaceful, authority," in such cases as come within its jurisdiction. To Wilson's imagination this idea opened up a magnificent prospect of the government of law, and of international peace based upon the existence of a court for the judicial settlement of international disputes. His dream of world peace was not only in terms of a hypothetical super-state but also in terms of a very real super-court.[44]

It is probably superfluous now to point out that the effectiveness of such a court would depend entirely upon the sense of law possessed by those who submit their cases to it. If the litigants in a

[42] Wilson, *Works*, I. 377.

[43] See R. I. vs. Mass., 4 How., 491, and Va. vs. Tenn., 148, U. S., 503, 522–4.

[44] Wilson, *Works*, I. 380. Cf. Duguit, *Law in the Modern State*, p. 89.

controversy felt that the law thus administered was merely the dictate of a superior, and if the actions of the court were such as to justify that opinion, the court would have little value. If on the other hand the litigants possessed the spirit of fair play and a willing-ness to abide by rules because of their personal interest in the making of those rules, and if the court were actuated by a like motive, Wilson's dream was not a vain thing. But the whole question depends upon the acceptance of his original and fundamental legal theories.

8

LIMITING AND DIVIDING SOVEREIGNTY

B ROADLY SPEAKING, the British imperial problem was, and is, the task of reconciling two jealous tendencies. How can the existing limitations upon the independence of the dominions be relaxed, while at the same time a sufficient bond of unity is maintained to impel the communities that compose the empire-commonwealth to behave like gentlemen in the league of nations to which they belong? How can sufficient latitude of action be allowed for the unfettered growth of the individual community, while preserving at the same time a sufficient degree of respect for the central authority to insure the reference of differences to the arbitrament of tribunals rather than to the wager of battle, so that the framework of the empire-commonwealth may not be injured and thus incapacitated for performing its beneficent functions?[1] Broadly speaking, this is the task of any league of nations, whether, as in the case of the Britannic Commonwealth, we begin with the one and work toward the many, or, as in the case of a more universal league, we begin with the many and work toward the one. The separate identity of the one and of each of the many must be preserved, else the problem is not solved.

Now in all this the chief problem of thought lies in what the books call "sovereignty." Your philosophical thinker will inquire of the imperial and international political engineer, how sovereignty is to be preserved. Your unphilosophical thinker will ask practically the same question when he wonders what is to become of independence. Therefore, no study of the political thought of the Ameri-

[1] A. B. Keith, *Imperial Unity in the Dominions*, p. 25.

can Revolution can leave this question out of account. But let none be deceived. Few thinkers of this or any other age can really think clearly in terms of sovereignty, and we ought to bear in mind that the men here to be considered are the exceptions. Not exceptions in the sense that they thought differently from the majority, but exceptions in the sense that they thought at all. As the political thought of the Revolution unfolds, we observe that thinker after thinker drops by the wayside as the problem approaches this question of sovereignty.

When Governor Hutchinson announced to the Massachusetts General Court that he knew of "no line that can be drawn between the supreme authority of Parliament and the total independence of the colonies," he touched the heart of this problem.[2] Had he been able to draw that line, he would have been in the possession of the theory for mediation between absolute dependence and absolute independence, which, as has been observed, is not only the problem of the Britannic Commonwealth but of all international organization. Yet Englishmen are certainly among those whose history supplies material for the formulation of such a theory. It is more and more coming to be recognized that the rise of the British Empire can to a very large extent be traced in terms of chartered trading companies. What were these companies? Attention has already been called to the fact that the science of corporations is akin to the science of commonwealths. Perhaps it is not going too far to call these trading corporations embryo commonwealths, as their charters have been designated embryo constitutions.[3] For example, the charters of the Merchant Adventurers, that great company for the export of English woolen cloth to the continent of Europe, were, in so many words, grants of power and authority for the better government of English merchants dwelling in the Low Countries, to insure order and justice among them. One can hardly read the successive charters of this organization without being struck with the idea that here is a trading corporation possessing a degree of governmental authority which practically made it a subsidiary government in some kind of a federation. Some of these companies, of which the Merchant Adventurers is but one example, obtained certain extra-territorial privileges in the countries in which they

[2] *Mass. State Papers*, p. 340.
[3] W. Morey, "Genesis of the Written Constitution," *Ann. Amer. Acad.*, I. 531.

operated. That is, their members were exempt from the jurisdiction of local tribunals in a great many cases, and subject to their own company court, a situation somewhat analogous to the "capitulations" of international law. Such, for example, was the case of the Muscovy Company.[4] These companies did in fact constitute little "imperia in imperio," little states within a state, which the orthodox political scientists so abhor, but which persist, nevertheless. These companies existed by virtue of the charters which conditioned the exercise of jurisdiction on their part and delegated to them certain of the powers which otherwise belonged to the King in Parliament.[5] Authority was thus divided, and the measure of that division was the charter, a set of rules which limited the power of both grantor and grantee.[6]

Broadly speaking, the first Britannic self-governing dominions sprang from similar companies, and from their charters sprang the first constitutions. If, in these dominions, these colonial communities, any line was to be drawn between the authority of the King in Parliament and the authority of the dominion, an examination of the charter was certainly a material aid to one who wanted to draw that line. Now the objection must inevitably arise that since the King, or the King in Parliament, granted these charters, the companies or the colonies must necessarily in fact be subject to the power of the grantor. But this is no necessary consequence. The British Parliament passed the British North America Act; does that make Westminster supreme over Ottawa? It may be so in theory, but where is the Englishman who would take it upon himself to announce that fact from the housetops? If a line can be drawn between the respective fields of jurisdiction of the British Government and of a trading company, or embryonic commonwealth, the rules found in the charter played a very large part therein. Is not this placing a limitation, by a set of rules, upon the so-called sovereignty of either group? Anyone who would rationalize the doctrine of sovereignty in interstate relationships will find valuable food for thought in the British imperial relationships, and insofar as the

[4] C. P. Lucas, *Beginnings of English Overseas Enterprise*, p. 123. A. J. Gerson, *Organization and Early History of the Muscovy Company*, pp. 47, 75.

[5] W. E. Lingelbach, *Merchants Adventurers: Their Laws and Ordinances*, pp. 218, 221, 229.

[6] E. P. Cheyney, *History of England from the Defeat of the Armada to the Death of Elizabeth*, I. 337–8.

struggle over the British imperial problem that we know as the American Revolution threw any light on that doctrine, it would be a very incomplete study of the political thought of the American Revolution which would omit it.[7]

"The American Revolution broke out, and the doctrine of the sovereignty of the people came out of the townships and took possession of the state."[8] A little reflection on De Tocqueville's comment may make clear both the doctrine of sovereignty and the theory of the state as it appears in the ideas of the Revolutionary period. The sovereignty of the people was said to take possession of the state; the state was not said to take possession of sovereignty. Now it may be correct to say that after all "the political theory used by the Americans in the Revolutionary struggle was similar to that of the English revolutionists of the seventeenth century, as best stated by Locke,"[9] though the record shows that the eighteenth century English heirs of the Locke tradition had some difficulty in squaring their thought with the American adaptation of the Lockeian ideas. But let us make our terms clear. The philosophers tell us that "Bodin was the writer to whom is due the first clear enunciation of the doctrine of sovereignty,"[10] and upon turning to that author it is discovered that "sovereignty is the supreme power over citizens and subjects unrestrained by laws."[11] Even Grotius had admitted that sovereignty inheres in general in the state, so by the time of the American Revolution it was pretty well established in political thought that in every state there must reside somewhere a paramount power to which all must bow, which was above all positive law, and, indeed, the source of that law.[12]

Gierke's illuminating study has shown the position of sovereignty

---

[7] It is interesting to observe the interchangeability of terms to which the emergence of corporations into commonwealths in America gave rise. On Jan. 19, 1775, a colonial paper remarked, "The people of Marblehead met today and resolved that as a number of the individuals of the town may soon be called forth to assist in defending the *charters* and *constitutions* of the province" it were well that they be instructed in the art of war. Moore, *Diary of the American Revolution*, p. 12.

[8] De Tocqueville, *Democracy in America* (Gilman Ed., 1898), I. 70.

[9] C. E. Merriam, *History of the Theory of Sovereignty Since Rousseau*, p. 159.

[10] H. Sidgwick, *Development of European Polity*, p. 328.

[11] J. Bodin, *De Republica*, Bk. I. ch. VIII.

[12] *De Jure Belli ac Pacis*, Ch. III. Sec. 8.

in its younger days before it was old enough to command the worship which later marked its progress. He has outlined clearly the notion which seems to have been prevalent in the middle ages, that the sovereignty of the state found its position somewhere below divine law (natural law) and somewhere above human law (positive law).[13] It is indeed hardly fair to call it sovereignty in this early stage, for the pyramided nature of the mediæval politico-social structure hardly admitted as yet of the idea of a national state as it developed later. In this earlier stage, the idea of sovereignty can be observed as apart from the state, and hence as yet uncontaminated by the idea that it could be the exclusive possession of a semi-juristic group, standing in a constant state of nature and at war with numerous other similar groups, each possessing a similar chattel of which it is equally a jealous guardian. Here, in its separate condition (if, indeed, sovereignty can have any separate existence at all), we find that, as far as mediæval thought can be said to exhibit any degree of uniformity, thinkers were fairly unanimous that there was a natural, divine law of God, below whose rules stood the power of the state, and that power stood in turn above the human, man-made, positive laws.[14] In an age which produced this kind of thinking, Bryce has shown how mediæval theory constructed the civil on the model of ecclesiastical society, "how the Holy Roman Empire was the shadow of the popedom, designed to rule men's bodies as the pontiff ruled their souls. Both alike claimed obedience on the ground that Truth is One, and where there is One Faith there must be One Government."[15] This principle of formal unity was what the reformation overthrew, and hence we can detect political theories emerging from the middle ages as Gierke has outlined them, while at the same time we observe the idea of a separate state beginning to be applied to those national groups which the modern age has developed into the nation-states of modern Europe. Thus Bodin's sovereignty, though in essence the idea may

[13] A "positive" law will be understood as a human rule which is contra-distinguished from what James Wilson called "natural" or "divine" law. This satisfies Austin's usage. See *Lectures on Jurisprudence,* I. 89. It does not exclude the lawyer's definition of law as any rule which the courts will enforce. See A. V. Dicey, *Law of the Constitution,* (8th Ed: 1915), p. 38.

[14] Otto Gierke, *Political Theories of the Middle Ages,* trans. by F. W. Maitland, (1900), pp. 78, 93.

[15] Bryce, *Holy Roman Empire:* (Ed. 1911), Chapter VII. of course, but see also p. 99n and 380.

be as old as Aristotle, became the accepted theory of the supreme power which existed in any socio-national group. "There was," writes Gierke, "a steady advance of the notion that the state was an exclusive community. In phrases that tell of the antique world, men spoke of the state simply as 'human society.' The state is the all comprehensive, and therefore the one and only expression of that common life which stands above the life of the individual."[16] But taking an exclusive and potentially tyrannous authority from a pope or an emperor and giving it to certain national units did not solve all political problems, for there was so close an identification of the state with its government in the days of the absolute monarchs that the practical problems connected with sovereignty remained to be worked out in a series of revolutions which, in the case of central and eastern Europe, have lasted to our own day.

Even the earliest of the revolutions, that of England, shows in its most representative spokesman, John Locke, a curious confusion of concepts of community, state, society, and government. It may be in some respects fair to base the American Revolutionary thought upon the teachings of Locke, but in another sense it is misleading, for Locke did not always make that distinction which appears so forcefully in the writings of John Adams and Thomas Paine, that the community, or society, may have a will apart from the government, with a consequent corollary which would protect the rights of man and the rights of the minority against the whim of the majority who control the government.[17]

At the threshold of the temple of sovereignty, we pause to distinguish more clearly the image of the triple-headed god within.[18] Today one of the heads is missing. For one of the senses in which

[16] Gierke, *Political Theories of the Middle Ages*, p. 94.

[17] John Locke, *Two Treatises on Government*, Bk. II. Sec. 95–101. "When any number of men have so consented to make one community or government, they are thereby presently incorporated and make one body politic wherein the majority have the right to conclude the rest." Sec. 95. On the other hand see John Adams: "Rulers are no more than attorneys, agents and trustees for the people; and if the cause, the interest and trust is insidiously betrayed or wantonly trifled away, the people have to revoke the authority they themselves deputed and constitute abler and better agents, attorneys and trustees." *Works*, III. 456–57.

[18] Following the three different senses in which Merriam's analysis demonstrates that the word has been used, *History of the Theory of Sovereignty Since Rousseau*, pp. 222–4.

the word was used is no longer of much consequence; in the sense of "a position of privilege held by the monarch of a state," the thought of the American Revolution definitely rejected sovereignty. It will be remembered that among those active in the decapitation was Thomas Paine, whose *"Common Sense"* was a violent attack on the idea of sovereignty as resident in an heredity monarch. Nevertheless the image has two other heads which are still the recipients of the homage of the votaries at its shrine. "Sovereignty which is internal as paramount over all control from within any given state and sovereignty which is external as independent over all control from without," are two senses in which the word has been and is used.[19] At first we are concerned with the former of these two, with internal, political sovereignty. Bodin in the sixteenth century seems to have identified the residence of sovereignty with the *de facto* sovereign, and used the word "prince" when discussing it.[20] Such a sovereign was whomsoever the accident of birth left upon the throne of France. Hobbes registered the advance of the next century, the seventeenth, by placing sovereignty "in him or them, on whom the sovereign power is conferred by the consent of the people assembled."[21] Finally in the writings of Locke and Rousseau sovereignty was found deposited with the people, and the theory of sovereignty for politically revolutionary purposes was enunciated.

But Englishmen had seized upon that phase of Locke's writings in which he had emphasized that in any government the legislative is supreme; there appeared the doctrine of the supremacy of the High Court of Parliament. That is one reason why it is not fitting to dismiss the whole political thought of the American Revolution as a mere adaptation from John Locke, because even if it was in one sense such an adaptation, it adapted a phase of the Lockeian philosophy which had been neglected in England. Since we are not concerned so much with the origin of ideas as with their reappearance, American thought becomes an even more distinctive thing in the light of the application made of those principles. If Locke enun-

---

[19] T. E. Holland, *Elements of Jurisprudence*, pp. 47–8, and Cf. R. T. Crane, *Sovereignty in Constitutional and International Law*, which distinguishes the two almost mutually incompatible senses of internal and external sovereignty which, nevertheless, persist in political thought, pp. 7–11, 73–4.

[20] *De Republica*, Bk. I. Ch. X.

[21] Hobbes, *Leviathan*, Ch. XVIII.

ciated them, so did Marsiglio of Padua, and Aristotle, too, for that matter, but none of those had the great opportunity of thinking the right thoughts at the right time which was vouchsafed to the philosophers of the American Revolutionary period.

There is yet another reason why the thought of the American Revolution is a proper subject for investigation independently of the intellectual tradition to which it happened to fall heir. Locke and Rousseau, it is true, enunciated the doctrine of popular sovereignty. For nearly two centuries two conflicting schools had waged a battle on the subject. Those who claimed that sovereignty was in its nature unlimited and the prerogative of the monarch fought with those who contended that man is endowed with natural rights which the state can not legally invade. The American Revolution marks a victory for the latter party, but since that victory a very strange thing has happened. As President Lowell of Harvard has pointed out, the victors have adopted the principles of the vanquished which they had struggled so long to overthrow.[22] Sovereignty, supreme power unrestrained by law, was a menace in the hands of kings who might wield it as they would. But after the people had gained it for themselves, they gave it away again to the state and have learned to their sorrow the danger of enthroning the sovereignty of the state above positive laws. Anglo-Saxonwise, we would not part company utterly with the past in reconstructing the theory of the state. It seems, therefore, that it would be hard to find a more illuminating period for study than that opportune moment between the victory of the natural rights school over the divine rights school and the beginning of the modern doctrine which has revived the organismic theories of the state and has endowed the organism with supreme power, sovereignty, potential tyranny, and absolutism, which mankind had striven so long to wrest from kings and princes. For after all, the natural rights school, to which our Revolutionary thinkers belong, could not think in terms of absolute, unlimited power anywhere outside of the deity, because the natural rights, themselves, were things which limited the powers of governments and states.

---

[22] "But now, just at the moment when democracy is carrying everything before it and the advocates of natural rights of man appear to have triumphed, there has come a sudden change of principle, and the victors, adopting the opinions of the vanquished, are almost universally convinced that the authority of the sovereign from its very nature can be subject to no limitation of restraint." A. L. Lowell, "Limits on Sovereignty," 2 *Harvard Law Review*, 70, ff.

The rebellion of the thinkers of colonial America against an omnipotent sovereign dwelling thousands of miles away is a fact which it is interesting to associate with the fact that American thought emerged in an atmosphere of religious non-conformity. Now one of the groups which throughout history seem successfully to have challenged the claim of the state to paramount authority is the group to which, without designating any particular sect, we can give the name of the church. From the struggle over the investitures to the Kulturkampf, there are examples of it that would make him a bold historian who asserted that the state has been victorious in every instance.[23] Yet to make good its claim to sovereignty the state would really have to be sovereign, i.e., the paramount authority. Hence there is nothing very strange in the sight of the descendants of men who asserted the right of their group against the superior claims of the so-called sovereign state, undertaking to assert their rights again in another group capacity, this not a religious group but a frankly political one.

Britons conceived the empire as a unicellular state wherein sovereignty was possessed, according to the Lockeian dogma, by the legislative, that is, by the High Court of Parliament at Westminster. Britons talked about "our sovereignty" over the colonies. Benjamin Franklin finally burst out, "I am quite sick of *'our sovereignty'*."[24] To his mind the empire was not unicellular, and it was high time that Britons came to recognize that the communities across the seas were equal in rank and dignity to the island off the coast of Europe which arrogated to itself the headship of the empire. Bryce[25] and Dicey[26] have tried to solve the riddle of sovereignty in Britain by distinguishing the "legal sovereign" (Parliament) from the "political sovereign" (the electorate). Franklin's remark epitomizes what the colonials felt about the existence of a "legal sovereign" in the empire. Put more clearly and in practical terms by Samuel Adams, it was declared that, "By the charter of this province, the legislative power is the Governor, who is appointed by the King, the Council and the House of Representatives. The legislative of any commonwealth must be the supreme power."[27] Following Locke's lead as to

---

[23] Cf. H. J. Laski, *Problem of Sovereignty*, Chs. II, V.

[24] *Works*, (Bigelow Ed.), IV. 316.

[25] James Bryce, *Studies in History and Jurisprudence*, p. 505.

[26] A. V. Dicey, *Law of the Constitution*, (8th Ed. 1915), p. 425.

[27] *Valerius Poplicola* to the *Boston Gazette*, 28 Oct., 1771, S. Adams, *Works*, II. 260.

the legal or governmental sovereign, as opposed to the practical or political sovereign, there were as many sovereigns in the British Empire as there were constituent parts of it. There could hardly be anything very awe-inspiring about a sovereignty which was not only divisible, but divisible into so many pieces. As to its limitability, such a sovereign was merely the creature of society, limitable and changeable and even destructible at the will of society. The Jeffersonian view held that governments, legislatures, as Locke would have said, were merely agents "instituted"[28] or "framed"[29] among men, and not set irretrievably above men, as a power "unrestrained by laws." On the contrary, Jefferson came continually back to the proposition that the legal sovereign, as Bryce and Dicey, following the lead of Locke, would call it, was very much at the mercy of the people.[30]

But in the field of the practical or political sovereign, we have a more serious problem. Locke started with a state of nature, from which mankind emancipated itself by establishing, first, political society, which in turn instituted government.[31] This involved a surrender of such natural rights as the common good demanded should not be exercised irresponsibly by private individuals. But Locke's confusion here of "community" and "government" would warn one not to draw too specific a conclusion as to how political society instituted government.[32] Yet that government contained the sovereign power which, we have observed, Bryce and Dicey have rationalized as the *de jure* or legal sovereign. "In all cases whilst government subsists the legislative is the supreme power."[33] From such a theory grew naturally the doctrine of Parliamentary supremacy. But despite this outspoken statement, Locke admitted that behind the government stood the community, at whose pleasure government existed. At this point we seem to have the whole American idea. But one must move cautiously. This community, or society, apparently never registered its will nor acted in its sovereign capacity except for the purpose of overthrowing a government and the institution of a new one, for "whilst government subsists, the

---

[28] *Declaration of Independence.*
[29] Jefferson, *Works,* (Ford Ed.), IV. 475.
[30] Jefferson, *Works,* (Ford Ed.), IV. 362–3, 465–7.
[31] *Two Treatises on Government,* Bk. II. secs. 95–9.
[32] Ibid., Secs. 95, 97.
[33] Ibid , Sec. 150.

legislative is the supreme power." Yes, "the community may be said to be in this respect always the supreme power, *but* not as considered under any form of government, because this power of the people can never take place until the government be dissolved."[34] It is not at all fair to say that Locke did not, upon occasion, distinguish society from government; he certainly did. But the thing he does seem to have difficulty in conceiving was an expression implying a manifestation of the social will independently of the will of a particular government and during the existence of a particular government. The constitution of the "legislative" was the first and fundamental act of society, and this creation of society then became "the soul that gives form, life and unity to the commonwealth."[35] A government once made, its will is law until another government comes along and makes another law, and in each case the minority have no rights which the majority cannot in the last analysis invade. If a particular government be unrepresentative, during its tenure society must needs be dumb.[36]

Rousseau has little more to offer. Although in no sense can he be said to have been as influential on the thinkers of the American Revolution as was Locke, yet he is commonly thought of as representative of the school of thought which also embraces the Americans. He predicates a general will which dictates what the supreme power shall do. This is slightly different, it will be observed, from Locke, who identified his sovereign with the supreme power rather than with the will which guided that power. But for our purposes the distinction is little more than academic. Sovereignty, "being nothing but the exercise of the general will,"[37] was a thing which Rousseau would have us differentiate from the "will of all."[38] "There is often a great deal of difference between the will of all and the general will; the latter regards only common interest, while the former has regard for private interests, and is merely the sum of particular wills, but take away these same wills, the pluses and minuses will cancel one another, and the general will remains as the sum of the differences."[39] Hence it was easy to say that "the

[34] *Two Treatises on Government,* Bk. II. Sec. 149.
[35] Ibid., Sec. 211.
[36] Ibid., Sec. 212.
[37] J. J. Rousseau, *Le Contrat Social,* (not published till 1762).
[38] Ibid., Bk. II. Ch. I.
[39] Ibid., II, iii.

general will is always right and always tends to public advantage; but it does not follow that the resolutions of the people have always the same rectitude." All this leads directly to the conclusion, "as nature gives every man an absolute power over all his limbs, the social pact gives the body politic an absolute power over all its members, and it is this same power, which when directed by the general will bears, as I have said, the name of sovereignty."[40] Such a conception of sovereignty would seem to be a thing which knows neither law nor limitation, for "It is admitted that whatever part of his power, property and liberty each one alienates by the social compact, is only part of the whole of which the use is important to the community, but we must also admit that the sovereign alone is the judge of what is important." Under these circumstances we certainly do Rousseau no injustice by calling attention to his proposition that "It is contrary to the nature of the body politic for the sovereign to impose upon itself a law which it cannot transgress."[41]

The mediæval theory left sovereignty above positive law, and it is difficult to see where either Locke or Rousseau made very much of an advance upon that theory. True, the new popular sovereign was perhaps more democratic than Hobbes' sovereign. If Hobbes absorbed the government in the sovereign, one is tempted to concur that Locke and Rousseau, and particularly the latter, absorbed the government in the people and left them as unrestrained by law as Bodin's sovereign had been. Turning now to John Adams' *Dissertation on the Canon and Feudal Law*,[42] we find one of the most searching sketches on the theory of politics which appeared in America in this period. It is not a complete statement of theory or a consistent and well rounded presentation. Rather is it a series of penetrating comments which would furnish as much food for thought as many lengthy and didactic works which consume three or four times as much paper. In a sense it contains the answer to Sydney Smith's query, "Who reads an American book?" The answer is, "Englishmen."[43] Popular sovereignty, the sovereignty of the people, sovereignty resident in the people, the supreme power dwelling in the mass of the people, or whatever term anyone wishes

[40] J. J. Rousseau, *Le Contrat Social*, II. iv.

[41] Ibid., I. vii or II. i.

[42] Published in August, 1765, in the *Boston Gazette*.

[43] Reprinted in London and printed in book form in England twice before it was published as a book in America in 1783. John Adams, *Works*, III. 445.

to employ to express the concept of sovereignty held by the men of the Revolutionary period in America, was viewed here as the culmination of an age-long struggle in which that power was wrested by the masses from the classes. Later in the nineteenth century John Adams might have explained this as the "evolution" of sovereignty from the private possession of a priest or prince to the public possession of the co-contractors who composed society and instituted government. At one time there had been a monarch with many rights and a people with many duties; now there was a monarch with many duties and people with many rights. Rightly or wrongly, he interpreted the mediæval political thought as a dull thing in which the twin tyrannies of priests and princes maintained the supreme power in given administrative areas, by force, fear and fiction. The modern age had shown people where the real weight in numbers, and hence the real force, lay, and it had removed their fear by destroying the fictions of canon and feudal superstition. "In the middle ages," says Maitland, "land law is the basis of all public law."[44] John Adams seems to have been on the track of some such thought in this essay, and in it he saw half the explanation of what he regarded as the tyranny of the middle ages. The other half of the explanation was to be found in the church and its canon law. This twin confederacy of the canon and feudal law exercised a temporal and spiritual tyranny which was, in fact, the "supreme power" over the people of the middle ages.[45] The Reformation was simply an effort to loosen the shackles of this sovereign. "It was this great struggle which peoples America."[46] Not merely "Puritans" seeking religious freedom were they who settled America, but men who sought refuge from the oppressive European public law which was based upon land tenure, and which presumed that primarily one person "was vested with the propriety of all lands within the territory."[47] How far this is a correct conclusion, or how far the Americans got away from these oppressive sovereigns, is a question into which it is not our province to enter. But they did think that they had emancipated themselves from the bonds of canon and feudal law, and the point which it is interesting to observe is that

[44] F. W. Maitland, *Constitutional History of England,* (1906), p. 38.
[45] John Adams, *Works,* III. 450.
[46] Ibid., III. 451.
[47] Ibid., III. 450.

John Adams thought of these bonds in terms of systems of laws as well as in terms of persons.[48] The feudal sovereigns were accompanied in his thought by the oppressive systems of law whereby that sovereignty was made manifest. To take the place of the old sovereigns and their old law what had the thought of colonial America to offer? They had to offer not only the sovereign people, but the law of the Constitution. The Constitution was the articulate expression of the sovereign people which insured their liberty. This involved not only the setting up of government to secure the rights of man, but the enunciation of principles which conditioned human association. One of the chief of those conditions was, of course, the preservation of those natural rights which men did not surrender upon their entrance into political society. Now those rights, which the Constitution was designed to insure, form the connecting link between natural (divine) and positive (human) law in the thought of this period. The discussion at this point transcended the bounds of what is ordinarily called public law, and some of the keenest thinkers, like John Adams, Alexander Hamilton, and John Dickinson, are found associating the natural rights of men with both the British Constitution and divine law. The British Constitution is held to be not the origin, but the expression of preëxisting rights, emanating in the last analysis from what Hamilton called "an intelligent, superintending principle who is Governor and will be the final judge of the universe."[49] In some such sense as this must be understood Adams' declaration that "British liberties are not the grants of princes or parliaments, but original rights, conditions of original contracts, coequal with prerogative and coeval with government; that many of our rights are inherent and essential, agreed on as maxims and established as preliminaries even before a parliament existed."[50]

Supplementary to John Adams' *Dissertation,* Hamilton's replies to the *Westchester Farmer* carry the idea of a discoverable natural law (divine law) on to its application. He is prone to identify natural law with what he calls the spirit or genius of the British Constitu-

[48] *Essay on the British Constitution,* John Adams, *Works,* III. 479.

[49] *The Farmer Refuted; or a More Comprehensive and Impartial View of the Disputes Between Great Britain and the Colonies:* [Alexander Hamilton] (New York: February, 1775), Hamilton's *Works,* (J. C. Hamilton Ed.), II. 43.

[50] John Adams, *Works,* III. 463.

tion.[51] The rights of men which exist under this natural law "are not to be rummaged for among old parchments or musty records. They are written as with a sunbeam, in the whole volume of human nature, by the hand of the divinity itself; and can never be erased or obscured by mortal power." Hamilton believed that the law which secured these rights was a thing which resisted and restrained men while still in a state of nature and that upon their entry into political society and their institution of government, it became a part of the constitution. He pilloried the *Westchester Farmer* as a disciple of Hobbes, ranged himself on the side of Locke, and applied as principles of public law, doctrines which he believed subordinated all men, whether in society or out, to those principles.[52]

The final link in the chain connecting natural law with the law of the Constitution is supplied by Samuel Adams' *Natural Rights of the Colonists*.[53] "Just and true liberty, equal and impartial liberty, in matters spiritual and temporal, is a thing that all men are clearly entitled to by the eternal and immutable laws of God and nature, as well as by the law of nations, and all well grounded municipal laws, which must have their foundation in the former."[54] How natural law gets adopted into the British Constitution is explained by his conception of the nature of Magna Carta, which he regards as a "constrained declaration or proclamation and promulgation in the name of King, Lords and Commons of the sense the latter had of their original, inherent, indefeasible natural rights, as also those of free citizens equally perdurable with the other."[55] The point where Samuel Adams seems to advance on Locke or Rousseau is in pointing out that these natural rights are not held at the whim of the majority, but are the permanent possession of men in society. "In short, it is the greatest absurdity to suppose it in the power of one or any number of men, at the entering into society to renounce their essential natural rights, or the means of preserving those rights, when the grand end of civil government, from the very nature of its institution, is for the support, the protection and de-

---

[51] *The Farmer Refuted;* Hamilton's *Works,* II. 80, 96. See also, Hamilton, *Full Vindication of the Measures of the Continental Congress from the Calumnies of their Enemies,* (New York: 1774), *Works,* II. 4.

[52] Hamilton. *Works,* II. 43.

[53] Wells, *Life and Public Services of Samuel Adams,* I. 502–7.

[54] Ibid., I. 502.

[55] Ibid., I. 505.

fense of those very rights; the principal upon which, as is before observed, are Life, Liberty and Property. If men through fear, fraud or mistake, should in terms renounce, or give up any essential natural right, the eternal law of reason, the grand end of society, will absolutely vacate such renunciation."[56] These ideas merit some consideration as the reappearance in another form of concepts which foreshadow the American doctrine of constitutional law. Here, indeed, applied on a wider scale, we have the idea that there is a law which limits the actions of men acting collectively. In the former discussion, it was apparent that man acting collectively in government was restrained by law; now Samuel Adams would lay down the proposition that man acting collectively even in society is equally restrained by law. This time the law was not such an easily discoverable thing, indeed, one can hardly be blamed at first glance for accusing the thinker of confusing natural and positive law. But the discovery of natural law through the mediumship of the constitution is an attempt to answer even this. Where now lies sovereignty?

Before answering that, we must recur to Wilson and observe the thought of this most enthusiastic exponent of popular sovereignty. His "Lecture on Municipal Law" attacks the problem of sovereignty directly. The "celebrated Grotius," he tells us, "introduces what he says concerning the interesting doctrine of sovereignty with the following information: 'Learned men of our age, each of them handling the argument rather according to the present interest of the affairs of his country, than according to truth, have greatly perplexed that which in itself is not very clear.' In this the learned men of every other age have resembled those of the age of Grotius."[57] "Indeed it is astonishing in what intricate mazes politicians and philosophers have bewildered themselves upon this subject. Systems have been formed upon systems, all fleeting because unfounded. Sovereignty has sometimes been viewed as a star, which eluded our investigation by its immeasurable height; sometimes has been considered as a sun, which could not be distinctly seen by reason of its insufferable splendor. Always magnificent, always interesting to mankind, it has become alternately their blessing and their curse. Its origin has often been attempted to be traced. The great and the wise have embarked in the undertaking; though seldom, it

[56] Wells, I. 504.
[57] Wilson, *Works*, I. 231; *De Jure Belli ac Pacis*, I. iii. 5.

must be owned, with the spirit of just inquiry; or in the direction which leads to important discovery. The source of sovereignty was still concealed beyond some impenetrable mystery; and because it was concealed, philosophers and politicians in this instance have gravely taught, what in others the poets have fondly fabled, that it must be something more than human; it was impiously asserted to be divine. Lately the inquiry has been recommenced with a different spirit and in a new direction; and although the discovery is nothing very astonishing, yet the discovery of something very useful and true has been the result. The dread and redoubtable sovereign when traced to his ultimate and genuine source has been found as he ought to have been found, in the free and independent man. This truth, so simple and so natural, and yet so neglected or despised, may be appreciated as the first and fundamental principle in the science of government."[58] What meaning had such a pronouncement in the words of James Wilson that perhaps it might not have had in the words of Locke? True, Wilson observed, "Mr. Locke and other theoretical writers have held that there remains still inherent in the people a supreme power to remove or alter the legislative, when they find the legislative act contrary to the trust imposed in them; for when such trust is abused it is thereby forfeited, and devolves upon those who gave it."[59] Though whatever Mr. Locke and the theoretical writers might maintain, Blackstone could still reply, "But however just the conclusion may be in theory, we cannot practically adopt it, nor take any *legal* steps for carrying it into execution under any dispensation of government now existing."[60] But Wilson was of a nation that did "practically adopt it," and take "legal steps for carrying into execution" the sovereignty of the people as opposed to the sovereignty of government. He took an active part in the convention which framed the government wherein much of the Lockeian theory became a legal practice.[61] He not only joined Samuel Adams in denying the sovereignty of a particular government at a particular time, he denied the sovereignty of any government at any time.

Wilson's views on this subject were the same as those held by one

---

[58] Wilson, *Works*, I. 25.

[59] Locke, *Two Treatises on Government*, II. Secs. 149, 227.

[60] I. Bl. Com: 162.

[61] Farrand, *Records of the Federal Convention*, II. 73, 391; McMaster and Stone, *Pennsylvania and the Federal Constitution*, p. 354.

of the best known political scientists in contemporary England, James Burgh. This author has shared the fate of Camden in the oblivion to which English writers have consigned him. Yet his "Political Disquisitions" were in their day regarded as a mine of information and inspiration by those Englishmen who took the Americans seriously and insisted that if Boston was going to talk about representation, so should Manchester and the other victims of the rotten borough system. From the publication of his most notable work till 1832, Burgh's influence was felt and acknowledged. He sympathized entirely with the Americans in their position on taxation;[62] he quoted Bolingbroke to the effect that "there is something which Parliament cannot do,"[63] and, as to Blackstone and sovereignty, he remarked, "The truth is, therefore, that the learned judge has placed sovereignty wrong, viz., in the government; whereas it should have been placed in the people, next and immediately after God."[64]

One should observe Blackstone's language carefully in his statement, "How the several forms of government we now see on earth actually began is a matter of great uncertainty, and has occasioned infinite disputes. It is not my business or intention to enter into any of them. However they began, or by what right soever they subsist, there is and must be in all of them a supreme, irresistible, absolute and uncontrolled power, in which the *jura summi imperii,* or rights of sovereignty, reside."[65] Here Blackstone was talking about the sovereignty of the government, or what has been called "legal" sovereignty, and he found it in Parliament.[66] The Massachusetts proclamation of 1776 had employed similar language and reached a totally different conclusion: "It is a maxim that in every *government* there must exist somewhere a supreme sovereign, absolute and uncontrolled power; but this power resides always in the body of the people, and it can never be delegated to one man or to a few, the Great Creator having never given to men a right to vest others with authority over them unlimited either in duration or degree."[67]

[62] James Burgh, *Political Disquisitions, or An Enquiry into Public Errors, Defects and Abuses,* (London: 1774), 3 Vols., II. 274–81.

[63] *Ibid.,* III. 442.

[64] *Ibid.,* III. 278.

[65] 1 Bl. Com. 48–9.

[66] 1 Bl. Com. 51.

[67] Force, *American Archives,* 4th Ser., IV. 833.

However representative the Massachusetts proclamation might be, it is at least assailable. Blackstone, thinking of the legal sovereign, placed it in the law-making body. The Massachusetts proclamation, thinking of the same thing, had then confused it with political sovereignty.

But James Wilson's lecture on municipal law subjects the Blackstone doctrine to an interesting analysis in which he uncovers the American doctrine. Both Blackstone and the Massachusetts proclamation had said that supreme power must reside somewhere in government. Wilson said, "I agree with Blackstone that supreme power must reside somewhere in the *state.*" Now Blackstone had said not *state,* but *government.* For the rest the lecture on municipal law is not so much a valid attack on the Commentator as it is a clear statement of the position of the Americans. Legal sovereignty simply did not exist. Political sovereignty was resident in all the people and by definition could not possibly be the "absolute, uncontrolled, unlimited and indivisible" thing which appears in the books from Bodin to Burgess. In fact what the philosophers of the American Revolution did with sovereignty was just this: they scrapped it, as far as the ordinary meaning is concerned. The succession of steps in the philosophy of the Revolution was something like this: First, men got together in society, then society formed a government. Now, said the Europeans, from Puffendorf to Blackstone, we are ready to take the third step and confer sovereignty on someone. Wilson asks, why take the third step? "I see no necessity for it, I see no propriety in it; it is derogatory in my humble judgment from the general principles of legitimate sovereignty, and inconsistent with the best theory and the best exercise, too, of supreme power."[68] Now if sovereignty was a power "unrestrained by laws," what was *legitimate* sovereignty? Wilson's theory of the relationship of government to society throws some light on this. "By the term constitution, I mean that supreme law, made or ratified by those in whom the sovereign power in the state resides, which prescribes the manner according to which the state wills that the government should be instituted and administered. From this constitution the government derives its power, and by this constitution the power of the government must be directed and controlled; of this constitution no alteration can be made by the government, because

[68] Wilson, *Works,* I. 185–8.

such alteration would destroy the foundation of its own authority."[69] In other words, the state, or society politically organized, was not an entity with a separable existence from the society which composed it. Hence that later creation which conferred the sovereignty of the people upon the state was what Wilson would have regarded as "derogatory from the general principles of legitimate sovereignty." Indeed, the eighteenth century with its doctrine of the rights of man upon which government could not trespass could hardly have thought otherwise.

Perhaps it is not unfair to say that the Bodin-Burgess kind of sovereignty was, as far as the eighteenth century was concerned, rendered innocuous and relatively meaningless. The "active principle" of sovereignty, that is, government, far from being "unrestrained by laws," was definitely harnessed by the law of the constitution. The passive element, the electorate, simply absorbed sovereignty, yet even they were limited by those aspects of natural law which were embodied in the law of the Constitution. If society acted "ultra vires" its action was, in the words of Samuel Adams, "vacated."

What, then, were the theory of the state and the doctrine of sovereignty which the thinkers of the American Revolution had to offer? The answer, it seems, is something like this: They had no theory of the state. They had a theory of society and a theory of government, and a theory of the relationship of the one to the other. But of the state in the modern sense, they knew little. Those who have followed the theories on into the next century show how, instead of the sovereignty of the people taking possession of the state, the people surrendered sovereignty to the state.[70] Whether one large element in the nineteenth century thought may not have been a compromise between democracy and nationalism, is a question which it would be difficult to answer. Being willing to discover sovereignty in the people, it was not necessary for the men of the Revolution to compromise halfway and erect a semi-metaphysical organismic entity called the state and endow it with sovereignty. Perhaps their thought is barren without that element which the

<hr>

[69] Wilson, *Works*, I. 417.

[70] "With the reaction against the eighteenth century political theory came the development of a doctrine of the organic and personal nature of the state, which was impossible under the dominance of the revolutionary ideas." Merriam, *Hist. of Sovereignty etc.*, p. 90.

modern age has so industriously tried to isolate. But their ideas enabled them to avoid the snares with which the modern world has associated the idea of sovereignty in its third great sense, that of external sovereignty. Willing as they were to remain within the circle of the Britannic Commonwealth, while being in effect and in name free and independent states, the problem of external sovereignty had no terrors for them. As to their solution of the doctrine of sovereignty in its internal sense, there is an interesting clue in Maitland wherein he discusses the claimants to sovereignty in the time of James I.[71] It will be remembered that attention has been called to the fact that this was the period in which the English law was being transplanted across the Atlantic. Maitland reckons with Coke's doctrine of the supremacy of the law over Parliament. It will also be remembered that Coke's doctrine exercised considerable influence in shaping the American doctrine of constitutional law, that there is no will of government above the law. The historian epitomizes Coke's doctrine by calling it the "sovereignty of the law," and then proceeds to illustrate how unworkable it is and to note its early demise in England.

Strictly speaking, the theory of sovereignty consciously dominant with the thinkers of the American Revolution was the sovereignty of the people. But James Wilson's ideas on this head were probably clearer than those of any of his contemporaries, and one cannot go very far into Wilson's writings without becoming acutely aware of the fact that the "sovereignty of the people" as he understood it, was a very different thing from the apparently similar theory worked out in the French Revolution. French thinkers, after worshipping for centuries the theory of monarchical sovereignty, suddenly discovered that by a simple verbal change they could substitute the nation for the king and blandly call themselves democratic because they now worshipped the "sovereignty of the nation."[72] But let none be confused by the analogy with American thought. Wilson's sovereignty of the people was not the sovereignty of the nation. It was the sovereignty of the people, and the people might act in the local, the national, or the international capacity, as far as he was concerned.[73] Wilson's friend, James Iredell, had put this more

---

[71] F. W. Maitland, *Constitutional History of England*, pp. 297–301.

[72] Declaration of the Rights of Man, Article III. Duguit, *Law in the Modern State*, pp. 10–15.

[73] This is also the opinion of my friend, Mr. B. A. Konkle, who has spent

clearly than anyone else in discussing the nature of the Britannic Commonwealth in 1774. He insisted that the question of conflicting jurisdictions should not arise, that the same people might be citizens of North Carolina, or citizens of the Britannic Commonwealth, and that in fact there was no need of worrying about the ever-present bugaboo of the *imperium in imperio*. Said he, there might be "several distinct and independent legislatures, each engaged within a separate scale, and employed about different objects." The American Federal system today as well as the federal systems in the self-governing dominions of the Britannic Commonwealth, are conclusive demonstrations of the truth of what Wilson and Iredell were talking about.[74]

But after all, the sovereignty of the people of American political thought could only manifest itself when the people spoke in their constitutional capacity, i.e., in the formation and amendment of their constitution of government. Only when the people make constitutional law is the sovereignty of the people really a thing of which one can take practical cognizance. This enables us once more to inquire whether it may not be worth while to see what appears when we examine the American theory of sovereignty as being sovereignty resident in law.

The logical mind at once sees a contradiction here, or at least the confusion of natural and positive law. Were not Americans placing a semi-human, semi-divine law above the power of persons and states? Was such a law really ascertainable and really enforceable

---

many years research on his forthcoming *Life and Writings of James Wilson.* The concept is a simple one: if the same people can be citizens of North Carolina, and citizens of the United States, without destroying the identity of either North Carolina or the United States, why cannot they with equal ease become citizens of a more inclusive Commonwealth of Nations, as indeed, a man today can be at one and the same time a citizen of New South Wales, a citizen of the Commonwealth of Australia, and a citizen of the Britannic Commonwealth. Superadding on this a League, or Association, or Conference of Nations would in nowise destroy the identity of any of the other political units. Indeed, the trend is all the other way, for the self-governing dominions tend to assert more emphatically their individuality, and more "colonies" are demanding the "dominion status." Surely this product of American thought is a contribution to our international political philosophy which is not to be despised. Vid. Wilson, *Works,* I. 333, Passim. Cf. H. G. Wells, *Outline of History,* II. 584, i.e., Ch.: "The Unification of the World."

[74] McRee, *Life and Correspondence of James Iredell,* I. 219; Wilson, *Works,* I. 25, 185–8.

in human tribunals? Locke had said that the supreme power of the people could not manifest itself without the dissolution of government, but the Americans demonstrated that positive law could register the will of society independently of government while government was in being and operation. Rousseau had denied that the body politic could restrain itself with laws which it could not transgress. But the Americans appealed to a law, which they seemed to think valid for political purposes and suitable for political usage, which was in fact superior to political society. As Hamilton had said, there are some laws, which are pertinent in political discussion, which the hand of mortals can not erase. James Wilson was perfectly right in stressing the sovereignty of the people, because he represented the reaction against the legal sovereignty of Parliament, just as Paine represented the reaction against the personal sovereignty of the hereditary monarch. But the sovereignty of the people explains only a part of the thought of the Revolution and gives an incomplete picture of it. Wilson clearly differentiated natural and positive law, but he did not distinguish their respective fields of jurisdiction. In this perhaps lies the explanation of the apparent confusion of the two. His course of lectures at the law school opens with a lecture on "Natural Law," a thing which would be strangely out of place in the modern legal curriculum, being relegated to the departments of Philosophy and Ethics.

Now it is to be remembered that in legal thought, down even to our own day, the only branch of law which is acknowledged to be above states and nations is what the eighteenth century called the "Law of Nations" and what the modern world calls "International Law." In the eighteenth century, as has been observed in the chapter on Wilson's legal theories, this law was still held by many to be a division of natural, or divine law. The explanation of this is to be gleaned from Gierke's assertion that "Since the constituted power in the Church and in the State had not created the law of nations, but received it, it was therefore held to partake of the immutability and sanctity of natural law."[75] Might it not very well be that the interpreters of the American Revolution, in their apparent confusion of natural and positive law, of the law of the constitution with rights secured under natural law, were actually groping towards the idea of a law which was not created by states, but which society had

[75] Gierke, op. cit., p. 76.

received and having found good by experience had bound itself to observe by its own consent? Such a law was so very real to the Americans that they proceeded in a small way to apply it in connection with their own constitutional law, a law which transcended governments. Viewed from this standpoint, then, it is probably not wholly wrong to characterize the American doctrine of sovereignty as being, in one sense, a doctrine of the sovereignty of law. There is nothing new or startling about such a conclusion; indeed Aristotle seems to have placed the sovereignty of law above every form of personal sovereignty.[76]

Thus, if the question were asked, and it might not improperly be asked, from what source this law is "received," the answer is that the thinkers of the Revolution were not so clear on this point. But was it all necessary that they should have been clear? The question of divine revelation is one upon which the learned doctors in temple have disagreed, and it would be asking a good deal of the practical politicians in the town meeting that they settle it. The fact that the political engineers got as far as being able to conceive a law by which all men, within the state or as a state (understanding a state as a portion of society), were in fact bound, is a contribution to political thought of no mean dimensions. Perhaps no greater contribution has been made to the problem of mediating between the idea of an absolutely independent and an absolutely subject state than that concept which would recognize the existence of a sovereign law. Such a sovereign would limit the independence of the one and prevent tyranny, as it would protect the other in its dependency. Such an idea would lay the foundation for rules enforceable in courts which would relieve the subject state from the position of being absolutely at the mercy of the state which had undertaken to include such subject state in its "protectorate," or "sphere of influence," or "mandate," or whatever term may be used to express the tutelage of an advanced over a backward state.

Perhaps, too, it is no accident which led Stephen Hopkins to employ the expression, "Sovereignty of the British Constitution," in his effort to find a theory which would fit in with the concept of an empire of semi-independent states.[77] So, too, perhaps Samuel Adams really meant what he said in the Circular Letter, "That the

[76] Aristotle, *Politics,* Bk. III. xvi. 5. Cf. W. A. Dunning, *Political Theories, Ancient and Medieval,* p. 71.

[77] *Rhode Island Records,* VI. 427.

Constitution ascertains and limits both Sovereignty and allegiance."[78] Certainly this expresses exactly the nature of that law of the British Constitution to which the colonists appealed in their efforts to make clear their position. Within any given state, the Americans believed that as between persons, sovereignty was resident in the people, and not in kings or parliaments. But this is not the whole story, for if that given state was to aspire to the name of "republic," then it must primarily be what Harrington had taught John Adams to think of as "an empire of laws and not of men."[79] If this formula could, in turn, claim to be a political principle, then its application was certainly not to be limited by the artificial frontiers of either human or physiographical construction, for it is hardly a thing which takes cognizance of frontiers. In an "empire of laws and not of men," principle, not people, was sovereign, by definition.

Under such an analysis of sovereignty, the supreme limitations upon human action are found resident in a set of rules which, for want of a better term, we denominate as law. The law found its practical expression in constitutions and charters, rules by which groups in the political system were bound by quasi-contractual obligations. As has been observed, this was, in essence, exactly what actually existed in the case of corporations which have played such a large part in the formation of the Britannic Empire-Commonwealth. Charters, sets of rules by which authority was delegated to Merchant Adventurers, Virginia Companies, or East India Companies, yet in which jurisdiction was delimited; such charters rationalized sovereignty by the subjection of all groups to law. The question of devising some theory of international coöperation, if referred to the students of the Science of Commonwealths and Corporations of the eighteenth century, discovers this answer: all groups must understand the theory of law by consent, and having understood it, must agree to sacrifice independence at the dictate of that law.

To approximate in such a law the principles of a higher spiritual law is a task which may, then, perhaps, be approached. But until the groups admit the existence and validity of any law at all, there is little use in exploring the higher realms. It would, indeed, be highly desirable to have all group problems solved by the principle

[78] The Circular Letter of Massachusetts Bay; Almon, *Prior Documents*, pp. 203–5.

[79] John Adams, *Works*, IV. 194.

which Hamilton called God, but until the groups can demonstrate their capacity to be faithful in the unrighteous mammon, they can hardly expect to have true riches committed to their trusteeship. As John Adams pointed out, there is no use advising people to depend for their safety, liberty and security upon hopes and blessings which we can hardly expect will fall to their lot. Hence the advisability of "some political institutions" upon which man may lean in the period of his unenlightenment.

9

THE RELATION TO MODERN THOUGHT

Few writers on politics seem satisfied until they have made the trip to Aristotle and back. In consideration of the vast difference between his day and this of wireless telegraphy and electrical motive force, it is a matter of some interest that principles which he enunciated have a relevancy today. But they have had that relevancy in many another day as well, and perhaps it is not going too far to say that what we have been observing here is not the creation of new ideas but merely the revival of these older ones. One may, as has been noted, trace Otis' pronouncement that an act of Parliament contrary to the Constitution is void, back to Vattel. But with equal propriety it might be traced to William of Ockham's doctrine that the commands of the sovereign "ultra vires statuentis" are also null.[1] Similarly one might say of the theories of John Locke and James Wilson, which discovered sovereignty in the people, that here is only another and yet another recurrence of the thought which Marsiglio of Padua expressed when he pointed out that the will of the people is the efficient cause of the law.[2] It is not so much with the origin of ideas that we are concerned, as with their emergence and re-emergence at some peculiarly appropriate moment in history. In the midst of the American reaction against the treaty of Versailles in 1919, one American senator to whom the example of the British imperial organization and its precedents had been cited, became so impatient that he said frankly he was tired of hearing about

---

[1] William of Ockham (Occam), Dial. III: tr. 2; 1, 2; ch. 20, 26, 28; cf. II. J. Laski, *Foundations of Sovereignty*, p. 9.

[2] Marsiglio of Padua, *Defensor Pacis*, Bk. I: ch. xii.

Australia, that the first families of Australia were the descendants of convicts any way, and hence he declined to take advice from Australia, preferring to follow the traditions of his own country.[3] Now since this was just the same reason that Dr. Johnson had given for declining to respect the Americans in 1774, we can see that the Tory, as well as the Whig ideas are emerging and re-emerging, and neither truth nor error is the exclusive possession of any particular generation.

It is hardly profound to pass upon the political theories of the American Revolution the historical judgment that they exhibit no originality. That a people exhibited a familiarity with an important principle at an important time is a matter of some historic significance. Even if we cannot credit the American thinkers with originating certain political ideas, we are probably paying them a higher compliment by saying that at a critical time they did display, with remarkable results, an acquaintance with those ideas. Among the doctrines of which they showed some appreciation was that involved in the distinction between society and government. Dr. Johnson's statement that in sovereignty there were no gradations was followed with the enunciations, "There may be limited royalty, there may be limited consulship, but there can be no limited *government*." In explanation he went on to say, "There must be in every society some power or other from which there is no appeal."[4] Now it will readily be observed that the second of those statements has no necessary connection with the first, because as a fact government and society are two totally distinct things. This is a principle which transcends in importance the whole controversy attendant upon and incident to the application of the theory of natural rights. To illustrate: It is sometimes taken for granted that the eighteenth century natural rights school played into the hands of the *laissez-faire* theorists and thus worked untold social injustice in the name of protecting the natural rights of factory and mine owners. However this may be, one should not confuse a fundamental principle with its application in a particular age. Aristotle's principles may be as true today as they were two thousand years ago, but no one would be so foolish as to apply them today as though the modern world were identical with Aristotle's. Similarly with Jeffersonian principles, which if applied in eighteenth century agricultural Virginia might have

---

[3] Senator L. Y. Sherman (Ill.) Cong. Rec. 66 Cong. 1st Sess. 8010.
[4] *Taxation No Tyranny.*

resulted in a certain distrust of the state and state action, yet in twentieth century industrial Massachusetts might have a totally different application. If, in the eighteenth century, society willed *laissez-faire,* it might equally today under the principles of the American Revolution, will socialism, or communism, or sovietism, as far as the fundamental principle is concerned. So it is with that convention of the constitution which is known as the judicial veto, the power of the courts to declare a law unconstitutional. If it be true, as some allege, that it has been converted into an instrument for blocking social legislation, that is unfortunate, but it is no necessary consequence of the principle that there shall be no government above the law. The cure is no concern of political philosophy, but merely one of administration.

In laying down the distinction between society and government, the thinkers of the Revolution do not rigidly adhere to the distinction between the state and the government which the more modern political scientists urge. But those whom President Wilson calls the "plain people everywhere" have a most annoying faculty of confusing state and government, largely because the state is known to most people only through the action of the government. The "society *vs.* government" distinction has at least the merit of being clear. The doctrine of the responsibility of government to society is likely to run afoul of prevalent theories about the supremacy, the uncontrollability, and sovereignty of the state. But it is just because the doctrine of the sovereignty of the state is now being subjected to some very searching scrutiny that the thought of the American Revolution seems peculiarly pertinent. Religious groups and labor groups seem to be derogating from the supremacy of the state from within; other states, international law, and leagues of nations seem to derogate from the supremacy of the state from without; where, indeed, is now the sovereignty of the state?[5]

The answer to that question involves yet another fundamental idea which reappeared in the thought of the American Revolution, namely, the principle of divided authority, which is the essence of federalism. It is quite immaterial whether that be a logical thing or not; it need only be workable. Only the logical mind worries itself with whether there is being created an *imperium in imperio.* In the pre-Revolutionary discussions one finds again and again the English-

[5] See H. J. Laski, *The Problem of Sovereignty,* ch. II–V, and his *Authority in the Modern State,* ch. I.

man saying, "You cannot draw any line between absolute depend-ence and absolute independence." "Cannot" is notoriously a bad premise. It is so often the herald of the preacher of the doctrine of standing still. Perhaps it is not entirely unfair to suggest that by cutting loose from that doctrine the thinkers of the American Revo-lution were on the track of the new doctrine of semi-independence in a league of states.

It has been my aim to show here that the best mentalities of the old British Empire were working on the problem of bringing the political machinery of the empire into a better adjustment with the conditions which did in fact exist in the last half of the eighteenth century (Chapter II). What result was produced by these efforts in the way of practical suggestions falls under the three heads of theories of colonial dependency, theories of imperial federation (Chapter III) and theories of imperial partnership (Chapter IV). The pos-sibilities of the last named theories are of much greater consequence in the twentieth century, both as regards British imperial and as regards international politics, and so it seems that the thought of a representative "Britannic" rather than "British" thinker is worth analysis (Chapter V).[6] All this made certain very definite contribu-tions to political theory, and especially to that important branch of political thought pertaining to international relations. I have sought to point out that the Britannic laboratory disclosed the principle for which so many international publicists are still groping, namely, that governments are subject to law (Chapter VI). This principle, however, must be jargon, unless it is clearly understood that what the statesmen of the American Revolution understood by "law" was as different from John Austin's theory as day is from night. (Chap-ter VIII). All this involves the theme which must hover in the background of all our group thinking, and that is the question of sovereignty. I have therefore sought to show how the thinkers of the Revolutionary period met that issue. One might properly feel reluctant to deal with this topic at all, because its treatment pre-supposes a greater mental equipment than either the average reader or the average writer possesses. It is, however, as F. W. Maitland pointed out, because Englishmen have been unwilling to, or unable to deal with this subject, that there is in their history the tragic

---

[6] Sir R. Jebb's useful distinction between the term embracing the insular and the term embracing the world interests of Britain. Vid. his *Britannic Question*.

chapter of Ireland. It is also, as a more recent writer has emphasized, this same unwillingness and inability which plague international politics, so that Mr. G. L. Beer has not scrupled to remark that "the stern obstacle to the political organization of the world is the sovereignty of the state."

The original demands, if we may use that expression, of the Revolutionary Americans did not insist upon absolute independence and a separate membership in the family of nations.[7] All they asked was that their identity be not lost in that of England. It is well to remember that when the first and second Continental Congresses met, their ideal was not a complete separation; perhaps this will aid one to rid himself of that halo of political divinity with which we are wont to surround the ideas of independence and the sovereign state. When a given political form can not be made to respond to the demands of an economic situation, it is not always the economic situation which is at fault, or which will be changed. The separate economic identity of the American colonies was a fact in the last half of the eighteenth century, and the empire was broken by its own rigidity. The economic interdependence of nations is a *fait accompli* today; shall nations continue to break themselves because of the inelastic character of their so-called sovereignty?

But, as has been observed, the new historian of the federal idea will be called upon to tell some other stories and take account of some other forces than those included under the head of past politics. History may be past politics, but it is several other things as well. For example, there may be numerous examples of federalistic systems in the world, but the historian will be called upon to discriminate between those in which authority has been divided and distributed to secure harmony and those in which it has been

[7] "But if we are all *one dominion,* or, as I understand him, members of one state, tho' so remotely situated, the kingdom from the colonies, as we cannot all partake of the rights of the supreme legislature why may not this 'irresistible, absolute, uncontrouled' and controuling 'authority in which the *jura summi imperii* or rights of government reside' be established in *America* or in *Ireland,* as well as in *Britain?* Is there anything in nature, or has Ireland or America *consented* that the part of this one dominion called *Britain* shall be thus distinguished? Or are we to infer her authority from her power? Let him view the kingdom and the colonies in another light, and see whether there will be a solecism in considering them as *more* dominions *than one,* or *separate states.*" Samuel Adams as *Candidus* to the *Boston Gazette,* 20 Jun., 1772; *Works,* II, 321.

divided so as to secure more easy economic exploitation. Where in the Britannic Commonwealth has the principle of divided authority meant freedom, and where has it meant slavery? Among what other groups than purely political ones is authority to be further distributed? Will the reaction against the state find expression in the recrudescence of the eighteenth century natural rights theory,[8] or in newer theories of groups and their rights?[9]

It is not to be supposed that the substitution of one word for another ever worked a miracle in human affairs. But a growing understanding which reflects itself in a change of terminology may be a very interesting phenomenon. It is quite obvious that for some time past interstate relationships have been getting away from the vocabulary of the political scientist. People still talk blandly about free and independent states without stopping to inquire whether in fact there is any such thing. Britannic statesmen use practically the same language when speaking of the self-governing dominions as Americans use when speaking of those South American republics whose separate membership in the family of nations is hardly disputed. Persia is assured that she possesses integrity and independence; if so, what shadow of justification can there be in employing those same terms in connection with the Argentine Republic? If Brazil be a free and independent member of the family of nations, is, or is not New Zealand also? Is any of them a sovereign state? Persia is limited by a treaty with Great Britain, New Zealand by being a partner in the Britannic Commonwealth, and Brazil is a member of the League of Nations.

In the thought of the American Revolution, states can only be sovereign in the sense that they are portions of society, groups of people. The group can only be called sovereign by virtue of being composed of people who are sovereign. This is a very long way from what is ordinarily meant by the expression sovereign state. With that "living personality," that self-existent organic entity which has a being apart from the people who make it up, the thought of the American Revolution had not much to do. Yet, even the people were not sovereign in the Bodin-Burgess sense of a supreme power unrestrained by laws. The groping for a commonwealth of nations which characterized the thought of so many Americans in the ten

---

[8] See T. Baty's interesting article, 33 *Harv. Law Rev.*, 358.

[9] E. Barker, op. cit., 175 ff.

years before the Revolution rendered the term "sovereign state" of doubtful respectability.

Such principles tend to shift the burden of responsibility which government assumes from the state to society. Even if the *suprema lex* be the *salus populi,* at least the *populi* are entitled to have some voice in what constitutes their *salus,* and they may not care to identify that with what a particular government regards as the safety of the state. There is no use in society getting indignant at the state; the task is to get possession of it. Upon the outcome of this effort depends very largely the discovery of the formula which will compromise between the old and untenable theory of an absolutely irresponsible and independent state and the servile theory of a subject and economically tributary state. In the Britannic Commonwealth we may observe the formula most clearly and beneficially worked out in the case of those dominions where the people have most effectively got control of the state, while the formula is least clear in those cases where the thousands of illiterates make it impossible for the people to capture the state. So it was in 1776; the colonials had worked out a formula. The question of independence might never have arisen but for Britain's insistence that no line could be drawn between absolute subjection and absolute independence. The federally thinking politician, whose mental processes moved in economic channels, must have recognized that the social and economic divergence of Britain and her overseas colonies had by 1765 become so manifest as to demand a reorganization of the empire based upon the facts of the economic world. But Englishmen seemed to find it difficult to grasp the ideas that authority must be distributed and that law must be sovereign.

BIBLIOGRAPHICAL NOTES

For an excellent source of books and documents about the Revolutionary era, the reader is referred to Chapter X in the *Harvard Guide to American History,* edited by Oscar Handlin and others, published by Harvard University Press, 1954.

I

GENERAL BIBLIOGRAPHICAL WORKS

There is as yet no good, complete, critical bibliography of the American Revolution. Besides the usual aids, such as Channing, Hart and Turner's *Guide,* G. E. Howard's *Preliminaries of the Revolution,* C. H. Van Tyne's *American Revolution,* Channing's *History of the United States,* Vol. III, there is a very interesting although very incomplete list at the end of M. C. Tyler's *Literary History of the American Revolution.* M. Chamberlain and Justin Winsor, who wrote chapters i and ii in Vol. VI of the *Critical and Narrative History* edited by the latter, supply some useful hints. The following have been of the greatest value for general reference:

EVANS, THOMAS: American Bibliography, volumes IV and V, covers the period under consideration here, and attempts to give the titles of all books published in America between 1765 and 1785.

SABIN, JOSEPH: Bibliothea Americana, A Dictionary of Books Relating to America, from Its Discovery to the Present Time. (N. Y., 1868-1892.) Vols. I to XIX and part of XX appeared containing an alphabetical list of all the books the editor could locate, published in either England or America. It is extremely valuable as a check list, but unfortunately incomplete.

CHARLES RICHE HILDEBURN: Century of Printing (Phila., 1885.) Vols. I and II, lists all the issues of the press in Pennsylvania from 1685-1784.

II

COLLECTIONS OF OFFICIAL DOCUMENTS, ETC.

ALMON, JOHN: The Parliamentary Register, Vols. I and II for 1774. (London, 1774.)

ALMON, JOHN: A Collection of Interesting and Authentic Documents Relative to the Dispute Between Great Britain and America, Shewing the Causes and Progress of the Misunderstanding from 1764 to 1775. (London, 1777.) Usually known as "Almon's Prior Documents."

AMERICAN GAZETTE, THE: Being a Collection of all the Authentical Addresses, Memorials, etc., on the Dispute Between Great Britain and her Colonies. (London, 1768.)

ANNUAL REGISTER, THE. (London, 1765-75.)

DOCUMENTS Relating to the Colonial History of New York. 13 vols. (N. Y., 1856-75.)

FORCE, PETER, ed.: American Archives, 4th Series, Vol. I. (Washington, 1837.)

GIBBES, ROBERT W.: History of the American Revolution, Consisting of Letters and Papers Relating Chiefly to the Contest in South Carolina. (Columbia, S. C., 1853.)

GRIFFITH, WILLIAM: Historical Notes on the American Colonies and the Revolution from 1754-1775. (Burlington, N. J., 1843.)

HANSARD, THOMAS CURSON: The Parliamentary History of England. Vols. XV, XVI and XVII. (London, 1813-14.)

JOURNALS OF THE CONTINENTAL CONGRESS (W. C. Ford ed.) (Washington, 1904.)

LETTERS of the Members of the Continental Congress, edited by E. C. Burnett, Vol. I. (Washington, 1921.)

MASSACHUSETTS STATE PAPERS: Alden Bradford, editor: Speeches of the Governors of Massachusetts, and Answers of the House of Representatives of the Same, 1765-76, and other Public Papers. (Boston, 1818.)

MOORE, FRANK: Diary of the American Revolution from Newspapers and Original Documents. (N. Y., 1860.)

NILES, HEZIKIAH: Principal Acts of the Revolution in America. (Baltimore, 1822.)

RECORDS OF THE FEDERAL CONVENTION OF 1787 (Max Farrand, ed. 1911.)

III

BIOGRAPHIES, MEMOIRS, COLLECTED WORKS

ADAMS, JOHN: The Works of. (C. F. Adams, ed.) 10 vols. (Boston, 1856.)

ADAMS, JOHN: Life of. By Charles Francis Adams, v. Works, supra.

ADAMS, SAMUEL: The Writings of. (H. A. Cushing, ed.) 4 vols. (N. Y., 1904-8.)

ADAMS, SAMUEL: Life of. By William V. Wells. 3 vols. (Boston, 1665.)

BARRINGTON-BERNARD Correspondence, The: (E. Channing and A. C. Coolidge, ed.) (Boston, 1914.)

CARLISLE, EARL of: Manuscripts of. Historical Manuscripts Commission. Fifteenth Report, Appendix, Pt. vi. (London, 1897.)

COLDEN, CADWALLADER: Papers of, in the New York Historical Society Collections, Vols. IX and X. (N. Y., 1888-95.)

DARTMOUTH, EARL of: Manuscripts of. Vol. II, American Papers. Historical Manuscripts Commission, Fourteenth Report, Appendix, Pt. x. (London, 1895.)

DICKINSON, JOHN: Life and Writings of, in the Memoirs of the Pennsylvania Historical Society, Vols. XIII and XIV. Life by Charles Janeway Stillé and Works edited by Paul Leicester Ford. (Phila., 1891.)

DRAYTON, JOHN: Memoirs of the American Revolution from Its Commencement in 1776 as Relating to the State of South Carolina. 2 vols. (Charleston, S. C., 1821.)

FITCH, THOMAS: Correspondence and Papers of, in the Connecticut Historical Society Collections. Vol. XVII.

FRANKLIN, BENJAMIN: The Works. (J. Sparks, ed.) 10 vols. (Boston, 1847.) The Complete Works of. (John Bigelow, ed.) 10 vols. (N. Y., 1887-88.) The writings of. (H. H. Smyth, ed.) 10 vols. (N. Y., 1905-9.)

GEORGE III: Correspondence with Lord North, 1768-83. (W. B. Donne, ed.) 2 vols. (London, 1867.)

HAMILTON, ALEXANDER, Works of. (J. C. Hamilton, ed.) 7 vols. (N. Y., 1850.) (H. C. Lodge, ed.) 9 vols. (N. Y., 1885-6.)

HANCOCK, JOHN: A Picturesque Patriot, by Lorenzo Sears. (N. Y., 1912.)

HOPKINS, STEPHEN: A Rhode Island Statesman, by William E. Foster, in the Rhode Island Historical Tracts, No. 19. (Providence, 1884.)

HOPKINS, STEPHEN: Correspondence of, in the Rhode Island Records, Vol. VI.

HUTCHINSON, THOMAS: The Diary and Letters of. (P. O. Hutchinson, ed.) (Vol. I, Boston, 1884; Vol. II, Boston, 1886.)

HUTCHINSON, THOMAS: Life of, by James Kendall Hosmer. (N. Y., 1896.)

IREDELL, JAMES: Life and Correspondence of, by Griffith J. McRee. 2 vols. (N. Y., 1857.)

JEFFERSON, THOMAS: The Writings of. (H. A. Washington, ed.) 9 vols. (N. Y., 1853-4); The Writings of (P. L. Ford, ed.) 10 vols. (N. Y., 1892-7.)

JOHNSON, SAMUEL: Life of, by James Boswell. (G. Birkbeck Hill, ed.) 4 vols.

LEE, RICHARD HENRY: Letters of. (J. C. Ballagh, ed.) 2 vols. (N. Y., 1912.)

NORTH, FREDERICK, Lord: Second Earl of Guilford, by Reginald Lucas. 2 vols. (London, 1913.)

OTIS, JAMES: Life of, by William Tudor. (Boston, 1823.)

PAINE, THOMAS: Works of. 4 vols. (M. D. Conway, ed.) (N. Y., 1894.)

PAINE, THOMAS: Life of, by Moncure D. Conway. 2 vols. (N. Y., 1908.)

QUINCY, JOSIAH: A Memoir of, by Josiah Quincy, Jr. (Boston, 1825.)

SHARP, HORATIO: Correspondence of. (W. H. Browne, ed.) (1888-95.)

SHARPE, GRANVILLE: Memoirs of, Composed from His Own Manuscripts and from Other Authentic Documents, Etc., by Prince Hoare. (London, 1820.)

SHELBURNE, EARL OF: Life of, by Lord Fitzmaurice. 2 vols. (London, 1912.)

SMITH, WILLIAM: Works of the Late Provost of the College and Academy of Philadelphia. 2 vols. (Phila., 1803.)

WASHINGTON, GEORGE: Writings of. (Jared Sparks, ed.) 12 vols. (N. Y., 1834-7); Writings of. (W. C. Ford, ed.) 14 vols. (N. Y., 1889-93.)

WILSON, JAMES: Works of. (Bird Wilson, ed.) 3 vols. (Phila., 1803); Works of. (J. D. Andrews, ed.) 2 vols. (Chicago, 1896.) A new edition of the "Life and Writings of James Wilson" by Burton Alva Konkle is announced to be published shortly. This work will supersede the two above.

IV

CONTEMPORARY LITERATURE

(In the search for this material it often occured to me that it would be useful if the compilers of bibliographies would in some way indicate where certain of the rarer pamphlets could be found. I have therefore indicated here where the pamphlet or other writing which I used in this class may be found. This, of course, does not imply that other copies may not exist in other collections or libraries. The following symbols are used: NL—The Newberry Library at Chicago. HSP—The Historical Society of Pennsylvania at Philadelphia. LCP—The Library Company of Philadelphia. LC—The Library of Congress. UPL—University of Pennsylvania Library at Philadelphia.)

ACCOUNT, An, of a Late Conference on the Occurrences in America, in a Letter to a Friend. (London, 1766.) LCP.

ADAMS, JOHN: A Dissertation on the Canon and Feudal Law. (London, 1768.) NL.

ADAMS, JOHN: Novanglus and Massachusettensis; or Political Essays published in the years 1774 and 1775 on the Principal Points of Controversy Between Great Britain and Her Colonies. (Boston, 1819.) LC.

ADAMS, SAMUEL: The True Sentiments of America: Contained in a Collection of Letters Sent from the House of Representatives of the Province of Massachusetts Bay to Several Persons of High Rank in This Kingdom. (London, 1768.) NL.

ANDREWS, JOHN: A History of the War With America, France, Spain and Holland, 1775-1783. (London, 1785.) [The author was an Englishman who came to America in 1770.]

APPLICATION, An, of Some General Political Rules to the Present State of Great Britain, Ireland and America in a Letter to the Right Honorable Earl Temple. (London, 1766.) LCP.

APOLOGY, An, for the Late Conduct of America from the London Gazetteer, April 7, 1774. (v. Force, Amer. Arch., 4th sec. I, 241.)

ARGUMENT, An, in Defense of the Exclusive Right Claimed by the Colonists to Tax Themselves, with a Review of the Laws of England Relative to Taxation and Representation. (London, 1774.) LCP.

BERNARD, FRANCIS: Select Letters on the Government of America and the Principles of Law and Polity Applied to the American Colonies. (London, 1774.) UPL.

BLACKSTONE, WILLIAM: Commentaries on the Laws of England. (Chitty, ed.)

BLAND, RICHARD: The Colonel Dismounted, or the Rector Vindicated, in a Letter Addressed to His Reverence, Containing a Dissertation on the Constitution of the Colony. (Williamsburg, Va., 1766.) LC. (v. Wm. & Mary Quar. Hist. Mag., XIX, 31.)

BLAND, RICHARD: An Enquiry Into the Rights of the British Colonies. (Williamsburg, Va., 1766.) LC. [E. G. Swem, librarian of the William and Mary College Library has edited and reprinted this rare pamphlet. (Richmond, 1922.)]

BOUCHER, JONATHAN: A View of the Causes and Consequences of the American Revolution, in thirteen discourses. (London, 1797.) NL.

BURGH, JAMES: Political Disquisitions, or An Inquiry Into Public Errors, Defects and Abuses. (London, 1774.) 3 vols.

BUSHE, GERVASE PARKER: The Case of Great Britain and America: An Address to the King and Both Houses of Parliament. (Phila., 1769.) LC.

CARTWRIGHT, JOHN: American Independence; the Interest and Glory of Great Britain. (London, 1774.) LCP.

CHALMERS, GEORGE: Political Annals of the Present United Colonies, from their Settlement to the Peace of 1763. (London, 1780.) [Chalmers was one of the few historians of his day who really wrote history from the sources. His official position gave him access to records closed to other authors.]

CHURCH, BENJAMIN: Liberty and Property Vindicated and the St——p—M—n Burnt. (Hartford, 1765.) LC.

CONDUCT of the Late Administration Examined. With An Appendix Containing Original and Authentick Documents. (London, 1767.) [Probably by Charles Lloyd, v. D. N. B.] HSP.

CONSIDERATIONS on the Rights of the Colonies to the Privileges of British Subjects. (N. Y., 1766.) LCP.

CONSIDERATIONS on Certain Political Transactions of the Province of South Carolina, Containing Views of the Colonial Legislature, with Observations Showing Resemblance to the British Model. (London, 1774.) LC.

CONTROVERSY between Great Britain and Her Colonies Reviewed; The Several Pleas of the Colonies in Support of their Right, etc., etc. (Boston, 1769.) LCP. [Probably by William Knox, v. D. N. B.]

COOPER, MYLES: An American Querist; or, Some Questions Proposed Relative to the Present Dispute Between Great Britain and Her American Colonies. (n. p., 1774.) LCP.

COOPER, MYLES: A friendly Address to All Reasonable Americans on the Subject of the Political Confusions in Which the Necessary Consequences of Violently Opposing the King's Troops and a General Non-Importation Are Fairly Stated. (N. Y., 1774.) LCP.

CRISIS, The: Or a Full Defense of the Colonies. (London, 1766.) [Probably by Samuel Cooper.]

DAY, JOHN: Remarks on American Affairs. (London, 1774.) HSP.

DICKINSON, JOHN: An Address to the Committee of Correspondence in Barbadoes, Occasioned by a late letter from them to their agent in London. (Phila., 1766.) LCP.

DICKINSON, JOHN: Letters from a Farmer in Pennsylvania to the Inhabitants of the British Colonies. (Phila., 1768.) NL.

DRAYTON, WILLIAM HENRY: Answer to Considerations on Certain Political Transactions of the Province of South Carolina. (London, 1774.) LC.

DRAYTON, WILLIAM HENRY: A letter from a Freeman of South Carolina to the Deputies of North America, Assembled in the High Court of Congress at Philadelphia. (Charleston, S. C., 1774.) LC.

DULANEY, DANIEL: Considerations of the Propriety of Imposing Taxes on the British Colonies for the Purpose of Raising Revenue by An Act of Parliament. (Annapolis, Md., 1765.) UPL.

ESSAY, An, on the Constitutional Power of Great Britain Over the Colonies in America. (Phila., 1774.) LCP.

EXAMINATION, An, of the Rights of the Colonies upon Principles of Law, by a Gentleman of the Bar. (London, 1766.) NL.

EXTRACT of a Letter from the House of Representatives of Massachusetts Bay to their Agent, Dennys de Berdt, with Some Remarks. (London, 1770.) LCP.

FEW, A, Political Reflections submitted to the Consideration of the British Colonies in America by a Citizen of Philadelphia. (Phila., 1774.) [Sometimes attributed to Richard Wells, esp. by M. C. Tyler and so designated in catalogue at HSP.] HSP.

FITCH, THOMAS: Reasons Why the British Colonies in America Should Not Be Charged with Internal Taxes by the Authority of Parliament; humbly offered for Consideration in behalf of the Colony of Connecticut. (New Haven, 1765.) LC.

FLETCHER, J.: American Patriotism. (n. p., 1777.) NL.

GALLOWAY, JOSEPH: A Candid Examination of the Mutual Claims of Great Britain and Her Colonies. With a Plan of Accommodation on Mutual Constitutional Principles. (New York, 1775.) LCP.

GALLOWAY, JOSEPH: A Reply to an Address to the Author of a Pamphlet entitled a Candid Examination, etc., by the Author of the Candid Examination. (New York, 1775.) LC.

GALLOWAY, JOSEPH: The Examination of Joseph Galloway, Esq., late Speaker of the House of Assembly of Pennsylvania before the House of Commons, in a Committee on the American Papers. (London, 1779.) LCP.

GALLOWAY, JOSEPH: Historical and Political Reflections on the Rise and Progress of the American Rebellion. (London, 1780.) LC.

GALLOWAY, JOSEPH: Plain Truth, or, a A Letter to the Author of Dispassionate Thoughts on the American War. (London, 1780.) LC.

GALLOWAY, JOSEPH: Political Reflections on the Late Colonial Governments, in which their Original Constitutional Defects are Pointed Out, and Shewn to have Naturally Produced the Rebellion which has unfortunately terminated in the Dismemberment of the British Empire. By an American. (London, 1783.) LC.

GENERAL OPPOSITION of the Colonies to the Payment of the Stamp Duty * * * and also A Plan for Uniting to this Kingdom, etc., in a Letter to a Member of Parliament. (London, 1766.) NL.

GORDON, WILLIAM: A History of the Rise, Progress and Establishment of the Independence of the United States of America. (London, 1788.)

HAMILTON, ALEXANDER: Full Vindication of the Measures of the Continental Congress from the Calumnies of their Enemies. (N. Y., 1774.) LCP.

HAMILTON, ALEXANDER: The Farmer Refuted: or, A More Comprehensive and Impartial View of the Disputes between Great Britain and the Colonies, intended as a Further Vindication of the Congress, in Answer to a Letter from A. W. Farmer. (New York, 1775.) LCP.

HOPKINS, STEPHEN: Rights of the Colonies Examined (Providence, 1765.) Reprinted as Grievances of the American Colonies Candidly Examined. (London, 1766.) NL.; v. also Rhode Island Records, Vol. VI.

HOWARD, MARTIN: A Defence of the Letter from the Gentleman in Halifax to His Friend in Rhode Island. (Newport, 1765.) LC.

HOWARD, MARTIN: A Letter from a Gentleman in Halifax to his Friend in Rhode Island, containing Remarks on a pamphlet entitled Rights of the Colonies Examined. (Newport, 1765.) LC.

HUNT, ISAAC: The Political Family; or, A Discourse Pointing Out the Reciprocal Advantages which Flow from an Uninterrupted Union between Great Britain and Her American Colonies. (Philadelphia, 1775.) LCP.

HUTCHINSON, THOMAS: A History of the Province of Massachusetts Bay. (London, 1838.) 3 vols., of which Vol. III covers the period under consideration.

HUTCHINSON, THOMAS: and Lieutenant Governor Oliver, The Letters of, (Boston, 1773.) NL.

HUTCHINSON, THOMAS: Strictures upon the Declaration of the Congress at Philadelphia in a Letter to a Noble Lord. (London, 1776.) LC.

IREDELL, JAMES: Address to the Inhabitants of Great Britain (n. p., 1774) reprinted in McRee, I, 205-20; The Principles of an American Whig (n. p., 1775), reprinted in McRee, I, 245-54; Unentitled Pamphlet on the Revolution (n. p., 1776), reprinted in McRee, I, 283-323.

JEFFERSON, THOMAS: Summary View of the Rights of British America set Forth in Some Resolutions intended for the Inspection of the Present Delegates of the People of Virginia now in Convention: By a Native and a Member of the House of Burgesses. (London, 1774.)

JENYNS, SOAME: The Objection to the Taxation of Our American Colonies by the Legislature of Great Britain Briefly Considered. (London, 1765.) LCP.

JOHNSTONE, GEORGE: Speech on the Question of Recommitting the Address Declaring the Colony of Massachusetts Bay in Rebellion. (London, 1776.) NL.

JOHNSTONE, GEORGE: Speech on American Affairs, on the Address in Answer to the King's Speech. (London, 1776.) NL.

JUNIUS: Including Letter by the Same Writer under Other Signatures, to which are added his Confidential Correspondence with Mr. Wilkes and His Private Letters to Mr. H. S. Woodfall. A New and Enlarged edition with New Evidence as to the Authorship and an Analysis by the late Sir Harris Nicholas. By John Wade. 2 vols. (London, 1890.)

KNOX, WILLIAM: The Claim of the Colonies to an Exemption from Internal Taxes imposed by the authority of Parliament, Examined in a Letter to a Friend in America. (London, 1765.) LC.

LATE (The) Occurrences in North America and the Policy of Great Britain Considered. (London, 1766.) LCP. NL.

LATE (The) Regulations respecting the British Colonies on the Continent of America considered in a Letter to a Gentleman in Philadelphia, from his Friend in London. (London, 1766.) HSP.

LATHROP, JOHN: Discourse Preached on March 5th, 1778. (Boston, 1778.) NL.

LEE, ARTHUR: Appeal to the Justice and Interests of the People of Great Britain in the Present Dispute with America, by an Old Member of Parliament. Nos. 1 and 2. (London, 1774.)

LEE, ARTHUR: The Political Detection, or, Treachery and Tyranny of Administration, both At Home and Abroad, displayed in a Series of Letters, signed Junius Americanus. (London, 1770.) LC.

LEE, ARTHUR: Speech Intended to have been Delivered in the House of Commons, in support of the Petition from the General Congress at Philadelphia. (London, 1775.)

LEE, CHARLES: Strictures on a Pamphlet entitled Friendly Address to All Reasonable Americans. (Phila., 1774.) LCP.

LEONARD, DANIEL: Massachusettensis, or a Series of Letters containing a faithful State of many important and striking Facts which laid the Foundation of the present Troubles in the Province of Massachusetts Bay; interspersed with Animadversions and Reflections, originally addressed to the People of that Province, and worthy the Consideration of True Patriots of this Country. By a Person of Honor upon the Spot. (London, 1776.) LC.

LETTER (A) in Defence of Mr. Fox and Others in answer to Cicero, Lucius Cataline, and Several Others to the Prince of Wales. (London, n. d.) NL.

LETTER (A) To The Right Honorable Lord M * * * * on Affairs in America from a Member of Parliament. (London, 1775.) NL.

LETTERS TO the Right Honorable, the Earl of Hillsboro from Governor Bernard, and Governor Gage. (London, 1769.) NL.

MACAULAY, CATHERINE: Address to the People of England, Scotland and Ireland on the Present Important Crisis of Affairs. (London, 1775.) NL.

MACCARTY, THADDEUS: Two Sermons Preached at Worcester in 1774. (Boston, 1774.) NL.

MADUIT, ISRAEL. (Israil.): Some Thoughts on the Method of Securing and Improving Advantages Which Accrue to Great Britain from the Northern Colonies. (London, 1760.) NL.

MARSHALL, JOHN: A History of the Colonies Planted by England on the Continent of North America, from their Settlement to the Commencement of that War which Terminated in their Independence. (Phila., 1824.)

MASERES, FRANCIS (Masseres): Consideration on the Expediency of Admitting Representatives from the American Colonies to the British House of Commons. (London, 1770.) NL.

MAYHEW, JONATHAN: The Snare Broken. A Thanksgiving Discourse Preached at the Desire of the West Church in Boston N. E., Friday, May 23, 1766, occasioned by the Repeal of the Stamp Act. (Boston, 1766.) NL.

OBSERVATIONS on the Reconciliation of Great Britain and her Colonies by a Friend of American Liberty. (Phila., 1776.) NL.

OTHER (The) Side of the Question, in Answer to the Late "Friendly Address to All Reasonable Americans." By a Citizen (N. Y., 1776.) NL.

OTIS, JAMES: Vindication of the British Colonies Against the Aspersions of the Halifax Gentleman in a Letter to a Rhode Island Friend. (Boston, 1762.) (London, 1769.) NL.

OTIS, JAMES: Rights of the British Colonies Asserted and Proved. (London, 1766.) (3rd ed.) NL.

OTIS, JAMES: Brief Remarks on the Defense of the Halifax Libel on the British American Colonies. (Boston, 1765.) LC.

OTIS, JAMES: Considerations on Behalf of the Colonists in a Letter to a Noble Lord. (London, 1765.) (2nd ed.) NL.

PAINE, THOMAS: Common Sense, Addressed to the Inhabitants of America, etc., with the whole Appendix. (Phila., 1776.) NL.

PARAPHRASE On a Passage in a Sermon by the Archbishop of York. (n. p., 1777.) NL.

PETITION (A) from the Assembly of Massachusetts Bay to the King with Several Other Papers. (Boston, 1768.) LCP.

PLAN (A) of Reconciliation between Great Britain and Her Colonies Founded on Justice and Constitutional Security, by which the Rights of Englishmen in Matters of Taxation are Preserved to the Inhabitants of America and the Islands Beyond the Atlantic. (London, 1776.) LC.

PLAN (A) of Union, by Admitting Representatives from the American Colonies and from Ireland to the British Parliament. (Phila., 1770.) LCP.

PLAN (A) or Articles of Perpetual Union, Commerce and Friendship between Great Britain and Her American Colonies: Founded on the Solid Basis of Justice and Proposed as a Medium between the Claims of Total Independence on One Hand, and Those of Legal Subjection on the Other. (London, 1780.) LC.

PLAN (A) of Reconciliation with America, consistent with the Dignity and Interest of both Countries. (London, 1782.) LC.

PLAN (A) to Reconcile Great Britain with Her Colonies and Preserve the Dependency of America, by "Cosmopolite." (London, 1774.) LC.

PLAIN TRUTH, Addressed to the Inhabitants of America; Containing Remarks on a Late Pamphlet Entitled Common Sense. Written by Candidus. (Phila., 1776.) NL.

POOR (A) MAN'S Advice to His Poor Neighbors: a Ballad to the Tune of Chevy Chace. (N. Y., 1774.) LCP.

POWNALL, THOMAS: Administration of the Colonies, wherein their Rights and Constitutions are Discussed and Stated. (London, 1768.) LCP.

PRICE, RICHARD: Two Tracts on Civil Liberty. (London, 1778.) NL.

PROPOSAL OF A PLAN toward Reconciliation and Reunion with the Provinces of America and for a Union with the Other Colonies, By One of the Public. (London, 1778.) NL.

PULTENEY, WILLIAM: Thoughts on the Present State of Affairs with America, and Means of Reconciliation. (London, 1778.) LC.

QUINCY, JOSIAH: Observations on the Act of Parliament Commonly Called the Boston Port Bill; with Thoughts on Civil Society and Standing Armies. (Boston, 1774.) LC.

RAMSAY, DAVID: A History of the American Revolution. (Phila., 1786.)

REGULATIONS, Lately Made Concerning the Colonies and Taxes Imposed Upon Them Considered. (London, 1765.) HSP.

ROBINSON, MATTHEW [Lord Rokeby]: Considerations on the Measures Carrying on with Respect to the British Colonies in America. (Boston, 1774.) LC.

ROBINSON, MATTHEW [Lord Rokeby]: A Further Examination of Our Present American Measures and of the Reasons and Principles on Which They Are Founded. (London, 1776.) NL.

SAYRE, F.: The Englishman Deceived. (N. Y., 1768.) LC.

SHARP, GRANVILLE: A Declaration of the People's Natural Right to Share in the Legislature which is the Fundamental Principle of the British Constitution of the State. (Phila., 1774.) LCP.

SMITH, WILLIAM: Sermon on the Present Situation in American Affairs. (Phila., 1775.) NL.

SEABURY, SAMUEL: Free Thoughts of the Proceedings of the Continental Congress held at Philadelphia, September 5, 1774, Wherein Their Errors are Exhibited, Their Reasonings Confuted, and the Fatal Tendency of their Non-Importation, Non-Exportation and Non-Consumption Measures are laid open to the plainest Understandings; and the Only Means Pointed Out for Preserving and Securing Our Present Constitution, By a Farmer. (n. p., 1774.) LCP.

SEABURY, SAMUEL: The Congress Canvassed; or, An Examination into the Conduct of the Delegates at their Grand Convention held in Philadelphia, September 1, 1774. Addressed to the Merchants of New York. By A. W. Farmer. (n. p., 1774.) LCP.

SEABURY, SAMUEL: A View of the Controversy between Great Britain and Her Colonies: Including a Mode of Determining their Present Disputes, finally and Effectually, and of Preventing all future Contentions. In a Letter to the Author of a Full Vindication of the Measures of Congress from the Calumnies of their Enemies. By A. W. Farmer. (N. Y., 1774.) LCP.

SEABURY, SAMUEL: An Alarm to the Legislature of the Province of New York, occasioned by the present Political Disturbances in North America: Addressed to the Honorable Representatives in General Assembly Convened. (N. Y., 1775.) LCP.

SEABURY, SAMUEL: The Republican Dissected, or, The Anatomy of an American Whig. By A. W. Farmer. (N. Y., 1775.) (Advertised for publication, but not known to have been published: v. Tyler: Lit. Hist. of Amer. Rev. II: 475.)

SEWALL, JONATHAN: v. Novanglus and Massachusettensis supra.

STEDMAN, CHARLES: A History of the Rise, Progress and Termination of the American War. (London, 1784.)

SUPREMACY OF the British Legislature over the Colonies candidly Discussed. (London, 1775.) LCP.

THACHER, OXENBRIDGE: The Sentiments of a British American. (Boston, 1764.) LC.

TUCKER, J.: Interest of Great Britain considered with regard to Her Colonies. (Philadelphia, 1776.) LC.

WHAT THINK YE of Congress Now? or, An Enquiry how far the Americans are Bound to Abide by, and Execute, the Decisions of the late Congress. (N. Y., 1775.) LC.

WILSON, JAMES: Considerations on the Nature and Extent of the Legislative Authority of the British Parliament. (Phila., 1774.) LCP.

WYNNE, JOHN HUDDLESTON: A General History of the British Empire in America. (London, 1770.)

ZUBLY, JOHN JOACHIM: The Stamp Act Repealed * * * A Sermon Preached at Savannah, June 25, 1766. (Charleston, 1766.) LC.

ZUBLY, JOHN JOACHIM: A Humble Inquiry into the Nature of the Dependency of the American Colonies upon the Parliament of Great Britain, and the Right of Parliament to Lay Taxes on the said Colonies: By a Freeholder of South Carolina. (n. p., 1769.) HSP.

ZUBLY, JOHN JOACHIM: The Law of Liberty: A Sermon on American Affairs, preached at the opening of the Provincial Congress of Georgia. (Phila., 1775.) LC.

V

MODERN CRITICISM

ADAMS, GEORGE BURTON: The British Empire and a League of Peace, together with an Analysis of Federal Government. (N. Y., 1919.)

BARKER, ERNEST: Political Thought in England from Herbert Spencer to the Present Day. (N. Y., n. d.)

BRYCE, JAMES: Studies in History and Jurisprudence. (N. Y., 1901.)

CHAMBERLAIN, MELLIN: John Adams and Other Essays. (Boston, 1898.)

CHEYNEY, EDWARD POTTS: A History of England from the Defeat of the Armada to the Death of Elizabeth. (N. Y., 1914.) Vol. I.

COXE, BRINTON: The Judiciary and Unconstitutional Legislation. (Phila., 1892.)

DeTOCQUEVILLE, ALEXIS: Democracy in America (Gilman ed.) (N. Y., 1898.)

DEWEY, JOHN: German Philosophy and Politics. (N. Y., 1915.)

DICEY, ALBERT VENN: Introduction to the Study of the Law and the Constitution. (8th ed. London, 1915.)

DUGUIT, LEON: Law in the Modern State. (Trans. by H. J. and F. Laski. N. Y., 1915.)

DUNNING, WILLIAM ARCHIBALD: History of Political Theories, Ancient and Mediæval, (N. Y., 1903); History of Political Theories, from Luther to Montesquieu, (N. Y., 1905); History of Political Theories from Rousseau to Spenser, (N. Y., 1920.)

GERSON, ARMAND J.: The Organization and Early History of the Muscovy Company. (N. Y., 1912.)

GIERKE, OTTO: Introduction to the Political Theories of the Middle Age. (Trans. and intro. by F. W. Maitland. London, 1900.)

HAINES, CHARLES GROVE: The American Doctrine of Judicial Supremacy. (N. Y., 1914.)

JEBB, RICHARD: The Britannic Question, (London, 1913). The Imperial Conference, (London, 1911).

JENKS, EDWARD: Law and Politics in the Middle Ages. (N. Y., 1897.)

KEITH, ARTHUR BERRIEDALE: British Imperial Unity and the Dominions. (Oxford, 1916.)

LASKI, HAROLD J.: The Problem of Sovereignty (Yale Press, 1917); Authority in the Modern State (Yale Press, 1919); Political Thought from Locke to Bentham (N. Y., 1920); Foundations of Sovereignty (N. Y., 1921).

LINGELBACH, WILLIAM EZRA: The Merchant Adventurers of England, Their Laws and Ordinances with Other Documents. (Phila., 1902.)

LUCAS, CHARLES P.: The Beginnings of English Overseas Enterprise. (Oxford, 1919.)

McILWAIN, CHARLES HOWARD: The High Court of Parliament and Its Supremacy. (Boston, 1910.)

McLAUGHLIN, ANDREW CUNNINGHAM: Courts, Constitutions and Parties (Chicago, 1912); America and Britain (N. Y., 1918).

MERRIAM, CHARLES EDWARD: History of the Theory of Sovereignty Since Rousseau (N. Y., 1900); History of American Political Theories (N. Y., 1903); History of American Political Ideas, 1865-1920. (N. Y., 1921.)

TYLER, LYON GARDINER: The Leadership of Virginia in the war of the American Revolution. (Published in instalments in the *William and Mary Quarterly Historical Magazine,* vols. XVIII and XIX.)

TYLER, MOSES COIT: A Literary History of the American Revolution. (N. Y., 1897.)

WALSH, CORREA M.: The Political Science of John Adams. (N. Y., 1915.)

INDEX